TANK

INIQUUS CERTIFIED CERBERUS TACTICAL K9
BOOK 3

FIONA QUINN

THE WORLD OF INIQUUS

Ubicumque, Quoties. Quidquid

Iniquus - /i'ni/kwus/ our strength is unequalled, our tactics unfair – we stretch the law to its breaking point. We do whatever is necessary to bring the enemy down.

THE LYNX SERIES

Weakest Lynx

Missing Lynx

Chain Lynx

Cuff Lynx

Gulf Lynx

Hyper Lynx

Marriage Lynx

Delta Force Echo

Danger Signs

Danger Zone

Danger Close

Cerberus Tactical K9 Team Bravo

Warrior's Instinct

Rescue Instinct

Hero's Instinct

Cerberus Tactical K9 Team Charlie

Guardian's Instinct

Sheltering Instinct

Shielding Instinct

Trusted Instinct

Acting on Instinct

Certified Cerberus Tactical K9

Beowolf

Radar

Tank

CIA Color Code

Red Line

This list was created in 2025. For an up-to-date list, please visit www.FionaQuinn-

Books.com

If you prefer to read the Iniquus World in chronological order you will find a full list at

the end of this book.

TANK

CERTIFIED

Cerberus Tactical K9

FIONA QUINN

THE PLAYERS

World Cares

- **Rylee Jones – Co-director Operations**
- Neesa Meesang – Co-director of Operations
- Sun Yu, lawyer
- Mandy, logistics
- Erica, PA
- George, lead Team Quebec
- Stew, security

FBI

- **Dakota Kayne with K9 Tank**
- Benny Burnett with wife, Martha Burnett
- Jasper Lee
- Kumar Singh with partner Veer

Iniquus

- Hailey Sterling, logistics
- Reaper Hamilton, trainer
- Halo and K9 Max, Charlie
- Hawkeye and K9 Cooper, Charlie
- Ares and K9 Judge, Bravo
- Mace and K9 Diesel, Bravo
- Nutsbe and K9 Beowolf, Panther Force

1

———

Dakota

Sunday

Dakota Kayne dropped the gunmetal grey duffle to the ground, a bright blue Cerberus Tactical K9 logo stamped on the side. He glanced toward his massive German shepherd, Tank, sitting expectantly in front of him. "Let's see what they've packed for us, hey boy?"

Pulling the zipper, Dakota reached in to retrieve a bundle of neatly coiled lines resting at the top. Underneath was a water bottle, energy pouches, a towel, a race number with safety pins, and two tubes of grease paint. He left those in place as he held the handful of webbing and bungee cords under his dog's nose. "Hey, Tank, have you done this before?"

Tank's whole body shifted to excitement mode as he leaned forward, tapped his nose on the webbing, then shifted his gaze up to lock with Dakota's. Big for a German shepherd, Tank was all muscle and enthusiasm. Tank's biggest muscle by far, though, was his heart. If Tank were doing it, he would give 100%.

This was the first time in almost two months that Dakota and Tank were together.

Dakota had been down in Colombia, working a Secret Service mission. For two months, Dakota missed Tank with the same intensity of homesickness he had fought down when he deployed to the Middle East back in his military days.

Dakota had only just arrived back in the States Friday night. He had spent his Saturday doing the domestic things that needed attention after a long time away—filling the fridge, chucking the dead house plants, and opening the doors wide, despite the March chill, airing out the stale, unused smells that expand in a home when a door never opens to let in a blast of wind or sunshine.

That night, while Dakota was busy emptying his suitcases and throwing a load in the washing machine, Reaper, the lead trainer over at Iniquus's Cerberus Tactical K9, had called to check in. "Hey, man, I know you're scheduled to come to the campus and work with Tank on Tuesday, but we're a man down on our race team. We'd appreciate it if you could run Tank for a good cause."

"How's that?" Dakota asked, pouring a capful of detergent into the washer tub. He'd get to see Tank earlier than planned, so whatever this was, the answer was an eager yes.

While Dakota was on mission, Tank had been living at Iniquus's Cerberus Tactical K9 kennels for advanced scent training and certification in printing ink detection, along with sharpening Tank's tactical skills to the razor-blade's edge of Cerberus standards.

"Grace Del Toro, one of the Strike Force wives, is on a team that's putting on a charity event for the children's hospital tomorrow, and things took a step sideways."

Dakota had no idea what his "Sure, I can help. What do you need?" was going to get him into.

But that's how he now found himself laced up in his trail running gear this bright Sunday morning, standing with all three Cerberus Tactical K9 teams—Alpha, Bravo, and Charlie—in the roped-off parking lot of some Virginia farm just off the highway south of D.C.

There must have been close to two hundred people with dogs of all shapes and sizes scattered around the lot. Most of the dogs had basic leashes clipped to their collars, not this crazy setup he'd pulled from the bag with what looked like straps that went around the thighs.

Like a garter belt, maybe?

That'll be a new sensation.

With a flick of his wrist, Dakota unraveled the rope system so he could see the length of the contraption.

Tank knew exactly what this was and exactly what came next. His tongue hung low as he panted in anticipation.

"Okay, good, that's one of us who has a clue." Dakota looked over as a couple of the Cerberus operators strapped their tethers around their hips.

"Here we go." Dakota put his foot into the loop. He tried to mimic how the men stepped into the center, pushed the wide panel low on the back of their hips, then secured it in place with the various straps. "You'll give me a heads up before I get tangled in this spider web of a contraption, right?"

Tank's yip could be anything from "Let's go!" to "You look like a fool, dude. You're wearing it backward."

Dakota would guess Tank probably meant that second one.

The goal for today's event was to raise money for the children's hospital project—building an accessible playground and a safe trail to get the kids off the pediatric floor from time to time and out into the sunshine and fresh air.

Who could turn down an opportunity like that?

The way the hospital was going about raising that money sounded genius. The event paralleled their hospital's end goal of gathering outside in nature to feel better and have fun in community.

The charitable committee had hired an outfit that put together K9 obstacle runs. Doggos from all over signed up to race five miles, running the hills, lizard crawling under netting, splashing through ponds, and climbing walls.

It was the kind of event that got lots of people posting about their cool experience.

Lots of rattle and shake.

Lots of eyes on the event would hopefully drive a steady flow of funds from far and wide to fill the coffers, and the project would get the funds needed to greenlight the playground.

The problem for the committee was that a pop-up outdoor concert by some new social media sensation was suddenly soaking up local interest, and the competition for eyeballs would overwhelm the charity event's pull. The hospital committee had really leaned into the idea of getting exposure from viral posts and influencer participation. And it didn't look like they were going to fill the spectators' ranks the way they'd anticipated.

Grace believed they needed a wow factor, not just Joe Blow running his chihuahua, Spike. Though, honestly, if Spike came in a tutu, Dakota could see how that might work just fine.

Grace decided that Cerberus was the secret sauce for success.

Phone calls were made.

Iniquus Command was thumbs up.

They invited Dakota to join, wondering if a Secret Service special agent could keep up.

And here they were.

Granted, Cerberus competed with their K9s in tactical events all over the world. It was how they built their international reputation for excellence. And that was why, after Tank proved he was qualified for a training position and his name was put on the wait list, Dakota had had to save for a year in order to afford Tank's training in their Cerberus certification program.

Worth every penny as far as Dakota was concerned. In a pinch, this training could save both their lives while working in the field.

And as for today, Dakota could see how the inclusion of the Cerberus teams could push the charitable algorithm into green.

Dakota reasoned it through this way: Who gave the most money to charities? Women.

And what do women want?

Given his track record of late, Dakota was the wrong

person to ask. But he'd assume ex-special forces operators in wet T-shirts with their war dogs, fighting to be the first over the finish line, might be something that would catch the female eye.

"Oy there, mate, you ready?" Halo, one of two Aussies on Cerberus, stopped beside Dakota and reached out to re-adjust Dakota's lines. "First time, hey?" He clipped the bungee lead between Tank's harness and Dakota's belt.

"I've done mud runs before, and I was in the military. But strapped to a fur missile this way? Yeah, this is a first. Any advice?"

"Well, mate," Halo's accent had a friendly ease, "I'd make sure you tell Tank to stop before he pulls you out of your runners."

"Please don't do that," Dakota told Tank. "We're here for the kiddos and to have some fun."

"Just a warning, then," Halo said, "We've been working with Tank on his water skills. When cold water touches his belly, he freaks out a bit." Holding the length of his long lead neatly coiled around his fingers, Halo used a hand signal to move his Malinois, Max, between his legs. "You didn't swim him when he was a pup?"

"I'm a triathlete. My swims are too long. So, no. I guess I messed up on that one." Dakota put his hand on Tank's head, "Sorry about that, buddy."

"No worries," Halo said. "Sure, he has a moment of freak-out when his chest gets wet. Just spin him around in the right direction and start swimming. He'll switch gears, and he's good to go."

"Thanks." Dakota lifted his hand as Halo and Max jogged toward the group of Cerberus Malinois. The Malinois were going to be the first to take off at the starting line. Mainly because Malinois could eat dog food and, by alchemy, transmute it into rocket fuel.

The German shepherds turned it into jet fuel.

Rockets launched first.

Though, to Dakota's way of thinking, it shouldn't really matter what kind of fuel they were burning. The dogs would be held back by their person's speed.

Hopefully.

If not, then they'd crash and burn.

"Fun times!" Reaper called out as he approached, hand extended. "Glad you could make it." They clasped in a welcoming shake. "Today, you can see for yourself what Tank's been up to lately as he gets ready for his final tests." He bent to scritch behind Tank's ears. "Word of warning, Tank knows what he's doing here. When he takes off running, he's going to pull you along—a blessing and a curse, right? You're going to be racing faster than you ever have over an uneven surface. It's going to feel disorganized in your brain. It's not unusual to feel out of control, even to panic a bit as your speed increases significantly. Breathe into the sensation. But you also need to communicate with Tank, so he doesn't pull you off your feet and drag you face-first. The road rash would be epic."

If Tank was setting the pace, Dakota was more concerned about having enough lung capacity than the road rash. "You've been through this course?"

"We ran it yesterday to test everything out for the organizers. We found a couple of places that seemed too dangerous for the weekend warrior types. So they had to re-engineer a couple of spots. All in all, it was a great time."

Reaper leaned down to scratch Tank's neck. "Word of warning, in past evolutions, the shepherds don't like that the Malinois are out front, so they try to prove they're in the same running league. They're not. Fact of life. But you may want to lean back pretty hard until the Malinois turn out of sight."

"Got it."

"You've carried him on your shoulders?" Reaper asked.

"I have, but he was a lot smaller."

"When you get to the obstacles that require a carry, and it's not working out, you can always hug him to your chest like he's a baby, front paws over your shoulder." Reaper pointed at Tank. "Just watch because he likes to keep running those back legs of his, and you're in shorts."

"Copy."

Tank weighed a good ninety pounds now. The last time Dakota had slung Tank over his shoulders, Tank was a worn-out pup. Now, Tank was a whole lot of dog to drape across Dakota's shoulders.

"Also, when you get to the wall, the sign says to leave the dog clipped to the side and go over by yourself. We're all carrying the dogs on our shoulders over the wall. There's an event photographer stationed there, and we're doing our best to get those viral shots online to bring in the money. At Cerberus, climbing walls with our dogs on our shoulders is part of our protocol. Tank knows the deal. But if you're at all worried, I'd follow the sign."

Yeah, right. Dakota was much too competitive to take the easy route. He liked the challenge.

"If you go over, there's deep sand all around, so everyone's legs are safe. There are a couple other spots where it will be easiest to pick Tank up to run the obstacle. There's a log over a mud bog, and they have another cameraperson posted there." Reaper grinned. "Choice is yours, run across with your K9 in your arms like a superhero, or fall in and make a splash for the camera. Either one should get the clicks and help the kiddos. And that's what we want."

"I'm starting to think that falling into mud is why you invited me along." Dakota was only half kidding.

Reaper grinned and clapped him on the back as he took off toward a petite blonde woman with her hand in the air and a grin on her face.

"I'll give it my best, buddy," Dakota sank to a squat next to Tank. "But since I've never tried throwing you over my shoulder to climb an eight-foot wall before, there might be a learning curve, is all I'm saying." He scritched Tank between his ears. "They do this for a living. We'll figure it out together. We have each other's backs." Dakota stood. "Be patient with me, okay? All those cameras. This is gonna be hella humbling."

"Gentlemen," Reaper called out, "gather 'round."

Dakota snatched up the duffel, and he and Tank jogged over to join the group at the back of the transport, where they stood on the edge of the pack of Cerberus shepherds.

There, Dakota spotted two labs, a blond and a black. And, unexpectedly, a mastiff named Beowolf with his handler, Nutsbe, wearing a Panther Force Tactical logo on his shirt, was running with bilateral prostheses.

Reaper raised his hands. "Thank you to all of those who came out on your day off. We're here with the best of intentions—helping kids in need. Today, we're going to be in the public eye." He pointed to a poster duct-taped to the side of the vehicle. "We want to do our best by our youngest and most vulnerable, but we still need to maintain our anonymity. You probably already found face paint in the duffels." He turned and tapped the poster. "These are the stripe patterns, positions, and color combinations that will thwart AI in recognizing your face and successfully putting you into someone's database. The dogs were entered by their race numbers. We're going to try to command them with hand signals and voice, but try not to use their names around cameras, for all the obvious security reasons."

The men nodded.

When Dakota was in the sandbox and out with K9 teams, they never used their dogs' names in public, lest someone overhear, call the dog to them, and hold a military war dog hostage. At $100,000 to get the canines operational, it would be a big financial hit. But it would be an even bigger emotional hit for the units. And should the dog be used against an allied team, well, that would just all kinds of suck.

Better to never use the dogs' names.

"All of your names were placed on the roster as your call signs. No last names." Reaper looked over at Dakota. "We haven't put you in yet. We didn't know what you went by."

"Raisin," Dakota said.

The Cerberus men turned Dakota's way with laughter in their eyes.

"Raisin," Reaper repeated. "Okay then." He tipped his head toward the transport. "Bottle of water in the back of the vehicle if you're feeling parched and need to plump yourself back up."

Laughter rippled amongst the men.

That was fine. Dakota was used to it. The guy with the mastiff was named Nutsbe because his last name was Crushed. Dakota would pick his moniker "Raisin Kayne" over "Nutsbe Crushed" any day.

"Alright, Raisin, and the rest of you. Pick a camouflage configuration from the poster. Have the guy next to you apply your war paint. Be efficient with time, put your bags back here." He pointed toward the back of the vehicle. "And then, head to the starting line. We're going to give the crowd a good show. Lots of publicity equals lots of donations. Let's give them exciting footage and make this day a win for the kids."

Hawkeye turned to him, sticks of face paint in Iniquus' gunmetal gray and royal blue in his hand. "Do you care which design?"

"Whichever you want." As Hawkeye smeared a line down the side of Dakota's nose, he thought that he should get a picture of the different patterns. He'd learned face paint for combat, but he'd done that training before AI technology made identification a touch of a computer button.

Hawkeye handed the paint sticks to Dakota so Dakota could return the favor. They flung their bags into the back, and Hawkeye looked over Dakota's harness configuration. "You're strapped in right. Your first time doing a cani-cross mud run?"

"First. I'm gathering advice."

"Move your feet as fast as you can." Hawkeye slapped him on the back, and like a school of fish, they made their way to the starting line.

Dakota moved Tank to the outside of the group, where

they might have a little extra maneuvering room, giving Dakota time to figure out how all this worked.

Tank turned his head and eyed him as if to say, "Oh, we're going for it."

A whistle blew, and a voice boomed through the bullhorn. "Heat One. Cerberus Tactical, take your places." The Malinois gathered along the start line, barking their agitation at being held back.

"We're going in THREE. TWO. ONE!"

The gun cracked the air. The crowd's cheers swelled around them.

And the Malinois were off!

2

Dakota

Sunday

Wow, this was a much bigger deal than Dakota expected.

The spectators lined up along the track and gathered in large crowds around the two challenges Dakota could see.

Tank was handling pre-race nerves pretty well. Though by nature, Tank had a kind of "prince on horseback surveilling the battlefield" demeanor. He would stand regally and look out at his subjects. But like in the monarchy of old, he liked to leap into the fray.

Dakota got it, he really did. His body was happiest when he was pushing his limits.

Which was a good thing.

Excellent, in fact.

About twenty yards from the starting line, concrete water ducts nestled side by side in a line that led to a creek bed.

Yeah, why not start from the beginning with wet shoes?

Having raced his fair share in storm conditions, Dakota had chosen running shoes made for water sports, and he'd wrapped his heels and big toes in duct tape as a potential reprieve from friction blisters. No guarantees.

As the Malinois class sprinted through the pipes, the humans had to scamper on hands and knees. Exiting, the Malinois, waiting for their handlers to get a move on, jumped from water to rock, back into the water. They looked down the tunnel, yipping at their partners, scolding them to hurry; there was fun to be had on the other end. Come on! Come on!

Dakota couldn't imagine what it was like tethered to a Malinois when they were in high gear. For that matter, Dakota had never been tethered to any dog. And this first time, with a snowplow of a K9 like Tank? Yeah, this was going to be something.

Dakota could hear the handlers, from inside the concrete pipes, calling out to their partners to sit and wait, but when a Malinois heard a gun go off, the race was afoot.

Dakota glanced down and caught Tank's gaze. "*Apaw*, if you will," he said for Tank's amusement.

Tank turned and looked at him with a single raised eyebrow.

Once the race was *apaw*, these working dogs had their adrenaline pumping, looking for the joy they got from going fast and hard.

The first Malinois teams through the cylinders were now sprinting down the creek bed as their handlers leaped rock to rock.

Dakota watched the teams' progress, trying to figure out which route looked most efficient.

Beyond that, where the trees opened up to pasture, throngs of people cheered the teams' approach. In just a moment, heat one would be out of sight.

The German shepherds were up.

The starting announcer called through the megaphone, "Second heat, take your positions!"

Dakota and Tank found their places behind the line.

"Ready? In Three. Two. One." He dropped his arm as he blew a whistle; there was no second gunshot.

The line of German shepherds charged forward, reaching the tunnels and scrabbling through.

"Here we go, buddy. In. Forward." Dakota signaled Tank as they took their turn. Tank shot through like a bullet from the barrel. Dakota dropped to a quadruped position and bear-crawled like a cartoon character as fast as he could. The cold, rough concrete scraped his back when his ass went up too high.

Tank had none of the ducking and scrambling. He raced through, stretching the bungee to its elastic limit, and now it was dragging Dakota forward from his hips. Not wanting to lose his teeth on a face plant, he, too, was calling out, "Hold."

This course and Tank's physical prowess were definitely going to humble Dakota.

Ah, to be a dog for just one day. Maybe if he gathered enough good karma points in this lifetime, he would reincarnate as a dog like Tank.

Goals.

As soon as he cleared the concrete edge, Dakota popped

to his feet and took off, leaping rock to rock on the path that he'd mind-mapped, only letting Tank have but so much freedom. Man, he wished he could cut Tank loose and meet him at the finish line.

Tank would have a much better time letting his full athleticism shine.

From Tank's point of view, this experience must be like the time Dakota ran the Thanksgiving Turkey Trot with his then-six-year-old nephew, Bo. Now, Bo did a great job, and it was a good bonding time, but Dakota spent most of the time jogging in place.

Dakota leaped just as Tank got his paws onto solid ground. The drag intensified, and for a moment, it felt like Dakota was airborne, a kite lifted by the wind. His foot hit the slope and slid right out from under him. Dakota stretched out his hands to catch his weight, and his hands slid out to either side.

Tensing his shoulder muscles to keep his hands in place, he called out. "Hold. Hold." The clay-covered hill, slick with water and churned by the first heat, proved difficult. Every time Dakota placed a foot or hand and pressed his weight into it, that limb slid out from under him. Dakota looked up the hill to find Tank staring down at him.

Dakota searched the hillside and saw that he might be able to find friction on the dappled vegetation and, with Tank's help, climb the slope like a rock wall. He gripped a tuft of grass with his fingers and found another clump of weeds for his toes. Lifting his voice, Dakota called, "Hey, buddy, go out. Go. Go."

This was either going to work, or Dakota was going to be slicked from head to foot in red clay. The benefit was that he'd be unrecognizable. Cerberus boys would be the only ones who knew about this sad performance, he thought with a chuckle.

Besides, the Labradors were at his heels. And if Rourou the Labrador puppy passed them, Dakota wasn't sure Tank would forgive him.

Dakota balanced his toes on a tiny tuft of weeds to get a modicum of traction and dragged at the few blades of grass. That, coupled with Tank's mighty pull, and Dakota got to the top, where the accomplishment was met with cheers and lots of cell phones pointed in his direction.

Raising a hand in appreciation of their clapping and encouraging calls, both Dakota and Tank rode the energy from the crowd. Dakota always ran his best times when there was excitement in the air—or danger.

Yeah, danger could get his feet moving pretty fast, too.

Tank and Dakota sprinted down the trail.

Tank was out in front of him like a husky dragging a sled across the Tundra.

Reaper had been right; Dakota was running at breakneck speed. And it felt wild in his body. He was moving at a frightening pace that demanded surrender and hyperfocus at once.

The harness seemed to wrestle gravity into submission as they flew down the hill and back up the next.

When he ran in triathlons, Dakota had a tempo that ensured he kept a steady power surge throughout the race, and he could jet across the finish line strong. He'd trained it into his body, so he had a good sense of what was required.

Did he have clue one now?

Not at all.

All he knew was that he was trying to give himself a bit of grace for doing this crazy event with zilch experience and, at the same time, have some fun while doing a good deed. That didn't mean that Dakota could shed his competitive nature. He hadn't seen another team for a while now. And Dakota was determined to catch up.

Out in front, Dakota could hear the Cerberus operators yelling their commands and saw sprays of water.

"Buddy—" Dakota tried, but it came out as a wheeze. Yeah, there was no way he was going to be able to call out commands and run full out like this. No way that he could warn Tank and talk him through this. But he reasoned that Tank had a miracle sniffer and keen hearing; he knew.

He knew, and yet he didn't let up.

Tank raced toward the deck without a break in his stride.

Maybe Halo worked through the water issues.

This looked like it was going to be fine.

Tank leaped into the air, stretching his front paws long.

He was glorious as he sailed through the air.

The bungee stretched out, dragging Dakota's hips forward, so he had no time to set up for a dive. All he could do was lift his feet and let Tank drag him forward.

But the drag stopped mid-jump, and Dakota had barely pushed off with his back leg.

He missed scraping his back down the platform edge by inches. It caught the very back of his head as he tipped, then plunged into the water.

It was deeper than Dakota thought it would be. His feet didn't touch bottom, and he was six-foot-four.

And cold.

Purple goose-fleshed cold. But he'd built his cold tolerance lying in the pounding surf on Coronado Beach, along with the other wannabe Special Warfare Combatant-craft Crewmen enduring hours in the freezing surf, monitored for hypothermia by a temperature pellet he swallowed at the start of the challenge.

But Dakota could understand Tank's wild-eyed shock of a freakout dance as his K9 dog paddled straight for him, scraping his claws against Dakota's skin as he tried to climb up onto Dakota's shoulders.

"Cold belly?" Dakota asked through a teeth-chattering grin. He would do nothing to make Tank think that this was anything other than a typical day, and he should just get on with the task.

As Halo instructed, Dakota caught hold of Tank's harness and pulled him around to point his nose in the right direction, then Dakota plunged forward, digging his hands in as he swam for the far bank.

Tank flew up the steep mud and stood shaking his coat dry as Dakota had to use the climbing web to get himself out.

His shorts clung in a way that might not prove modest in those photos folks snapped. And given how cold that plunge was, for sure, they wouldn't be flattering.

"I'll have to make up for my sad deficit with a winning personality," he told Tank as he bent to take a breath.

Tank lifted a single brow.

"Yeah, yeah," Dakota called, "I'm coming."

Though he wore running shoes that let water drain out through the holes, they didn't clean out the mud. Dakota could feel a mound of fine grains forming a pillow under his toes, throwing off his natural footfall. Those grains were between his toes and under his nails, and the whole experience felt like he was using sandpaper on his feet as tiny sharp cuts formed wherever there was shoe.

That didn't slow Tank as he followed the curving wooded trail, popping out in the next field where Dakota could see the next obstacle out in front of them, the wall.

They had a photo spot all set up and well-populated so people could ooh and ah over the feat.

"Let's get real here, buddy," Dakota huffed out. "I don't do what Cerberus does in daily training."

The crew at Cerberus made their living by going into disaster zones with their K9 partners to save and protect clients. Whether it was corporate, government, or universities, if something was going down, be it a coup or a lava flow, Cerberus would find a way in and find a way to pull their clients out. Sometimes it was a search-and-rescue, digging through volcanic ash; sometimes it was flanking a threatened diplomat and running for the bunker. They trained for everything and anything. So today's obstacle course was just another day at the office.

Dakota spent his days hunting down counterfeiters, a slightly different skill set.

He had his days when being a triathlete kept him alive on the job.

But that didn't mean he'd ever tried to carry Tank on his shoulders up and over an eight-foot wall.

That required technique.

Yeah, he was going to look like a dork on social media — but for a good cause. More clicks, more money. He was in it to win it, and the only win that mattered was money for kids.

Mojo and his handler, Levi, were just ahead. It looked simple enough.

After placing Mojo into a sit, Levi squatted beside his dog and made the call that, from where Dakota stood, sounded like "Ally-oop!"

Mojo put his paws on Levi's far shoulder.

Levi grabbed the harness buckle at the front, scooped his arm under Mojo's butt, shifting Mojo until he draped across Levi's shoulders. Fluid. Easy. Once he stood, Levi told Mojo to relax, grabbed the rope, and went up effortlessly.

"It's a nothing burger, easy peasy," Dakota told Tank as he signaled him around to sit at Dakota's side. "You trained this, right?"

Dakota squatted. He lifted his right elbow and said, "Ally-oop!"

And Tank snuck his head around to give Dakota a whole face tongue bath.

"Thanks, big man." Dakota pushed him off. "That's not what we're looking for here. Can you get up on my shoulders?"

Tank lifted his paws and tapped at him. He didn't seem to have clue one what he was supposed to do.

Dakota had Tank stand while Dakota squatted and tried to stick his head under Tank's belly, thinking he'd somehow maneuver from there.

And that was ridiculous.

Hawkeye and his K9 Cooper trotted up beside him. He put Cooper to his side, took a knee, then looked at Dakota. "The directive you're looking for is *'sur l'épaule.'*" As soon as he said it, Cooper draped himself across Hawkeye's shoulders, then Hawkeye pushed Cooper's butt until he lay balanced and steady, and then Hawkeye stood.

"French, then. Not allyoop."

"First time, right? Do you want me to lift Tank onto you?" Hawkeye asked.

"I'd like to see if we can master it before the mastiff catches up."

"Yeah, well, Beowolf's highest speed is lope." Hawkeye grinned as he reached out to grab the rope. With Cooper draped over his shoulder, Hawkeye planted his foot and started to walk the wall. Dakota watched Hawkeye's posture closely. He kept his cheek toward the wall, so his shoulders tipped slightly forward.

"Go ahead and try it out," Hawkeye called down from the top. "I'll check on you when I get down."

After a reset and the correct command, things flowed with ease.

All right, not with ease.

Tank was monster-sized, and there was a lot of fur in Dakota's face sticking to his grease paint. But Tank relaxed into the configuration, keeping his muzzle ahead of Dakota's shoulder, which helped Dakota maintain his balance.

Still, it was tippy.

"One foot, then another. Here we go. Up the wall," Dakota sang to Tank. At the top, Dakota threw his leg over and grabbed up the second line to descend. "The dogs were supposed to run around the wall, and the humans were to go over alone." He took all the weight into his arms as he swung the second leg over and positioned his feet. "Why are we climbing the wall with our K9s on our shoulders? Oh-yeah, we're big bad special forces types. Go big or go home, my man."

Dakota walked the wall back down. This time, he pulled his arms to his sides to get his head closer to the wall because it felt like Tank might slip off.

He wouldn't do this if he thought Tank could get injured. This wasn't a mission where danger was inherent.

Dakota was glad that there were broad sand pits on either side; neither of them should get hurt if push came to shove. Came to thump.

"No jumping, buddy. Trust me. We're relaxing together. Good times. We're doing this for the kiddies."

There were strategically placed knots all along the rope. Dakota wondered whether that was to help folks with the climb or to dissuade people from fast-roping down by locking their feet and sliding.

Down was down.

Dakota knelt to let Tank off his shoulders.

The wet dog muskiness that now enveloped them both would wash off in the shower. *Just look at Tank's face!* Joy filled his eyes. Tank was in his element. He took a step and turned to glance back at Dakota.

"Yup, let's get it." He and Tank took off. A little less than a sprint this time since Dakota was dealing with the weight and rub of a pillow of grit in his shoes. But still a pretty good clip.

He could at least see the distant backs of the Cerberus team.

They hit the muddy log over the water that Reaper had mentioned.

Tank was standing there, tail wagging, waiting patiently for Dakota to show up.

Yeah, Dakota was willing to make a big splash of things if he was falling over. "Let's leave it all on the field, right buddy?" But he thought with Tank's aversion to those first moments of wet belly, it would be best if Tank wasn't on his shoulders if they did take the plunge. Dakota prized his eyeballs, and he didn't want to take a panicked clawing to his face. "Hugs," Dakota said as he patted his chest.

Tank stood on his hind paws and stretched upward.

Dakota scooped under his bottom. This was a hold they'd done since he was a puppy. Tank didn't need to know a magical command to get this one in place.

Dakota had to hold Tank in one arm to keep his other hand free to help hoist himself up. Tank was only ninety pounds, but the foot placement was a bit finicky when he couldn't see over the fur ball draping across his chest.

The rounded surface of the log forced Dakota's ankles outwards, and Dakota ended up shifting Tank onto his hip like a toddler.

Tank didn't love that. He twisted this way and that, trying to see the end, anxious to have his own feet under him, drool dripping onto Dakota's ear.

As soon as they reached the end of the log, Dakota squatted so Tank could set his paws on Dakota's thigh, and he thrust off in a magnificent leap that brought cheers and whoops from the crowd.

Dakota jumped down quickly as the bungee tightened, dragging his hips forward. They'd just had a triumph; no point in slip-sliding face-first now.

Dakota had lost sight of Cerberus and was running full steam.

Tank was powering up the steep hill, up and away from the crowd.

"Not gonna lie, buddy, I'm appreciating the assist on this incline."

All in all, Daktota thought that he and Tank had given a fair showing. And he felt that as they ran the course together, learning at the same time, trust grew between them.

Yeah, today was a good day. Food for the soul.

Dakota stopped at the last obstacle of the run, a forty-pound bag of dog chow that he'd have to carry to the finish line.

In this part of the task, he and Tank were completely in sync. They often ran the park trails long, hard distances. Dakota almost forgot the bag of food draped over his shoulder as he caught up to the others.

"Oy, there you are, mate," Halo called out with a wave of his free hand. "We were afraid you got lost somewhere along the line. We were just having a chat about who would be on the search and rescue mission to go back and find you."

"Appreciate the concern," Dakota said as they passed the table one by one, where they dropped off the bag.

"No more pussy-footing around," Levi called out. "Last one across is buying the first round."

They were off, blazing across the finish line to a cheering crowd.

Dakota bent as that petite woman from the parking area stretched to place the completion medal around his neck.

"I'm Grace. You must be Raisin. Thanks so much for pitching in."

"Glad to help." Dakota huffed, then shuffled forward to be out of the path as he bent to put his hands on his knees and catch his breath.

There, Tank stared into the crowd. His whole body tensed as he focused on a man in a wheelchair with a young boy in a wheelchair to his side. The boy was waving sticks with pom poms attached to the ends. A woman with brown hair had her face turned as she watched the next wave of runners come over the hill.

Tank yipped his high-pitched, "Quick! Come look!"

The woman swiveled toward them and raised her phone to take pictures of the scene, then smiled and waved.

As the boy lifted his pompom, Tank dove forward.

"Hey, ho there, big guy," Dakota panted out. "That's not a toy, and it's not for you."

Tank took another leap forward. And this time, Dakota shifted his focus to try to understand what was enticing Tank to act this way in public. All three people in that grouping had locked eyes with Tank, and Dakota locked eyes on *her*.

Suddenly, Dakota felt oddly like there was no definition to his body. If someone were videoing him and, in the clip, he shifted from a solid to a state of floating particles, he would think that was about the right sensation.

"Oy there mate, come on," Halo called out. "We're heading back to the vehicles!" The sharp tone glued Dakota's atoms back together.

It was such an odd sensation that Dakota immediately classified it as a coincidence of focus, while his body freaked out from the heavy exertion and the succession of cold-water plunges.

Tank turned to catch Dakota's gaze and give him a stomp of dissatisfaction. "Do I smell strange to you?" Dakota asked Tank. "Low potassium? Maybe I need a banana." Dakota gathered the length of the lead, then signaled Tank to his side as he jogged toward the transport.

Tank's feet moved forward, but his gaze stayed on the family with the boy and his pompom.

When they got to the group, the men removed the harnesses and dropped them into a bag for cleaning. Then Dakota, still reeling, bent to unlace his shoes. "I mean, it was like a sci-fi movie or something. I don't think a human body is supposed to feel that way."

Tank looked up at him.

He held up his first shoe and tapped the glob of sediment onto the dirt.

"You don't think a brain-eating amoeba was floating in any of those ponds we were swimming in, do you?" he teased. "To be honest, I was out here to do a good deed, not to have my gray matter turn into Swiss cheese. You know?"

"Hey, you okay?" Hawkeye asked, sitting on the tarp, to peel off his mud-covered shoes. "You look a little shell-shocked."

Dakota rubbed a hand over his heart. "Yeah, don't know. This is a new sensation for me."

3

———

Dakota

Monday

Monday morning, Dakota stepped out of his cab at the Bureau of Engraving and Printing on 14th Street, slid his tie neatly in place, then buttoned his navy-blue jacket.

Dakota found that when he calculated the time and money he spent looking for and then paying for parking, it was a better deal to take a cab.

That, and hailing a cab with his phone slipped into the Faraday sleeve in his briefcase, helped to keep Dakota's movements out of someone's database.

Honestly? While his department did a lot with geo-tracking to hunt the bad guys, it was equally simple and becoming more accessible for the bad guys to find and pinpoint those who were trying to stop them.

The risk of doing his job grew exponentially year over year.

And from that risk, recruitment became more difficult for the various alphabets, as agents knew how easily their families could become targets of a warning or retribution.

Dakota would admit that he weighed that risk into his relationship calculus. As a result, he played the field and didn't commit to exclusivity. Some of that was because he traveled for long periods where he had to be no-contact, some of that was to keep the women safe so there was no bull's eye pinned to their back, but part of it was also that Dakota had not yet met the woman who made him feel like he could say, "Yes, I'll change to a desk job so that none of my professional baggage will hurt you."

Ideas like that had been circulating in his system since yesterday's race, which probably had something to do with his date with Rose today.

Dragging his phone from the bag and checking for calls, Dakota considered Rose for a moment. While Dakota had been in Colombia, he'd realized she never really came to mind. And when they were out together, their conversations were becoming strained. Smart lady, quick-witted, and funny, she also had a solid wall up, and that might have the texture of guilt on its surface. Maybe she was already seeing someone else, where it clicked, and she started to feel she wanted to focus her attention elsewhere. Good for her. He'd broach the topic with her at lunch and see what she wanted to do.

As he walked down the sidewalk, Dakota was grateful that this crap weather had held off an extra day. While Mondays were always a slug when they were cold and gray, yesterday's race would have seen fewer spectators if the sky had been spitting sleet.

The icy drizzle started with pings on his nose and in his hair. Not enough to pop his umbrella, but since the damp would make his wool suit smell like a wet dog, he did it anyway.

He strode past the line of tourists waiting to take a tour of the printing presses and the sheets of true-blue—well, green—currency rolling off the line.

Dollah, dollah bills, y'all.

It was rare for him to show up in these offices. Dakota was usually out in the field hunting down international counterfeiters, mainly working out of Colombia and Peru, where most of the U.S. counterfeit dollars originated.

Interestingly, he'd come across fifty- and hundred-dollar bills coming out of a state-sponsored program in North Korea. There, the currency was near perfection. Those North Korean bills were almost indistinguishable from real U.S. currency, even by currency machines. Though they couldn't fake their way past a counterfeit-scent sniffing K9, right now, the Secret Service's primary defense. Stopping North Korea wasn't something the Secret Service had figured out how to do yet, so they didn't talk about it much. Or at all.

For security reasons, when Dakota worked in states across the U.S., he often borrowed space at a field office. But he liked to steer clear of them as much as possible. The human brain is an amazing thing. It could make subtle adjustments to how a person dressed, spoke, or moved their body to meld with the institution. It was a survival technique.

At his first job for Uncle Sam, working for the Navy, Dakota learned to pay attention to the minutiae of local norms so his brain could translate local gestures into his own body language, helping him blend in. And if that didn't work—if Dakota didn't come off like a local—well, it gave his body such a wide-ranging body language accent (for lack of better term) that he'd be viewed as a mutt, and not say a member of the elite forces trained to a specific gait and posture by the United States Department of Defense.

But here he was right in the belly of the beast, Dakota dragged the door open and turned to shake his umbrella and collapse it.

Today, it was time to check in with one of Dakota's oldest and closest friends, Jasper Lee. They'd been buds since grade school. Their life paths had lined up in parallel and eventually landed them in basically the same job. The wool suits they wore were a long way from the BDU, sand-covered torture of Coronado.

Dakota badged himself through the side door and headed right for the elevators, stepping into a mostly-filled car just as the doors were sliding shut.

Since his jog had lasted longer than usual that morning, Dakota had missed breakfast, and he hoped there would be a hot pot of coffee when he reached Jasper's office.

Yeah, yesterday had disabused Dakota of his ideas about how fit he was. He'd thought he was in pretty good shape. He'd even looked into signing up for the Iron Man this year. But since he had to use the afterburners to keep up with the Cerberus operators yesterday, Dakota thought that maybe his racing contests weren't pushing him hard enough.

He needed stiffer competition.

Dakota wasn't going to consider that maybe the problem

with keeping up stemmed from celebrating his fortieth birthday in Colombia.

There were men still playing in the NFL who were over forty—the Steelers, the Bills, the Broncos.

Forty was young.

Dakota still had some hills to climb before he was looking over the top at the valley below.

He was good.

Maybe part of the problem was that while Tank was training with Cerberus, Dakota had been working out of Colombia and had been running solo.

When Tank finished up his certification with Cerberus Tactical, he would whip Dakota's butt into shape. Dakota would ask Reaper for Tank's training protocol and replicate it as best he could while still holding down his job. After all, training and deploying was Cerberus's day-to-day, right?

As the elevator dinged the sixth floor, Dakota stepped through the sliding doors and turned down the short end of the hall.

At the end of the corridor, Dakota tapped at the open door and lifted a hand in salute, "Jasper." Turning, Dakota found another colleague sprawled in a side chair. "Benny, good to see you, man." Dakota dropped his wet umbrella by the wastebasket, then extended his hand for a shake.

"I brought the office a present." Benny slid his hand through the air to showcase three hundred-dollar bills, resting on the surface of Jasper's scarred desk.

Dakota bent to inspect the bills. "These are seriously good," he murmured to himself.

Jasper reached into his bottom drawer, pulled out a white box of nitrile gloves, and dropped it onto his desk.

Dakota plucked out a pair so he could pick up the specimen without adding his fingerprints.

When he snapped them on, they covered his fingers and half his palm.

Jasper was five feet five and had proportionately sized hands. That wasn't to say that Jasper wasn't a powerhouse. He was the wiry, sinewy type of guy that filled out most of the U.S. special forces—the kind that were like self-winding clocks that never run out of go-juice. And frankly, there were some tight spots—both physical and metaphorical— where a smaller size than Dakota's basketball player's frame (and shoe size) would have been helpful.

The gloves weren't going to work.

"Nah, you don't need those," Benny laughed. "I have stacks of these samples. You need to feel them, anyway, to see how clever they are."

Dakota stripped the gloves off and tossed them into the garbage. "Where'd these bills come in from?" He picked up a specimen and held it to a light. He slid his thumbnail over Franklin's shirt and felt the bump. He focused on the crispness and the hand feel. "Yeah, real artistry here. Are these samples from North Korea?"

"Florida," Benny said, leaning forward. "The gal was a fine arts student who got tired of living in her van. She's detail-oriented and a true craftswoman for sure. She spent her summer vacation traveling around the United States, big city to big city, printing those off in a hotel room."

"Printed. Like off a basic office printer?" Jasper asked. "That's impossible. How did she get past the internal security that she could print that?"

"Layers. This gal sent them through over and over and over again. Each time, she layered a different file. She said they learned a lot of these techniques in her art classes. She was replicating a piece of art, and it wasn't that tough to figure out."

"So she'd like to run off a stack of say border and eyebrows, and then fill the tray with the printed pieces to send through to pick up lips and a number?" Dakota pulled the chair out to form a circle with his colleagues.

"Exactly," Benny said, then grimaced. "She said it was like doing layered gel printing, whatever the hell that is."

Dakota bent the bill back and forth. "The paper has a good feel. If I wasn't looking for it, I'd say it's just right."

"She glued two layers of Bible paper together. That's part of the reason she was in a hotel. Nice hotels too, since she was traveling as a single female, right? So she said she was worried about staying in one place too long because she was sure the Secret Service would be beating the bushes." He sent Jasper a wink.

"Which you were," Jasper said.

"Second, she needed to bribe the maids to let her buy their boxes of Bibles, so she could cut the blank pages out, then she'd leave the Bibles in the supply closet."

"No one figured it out?" Jasper asked.

"Why the Bibles?" Dakota asked.

"She could only buy that paper in large lots, and she didn't want anyone to be able to track the delivery to her. And she could bribe the maids with counterfeit money, so she wasn't losing anything. And, she left the Bibles behind when she was done. No one would get what that was all about."

Benny twisted his face into a grin. "Genius, that woman is a mad genius."

"There must have been a chemical stench, though," Dakota picked up a bill and sniffed it. "This doesn't smell right. It's actually pretty bad." He coughed into his elbow. "Yeah, that's really bad." He sniffed hard and put the bill down.

"How did you figure it all out?" Jasper asked.

"She got into it with a local drug dealer who somehow figured out his client was trying to pay in counterfeit money. He used the client to track back to the gal. They had words. She said she was leaving the state and not coming back. But the cops picked up the dealer that night, and he needed something to trade with the DA."

"Counterfeiter," Dakota said.

"Counterfeiter," Benny said. "It was a good trade." Benny leaned forward, picked up one of the bills, and waved it in the air. "She's teaching us her craft. Fascinating gal. Really dedicated to detail and out-of-the-box ways of getting things right so that all the normal warning bells never went off."

"Out-of-the-box for us, but she's learning all the tips and tricks in her undergrad." Dakota put the bill back on the desk and dropped into a chair. "What did you trade for these lessons?"

"We tell the judge she cooperated," Benny said.

Jasper leaned back in his chair with a grunt. "That'll shave off some years in the clink."

"Yeah," Benny reached up and rubbed his shoulder, "she'll get just enough to learn a new unlawful trade for when she gets out."

"I don't know, maybe she'll go legit." Dakota unbuttoned his jacket and leaned forward. "I mean, this is primo work. She's a smart woman. She has to be tenacious as hell, creative, clever."

"And she has a boyfriend who's equal parts surprised and angry as hell, but also proud of how far she got because that's, and I quote here, 'just nuts, like something from a movie.' It looks like he's the keeper kind and will be sticking this out. Hey," Benny focused on Dakota, "speaking of sticking it out, I hear you're about to head out with a new partner."

"Tank?" Dakota asked.

"How'd you come up with the idea of a counterfeit sniffing dog?" Benny asked.

"Chemical scent certified, you mean. Tank needed a job, and he has a stellar sniffer. Cerberus trained him to know what a minted U.S. bill smells like, and then he's been trained to find what they're using out of South America, the kinds of ink and finishing chemicals that we've collected from the raids and from the sample bills."

"North Korea?" Benny asked.

"Tank can't do that. I haven't been given any specimens." Dakota reached up to scratch his nail over his brow. "And I'm not sure where we'd look for them."

"How close is he to finishing up?" Jasper asked.

Dakota turned. "All but done. Reaper Hamilton, the lead trainer over at Cerberus, wanted to observe Tank and me in the field. So far, he's been doing simulations. Of course, a lot of those are trained on-site—banks, airports, shops. He's had some hits, but those were planted for Tank to find.

Reaper would like Tank out doing a real-world mission so that he can observe and correct."

"All right," Jasper said. "I'll take a look around and see if I can't get something lined up. But you know, these things spring out of nowhere. Timing might be an issue."

Dakota wrinkled his brow as he peered over at Benny. "Hey, you feeling okay?"

"Yeah, why?" Benny panted.

"I don't know." Dakota shook his head. "You just—your face went gray. You don't look your usual self."

"Heartburn." Benny pressed his knuckles into his sternum. "It's been three days of this damned heartburn."

"You think you should see a doctor?" Jasper asked. "I mean, your age and all," he said it like a joke. He wasn't pointing fingers or causing alarm, just planting a seed. "Dakota, you're seeing that nurse around the corner. Maybe she could slip Benny here into her roster today."

Benny lifted his hand to bat the idea away. "I've got my own doctor. If this doesn't go away by tomorrow, I'll give him a call. I'm a shit cook, and if I sent myself to the clinic every time I gave myself indigestion, I couldn't afford to keep up with the co-pays." He turned to Dakota. "A nurse, huh?"

"Rose. She's great, she really is. The timing's off on anything happening there."

"Why's that?" Jasper asked. "I mean, if nothing else, it's convenient that she works about a ten-minute walk from here. You don't have to fight traffic if you're meeting up for lunch or whatever."

Dakota checked his watch. "Speaking of which, I need to

get out of here by noon. Rose and I are taking advantage of that convenience and grabbing a bite to eat."

"See? Convenience in the city is half the battle," Benny said.

"But only half. She's a single mom." Dakota shrugged off his suit jacket, which had grown too warm in the tight space, folded it, and twisted to lay it across the back of his chair. Maybe the heat was why Benny looked sweaty. "She has young kids. Preschoolers. They're her main focus. Rightly so. It makes scheduling much outside of the occasional lunch difficult."

"You like the kids?" Benny asked.

"Neither one of us is comfortable with my meeting them, what with where our relationship stands. Right now, we're keeping each other company. Nothing big."

"Good guy here," Benny smacked his hand on Jasper's desk. "He's got his priorities lined up right."

Dakota shifted his focus to Jasper. "Right now, my priority is to get out there with Tank, let him get some on-the-job training, get his nose certified, and get out in the field."

"Turn you into a pair of mock pirates," Benny chuckled.

"How's that?" Jasper asked.

"Sending them off looking for fool's gold."

4

———

Rylee
Monday

The doctor's office was freezing cold.

Yes, it was March, and while one day smelled like spring and felt warm with burgeoning hope, the next smelled like a snowstorm was ice skating down from the north.

Yesterday, Washington, D.C., was glorious. Today? Not so much.

Rylee Jones had dressed appropriately for the ice-spitting drizzle. But here in the doctor's exam room, she sat as requested: stripped down to her underwear, a pink napkin of a "modesty garment" stiffly resting on her shoulders and wrapping her torso, sitting on the padded table, her bare legs dangling from the side. Honestly, the rooms should be warm enough to keep the patients' toes from turning purple and skin from stippling with goose bumps.

And, if nothing else, the doctor should be heading through the door to make the discomfort short-lived.

But no.

Rylee had been shivering for forty-five minutes now.

With her coat hanging up in the lobby, Rylee had resorted to draping her sweater dress over her legs and was deciding whether to go ahead and pull it over her head and run out real quick to grab her coat.

Honestly, the warmest Rylee had been was during this morning's trek from her office at WorldCares, where she'd parked her car, to the medical building. Though outside the ice was pinging, it was probably warmer than this icebox of a room.

Rylee was in a bad mood and grousing. The cold room was simply an easy reason to vent frustration. And if she ran out to get the coat at the same time the doctor popped in, she'd probably miss her opportunity to be seen and have to set a new appointment and go through this all again.

"Suck it up," she chided herself. "Power through." After all, Rylee had been through colder and for longer.

The determined conquered the day.

Turning to her phone, Rylee sank herself into a good doom scroll, immersing herself in a post from the Muddy K9 Charity Run she'd gone to with her dad and foster brother the day before. Videos of the athletes and their dogs streaking by took her attention from a clock that seemed as frozen as the tip of her nose.

When the tap finally sounded at the door, Rylee had been in her shiver-clench so long that her "Come in" was a staccato ratatat she forced through chattering teeth.

"I'm Rose, Dr. Blanch's nurse." Rose wore a turtleneck

and a thick fleece sweatshirt with the clinic's logo. Her hands still looked stiff with cold.

"It's ffff-rrr-eezing," Rylee said, because there should be some conversation about a patient's comfort. Unless, of course, they were trying to dissuade patients from coming in.

"The doctor's running a bit behind. I'll try to get you out of here fast. Can you tell me what's going on for you today?"

Rylee reached for the spreadsheet she'd prepared and was lying beside her. On it, Rylee had listed all the data points that had come up in the last couple of years from previous medical appointments with an ever-growing list of doctors who shrugged and walked away.

Every time she got a new question, she added another category to the printout: her exercise regimen, nutrition pattern, years of blood work, her symptoms, their frequency, their impact on her day-to-day life, her family history of Multiple Sclerosis, the family members' ages of onset and diagnosis, and their current level of disability.

Rose sat down with the papers and scanned them over. "Right now, you're experiencing tingling?"

"Toes and fingers."

Rose looked up. "And it feels like?"

"Like my hands and feet have started to go to sleep, and with some movement I could get the blood flow going again," Rylee said.

Rose nodded, "But you can't?"

"No."

Rose turned the page. "Not a vegan? So not a B12 deficit."

"I eat a high-protein diet because I lift heavy. The

protein comes from animals, and I take sublingual B12 daily. The B12 labs on the third page, you can see it's high normal range."

Rose turned to that page. "These are past labs, and your A1C is normal, so you're not experiencing diabetic neuropathy." She glanced up. "Have you ever been diabetic?"

"I've always had stable glucose numbers. So no, this isn't diabetic neuropathy."

"Ever hit your head?"

"No, ma'am. I have been on battlefields as a medic, so I was around blast concussions. But when I was with the Navy, I had an MRI to check for damage, and I was okay."

"How long ago was that MRI?"

"Twelve—no, thirteen years ago." Rylee lifted her thigh to unstick from the paper table liner so she could shift into a new position. "Up until the last doctor I tried, I was told these sensations were all in my head and that I should get a hobby that flexes my fingers. Have I considered taking up knitting? Apparently, if I'd move my fingers, it would make my toes stop tingling."

Rose held a blank face. "And the last one?"

"Told me that I probably have a pinched nerve, and I might consider chiropractic."

"Have you considered that?" Rose asked.

"No. Not my thing to get crunched around." Rylee lifted her hand and spread her fingers. "Each to their own. But I did go to a physiotherapist, and she did what she could for me."

"Helpful?"

"She concluded that none of my nerves were pinched." Rylee's physio had worked hard, trying all the tricks from acupuncture to infrared, from stretches to exercises, to massage. If it was in her care bag and could be dragged out and tried, it had been. But Rylee got no relief, and the therapist was genuinely concerned when Rylee couldn't move the needle. "She sent me to yet another doctor."

"And who was that?" Rose asked.

"Here, today. My physio said I should try Dr. Blanch, as he was good at figuring out difficult cases. She called them zebras. That and my office is a block away, so if I were working with Dr. Blanch, it would be convenient." Rylee adjusted her grip on the pink napkin top to make sure she wasn't flashing Rose. The paper had started to rip. "I don't think this is a case of me being a zebra in a herd of horses, what with my family history of MS and all." Rylee looked directly into Rose's eyes and said clearly, "I need to go through the diagnostic assessments for Multiple Sclerosis. I'd like to start that process."

Rose nodded. "This is very thorough and answers the questions I'd ask. You've been to a lot of doctors about this?"

"A lot. Yes."

"And what have they done?" Rose asked as she flipped the papers back to the front page and dropped her arm, letting the papers dangle by her side.

"Until the last doctor, they offered me anxiety medications because they said that my breathing was too shallow, possibly too fast. But I think my breathing is fine."

"Just sit comfortably. I'm going to count your breaths as I take your pulse."

It was hard for Rylee to breathe normally with her body shivering.

"Eleven." Rose put the pages on the exam table and

pulled out a pad, writing that number down. "That's athletic. You were breathing normally?"

"Page two," Rylee said.

A glance at page two, and Rose nodded, "Yes, good job on your dedication to exercising." She slid the pad and pen away and gathered the papers.

Rose lifted Rylee's document. "I'm going to scan these into your file, and I'll share this with Dr. Blanch. He should be in in a minute to see you."

As Rylee said thank you, Rose stood, tight-lipped and worried. She gave Rylee a nod and left.

Alone again, with nothing but a poster of the muscular system and a painting of a duck to look at, Rylee was once again aware of just how cold that room was. She turned her phone over and looked at the time.

An hour late.

The nurse's name was Rose. It was an unusual name. It was Rylee's middle name, Rylee Rose, because her mother liked poetry and letter sounds that repeated. Rylee Rose Jones. Five letters, four letters, five letters made her mother happy with the symmetry and pattern. And if her mother was happy, her father was happy, so he signed off on it.

Rylee was fine with it. It was a good enough name.

But the fact that her nurse was named Rose, too, had to be a good omen.

The delay and the inhospitable conditions were making her angry. Wasn't this what detectives did to people accused of a crime? They put the defendant into an extra-cold room to heighten their survival instincts and make them want to lash out? It was a tactic that included isolation, anxiety, and power imbalance. All of that might mean the defendant had less control over their emotions and their tongue. The same felt like it could apply here, but Rylee needed to keep a tight rein. So Rylee spent the next few minutes trying to convince herself that this boded well.

She couldn't account for the temperature of the room, but surely the delay in care meant that Dr. Blanch was thorough and listened carefully to his patients. Once he got to Rylee, he'd weigh her experiences and symptoms, and she'd start moving through the process of getting a proper diagnosis. A clear yes or no on MS was the most important. She needed it physically so she could start the meds that would slow progression, and to allow her to apply for the various drug trials she'd been researching for her next steps.

Rylee also needed it for her psychological health.

The medical gaslighting was an exhausting mental load.

It was embarrassing.

It was demeaning.

Frustrating.

Yes, Rylee was frustrated.

There was a tap at the door, and after Rylee called out, Rose came into the room, handed Rylee back her spreadsheets, and moved to stand by the counter, blank-faced.

Well, that didn't bode well.

Rylee turned to find a jowly man with reddish skin and orange-ish hair, dressed in a white lab coat with a stethoscope thrust into his pocket.

"I'm Dr. Blanch." He stood in the doorway, one foot in the room and one foot in the hallway, with the door pulled up to his rounded belly to shield Rylee—clutching her pink napkin shirt closed over her boobs—from anyone passing in the hallway. "You're here about a tingling sensation. Have you considered that this could just be where you are in your cycle?" Dr. Blanch asked. He retained his position as far away as he could be from Rylee, leaving a hand resting on the doorknob.

Rylee blinked at him. "My cycle?"

"Hormones and anxiety. Have you tried yoga and meditation?" He asked with his furry eyebrows lifted high.

"Yoga?" Rylee pronounced slowly as she shook her head with incredulity. "I have a family history of MS, three generations on my father's side." Rylee lifted her spreadsheets and thrust them at the doctor.

"Do you want some medication?" He dropped his eyebrows in confusion.

Rylee leaned forward and focused on the man with a look she used when she needed things done. "For what exactly?" The words were a hard-edged cudgel.

"Anxiety." He shifted his focus to the nurse. "Rose, figure out which one she wants, and we'll put it through." He turned back to Rylee. "You should try one of the meditation apps on your phone. Learn to breathe deeper." His fingers lifted from the doorknob he'd been grasping, and he used the flat of his hand to show Rylee how to breathe in and out. "You'll be alright," he assured her in a warm paternal voice.

And he walked out the door.

Walked right out the door.

Rylee blinked; her mind had gone blank.

The nurse said something, but Rylee just let her jaw go slack. It hung there, gaping in her astonishment. Rylee had felt so good about today, so hopeful. Years of doctors dismissing her concerns were about to be over. "Rylee?" Rose called more firmly.

Rylee turned to the woman and raised a finger. "I swear to god if you ask me which anxiety drug I want, I'm going to get loud and obnoxious."

"No, ma'am. I'm not." She pulled her notepad from her pocket and leaned over to write on the same page that held her breath count from earlier. "I'm giving you the name of a friend of mine who went through nursing school with me. She's now a PA for a neurologist. This is the office phone number and the name of the group. That second name is me. Tell her I gave you the number and that you need to be seen as soon as there's an opening. Leave a message on her voicemail. And let her know you were diagnosed with 'anxiety.' She'll make you a priority."

"A woman?" Rylee reached out for the slip of paper and turned it to see fat letters printed neatly in blue ink.

"Yes." Rose slid the pad and pen back into her pocket.

Rylee fluttered the paper. "Thank you."

"I hope you get the answers you deserve." She walked to the door and, in a voice Rylee could barely hear, Rose said, "My kids are in daycare next door. That's why I work here," then left, slicking the door closed behind her.

Rylee jumped down from the table, balled up the pink paper, and shoved it in the waste bin.

She sat down and started gathering her fleece-lined leggings with fingers that were warming with her anger.

Yes, Rylee understood that doctors knew very little about female bodies. Researchers were only required to include women in their medical studies since the mid-nineties. Mice models didn't include female mice until the NIH mandated it in 2015. That meant that when the meds were tested on human females in drug trials, they had previously only been tested in male animal studies. "Here you go, ladies, we have no idea how this will impact your cute little XX chromosomes, but surely not so different from an XY, hey? We're pretty sure it'll be good for the guys, and yeah, you never know, you might get some benefit."

It was bad to have a female body in today's global medical landscape.

Only recently had doctors acknowledged that women had nerve endings on their cervix and needed pain meds for surgeries down there. Though, honestly, doctors still needed prodding to issue the prescription.

Yep, in the world of anatomy, women's bodies were under-researched, and treatment was most likely a blindfolded dart throw. Everything from agreeing that women felt pain and should be given pain medications to men receiving their diagnosis many years before a woman would —more than two years earlier in cancer diagnoses, almost five years earlier for metabolic diseases.

She got that women were medically second-class citizens. Every woman Rylee knew got it.

But come on! She had a family history. She wasn't looking for them to pull the answer out of their asses; she was simply asking if they believed her when she said she was experiencing unaccounted for symptoms, and then to follow up with diagnostics.

Still, no. Instead, Rylee had found in her clinical notes that "WW" had been added to her presentation of "clean and appropriately communicative." Rylee had asked her gyno what it meant when that was written down. Her gyno had scowled, "Who did that?"

"Not you. But others."

"It means 'whiney woman'. It means that you went to the appointment complaining for no reason other than you wanted attention."

"People do that?" Rylee was genuinely confused. She would never put herself through the ice-box offices and indignity of the pink napkin unless she genuinely needed help.

And here she was again, the WW.

Yoga. Yep, that should fix things right up.

Rylee dragged on her tights, reached for her dress, and wrestled it over her head. Slipping her feet into her flats, she grabbed up her phone and purse, then scanned the room to make sure that, in her seething fury, she wasn't leaving anything behind.

Because she never wanted to see this place again. Ever.

5

———————

DAKOTA
Monday

DAKOTA PUSHED through the ground-floor door of his office building and back out into the blustery gray day. A glance skyward told him he could leave his umbrella in the messenger bag, hanging crossbody, but he turned up the collar of his suit and hunched against the wind, his hands shoved into his pants pockets.

It smelled like snow.

Benny was right; if anything was in the cards for a lasting relationship between him and Rose, this ten-minute walk would have been hugely convenient. He'd let her know at lunch that they needed some quiet time on the phone to talk things through privately. He wouldn't bring it up over a public lunch or mid-way through her hectic day.

Rose should finish up with her last patient and take the elevator down to meet him out front in the next few minutes. She only had half an hour to grab a bite, so they agreed to hit the place they'd gone a time or two, a little deli around the corner on the same block as her medical building. Since every eating joint was packed this time of day, Dakota had called in an order that morning for the same sandwich combo Rose had last time. If she wanted that today, that call saved them time. If she was in the mood for something else, he'd take that order home and eat it for dinner; fewer dishes to wash. Win-win.

The lunchtime rush filled the streets with jostling, impatient cars, riding bumper to bumper. Dakota's gaze searched through their windshields, taking in all the cameras posted on the front dashboards. Then he turned and scanned the street. How many cameras could he count along this short route?

Dakota had a new concern that had niggled at him since yesterday's race. When Iniquus put protocols in place, they were there for good reasons. That Iniquus had worked out the exact stripe configurations and grease paint colors required to thwart AI recognition meant they'd put resources into a threat.

He had his own criteria for keeping himself safe. He'd used it effectively for over a decade.

Technologies were constantly advancing.

Working in the sphere of counterfeit money, he didn't need a savvy criminal with the ability to print ungodly amounts of money to pay someone to look up their new contact and find Dakota's smiling, (probably) mud-covered face and his real name and home address.

Things were changing fast.

Dakota would have to ask Reaper what minimum

actions he could take to mess up AI recognition. On his cell phone, the security on the facial identification seemed to hold. It didn't open for Dakota's cousin, who, according to his grandma, was Dakota's "spitting image." It didn't even recognize Dakota if he contorted his face with laughter or a grimace—the grimace one turned out pretty bad the last time he tried to make an emergency call with a dislocated shoulder.

While Dakota raced under his given name in his triathlon competitions, his face was usually screwed up with exertion or distorted by goggles or sunglasses. Before the hospital charity run, he hadn't put it together with the danger this posed for him.

Yeah, if Iniquus was taking the precaution of war paint in public, he'd have to up his survival game.

In the field, Dakota worked under pseudonyms. The idea that those aliases could be pulled up on some kind of sheet and the touch of a bad guy's finger on the enter key: Here is Dakota Ryan Kayne AKA and his list of work names. Yeah, it wasn't quite a gun to his head, but it was a pistol wagging in his general direction.

What would cartels do to Dakota if they could figure out his job title?

So far, he hadn't needed to utilize his SERE—survive, evade, resist, escape—training, and he certainly didn't want to land in anyone's cabin far enough away that no one could hear his screams.

Just last week, he and Jasper had been talking about the short-sightedness of Uncle Sam contracting with a privately owned security network to provide a nationwide surveillance system that could track anyone, anywhere in the United States by linking house cams, street cams, toll cams, and phone pings.

Texas police recently tracked a woman seeking a legal abortion in another state using over eighty thousand automated license plate readers as they tracked her state-to-state, even in states where tracking women seeking abortions was illegal.

Interestingly, a young woman disappeared in Texas, and the family filed a missing person's report. The surveillance systems were not used to find her. They simply asked neighbors to check their doorbell cameras and see if they picked up anything.

Different circumstances, sure, and in that case, the lack of a license plate was probably the missing link.

But that was what Dakota and Jasper debated the other evening: Who decided which cases got the full capacity of the system for good or for bad? Unfortunately, men in law enforcement had a sky-high rate of domestic abuse. And there was also a strong brotherhood that closed ranks to protect their own.

Police officers went largely unpoliced.

How easy would it be for powerful people to make a phone call and abuse the system—politicians with an eye to punishing their enemies, the monied wanting to manipulate the market?

The federal law enforcement now had a contract with two private companies that could digitally lasso an area and track anyone's phone from home to work to the shop to the gym. The surveillance was conducted without even a nod to Fourth Amendment rights and without a warrant.

It was also predictive.

So, if you got on the wrong side of the wrong guy and they had X amount of money to give to the private business, the bad guy could get a literal roadmap to where the subject would be and when.

And that's why Dakota used a burner that he changed out monthly and slipped his phone in a Faraday bag as often as possible.

It wasn't paranoia; it was self-preservation.

And Dakota thought the surveillance state in China was bad.

In China, surveillance was state-owned and used by the government.

In the United States, the fact that a private company ran the system meant that data on every citizen could be bought and sold to the highest bidder and fed into algorithms to manipulate and target.

Would the data centers only sell to other Americans or to American companies? Or was this data available on the international market?

Already, data collection had gotten so bad that grocery stores could predict what a given person would be willing to pay for any item and raise the price for that person. Three different people in the same store at the same time could see three different prices on a carton of eggs.

Dakota was pretty sure that didn't happen with citizens' data in China.

He wanted to keep himself out of the engines as much as possible, and it was getting harder and harder. It meant using burner phones for the most part, with only a household and an office number that remained constant. It was a whole lot of hoop-jumping, baseball-cap-wearing, and mirrored aviator glasses that covered much of his facial bone structure.

His phone rang, "Dakota here. What's up, Jasper? Miss me already?"

"Yeah, my heart aches," Jasper deadpanned. "Are you private right now?"

Dakota chuckled. "I was just wondering if I will even be private again. I'm walking to Rose's work. Why? What have you got?"

"Two things. I might call you in a minute. I was talking to Kumar about Tank to see if he had anything you could use to get him real-world experience. He said there's a charitable group of first responders coming in from the Colombian landslide. Since that's a vector for counterfeit, and since we've been seeing an uptick in counterfeit U.S. dollars in global disaster spots, he's working on getting search warrants together so he can look at any cash they've got on them. I told Kumar I wanted to come along and loop you in so we can test Tank's snoot. He said no problem. We need to wait on the judge's signature, then it's a go."

"What are you thinking?" Dakota asked.

"We stand to the side as the passengers walk by one at a time. If there are any hits, Kumar takes control of them. Then you and I go down to the luggage. You and Tank sniff the bags as they come off the conveyor. I take control of those that Tank indicates on. The rest head on through customs. We take anyone with a suspicious scent to a little room and do a search. Even if Tank doesn't get a hit, Kumar's going to signal to customs that we need to search the group."

"When is this?" Dakota asked.

"I need to get more details."

"I'm game," Dakota said. "Once we have a plan, I'll call over to Cerberus to check in. Tank is training today."

"In the meantime, your target's in the paper. The Colombian police took him into custody. Well done. I'm sending you the article. Read it, then give me a call."

Dakota's text pinged with a link, and Dakota stepped out of the path to lean against a bare-branched tree as he read that the attorney general's office in Colombia had arrested Carlos Diaz, the leader of a transnational counterfeiting group. This was the guy Dakota had been after for years, gathering data and evidence, and on that last trip to Colombia, he'd handed it all over to the government, hoping protection schemes wouldn't make it all disappear.

Since Diaz had been seeding their fake money in Colombia, Ecuador, and the U.S., Dakota had sent the same information to Ecuador as a back stop to the kind of corruption that exists to some degree in governments worldwide.

Dakota wished they could extradite Diaz to the U.S. and try him in American courts, but it was always easiest if the country of origin charged first, and the guy went through their system.

Dakota rang Jasper back. "Damn, they seized fifty plates, three machines, over a million in counterfeit bills, and they cut off the head of the chicken, leaving the group leaderless."

"A good day. If the airport doesn't pan out, you're back in the office?" Jasper asked.

"Yeah, right after lunch. We're just going to the deli down the way. You want me to bring you something back?"

"Me? I'm good. I brought my lunch. I'm putting you on speaker phone. Benny, hey, Dakota's grabbing a bite at the deli. You want something?"

"Nah, this heartburn's still terrible. I'll be drinking the pink bottle for lunch. It's my fault for all the pizza. I was watching basketball and got overexcited. Sometimes you gotta pay the fiddler."

"All right. Just text if you guys change your mind. Out." Dakota checked the time and slid his phone into his pocket, picking up the pace to make sure Rose wasn't waiting in the cold.

Arriving at Rose's building, he moved to the alcove out of the wind and waited between the medical office and the florists. In the window, beautiful bouquets were on display. Considering them, Dakota wondered if he should buy one for Rose. She'd been in a funk this last week, and flowers might cheer her up. The roses would be a no-go. Rose hated roses; every man in her life leaned into the play on her name, and she announced straight off that she thought that was low-energy and lacked creativity or a sign of genuine interest.

Noted.

But the bouquet next to the roses was tropical and unusual, with bright, upbeat colors. Maybe those?

His cell rang again. And he put his phone to his ear. "Yeah, man. You change your mind about lunch?"

"Kumar's back with the search warrant in hand." Jasper's voice rang with excitement. "The search covers anyone on the flight, but our target is WorldCares."

"They have their directors' suite up right up the street near Lafayette. That's convenient if there's an investigation."

"And who doesn't love convenience? They've got their team coming in on a direct flight, landing at two, but it looks like they're delayed an hour. Can you get Tank and get in place? I'll meet you over there."

"WorldCares. We need to tread lightly, there. They're an internationally renowned, a world leader in disaster relief with an impeccable reputation," Dakota said. "They have tight control over their accounting. I guarantee it. And we need to make sure we're not somehow getting them bad press."

"I'm not accusing them of anything. We don't suspect the WorldCares workers. We're simply trying to prove a theory. Kumar has the search warrants in case our 'please' and 'thank you' aren't enough for those folks."

"Putting pins into a corkboard?"

"Exactly," Jasper said. "Kumar's tracking natural disasters, and which NGOs," Jasper used the acronym for non-profit organizations that operated independently from the government, "might have come into contact with counterfeit bills. It's worth a look-see. And you said you needed a real-world field operation for Tank. That's what I came up with. I agree with you. There's little chance Tank will get a hit. But it's something."

"Appreciate it. We'd need to be there in advance, so meet by two?" Dakota asked. "Now that I have the time frame, I'll call over to Cerberus and see if that works on their end. Reaper wants to come along and observe to refine my techniques."

"Give him a call. With or without Tank, I want you there too. You have the best eye for Colombian-produced counterfeit currency."

"Yup. I'm on it. Text me a meet-up site, and I'll catch up with you there." Dakota pressed the button to end the call and looked up at the office building.

Rose was late.

His next call was to Reaper, who was jazzed about the idea of a real-world scenario and was en route.

Dakota checked the time. He could have a quick meal, explain that duty called, take a cab to his condo, get his car, and head to the airport.

Could he do it all? Calculating for traffic?

Possibly.

But a stressful lunch with his mind elsewhere wasn't good.

He glanced at the florists and hustled through the door, dragging his credit card from his pants pocket. "Hey, quick sale, please. I need this bouquet in the window, please."

The woman bustled over, pulled the flowers from the bucket, and took the credit card Dakota extended out.

"A choice of ribbon, sir?" She pushed the flowers into a helper's hands, and the helper was tearing paper and folding it neatly.

"Whatever you think would be nice."

"A note?"

"I'll say it in person," Dakota said. He was terrible at finding the right written words to express his sentiments. "Sorry for your gray mood," seemed like a bad idea.

When Dakota had said 'quick', these women took it to heart, and he was out the door moments later, bouquet in hand.

He planned to apologize for breaking their date, hand Rose the flowers, tell her about the lunches he'd ordered and paid for waiting for her, and ask to talk to her that evening.

She just needed to show up.

Rose was sometimes late if they got behind with the patients. She must be having a hard day.

Still, Dakota felt the pressure of time and decided to give her a call.

"Dakota."

"You sound bad," he said. "Are you okay?"

"Not bad. Just … look, I'm not coming down. Last night, my ex and I had a long talk about the kids and us. We decided we're going to make a go of it because it's too hard to do alone. Too expensive. Too exhausting."

"That's great for you, Rose. I hope it works out the way you want it to."

"I'm sorry, Dakota. You're a really nice guy. I've enjoyed knowing you."

"Nope, not at all. I wish you well. Good luck." He slid his phone in his pocket as he stepped to the curb, scanning for a taxi.

Okay, that was that. Dakota could trust his instincts; it was the conversation he'd felt looming.

He looked down at the flowers.

How did he feel about the end of his knowing Rose?

He enjoyed her company, and he was going to miss that. But there was always a barrier she set: this much and no more. She wasn't inviting him into her life. When his couple-friends started talking about their different love languages, Benny winked at his wife, Martha, and said, "Physical touch, that's mine."

And she'd countered with "You mean quality time."

"Yeah, that one." Benny chuckled. "Same thing, right? Tomato—tomahto?"

Martha gave him the stink face, then turned to Dakota. "And yours?"

Dakota's way of showing love—love for a woman, a friend, the community at large—was through acts of service. He felt happiest when he knew that his actions were making someone's life better, that he'd relieved a burden, taken something onerous off the table.

Rose hadn't allowed that.

He was all for strong, independent women. If he had a type, that was what he found attractive. But that didn't mean there weren't ways to help. For one woman he dated, she despised pumping gas. So he made sure that when she was driving them, they stopped by the gas station so he could do it for her. Same with coffee, she didn't hate making coffee, but when he was over at her house, he'd set up the coffee pot for the next morning, so it was ready when she woke up. She said that gesture had made her feel cared for.

Big was good; little was just as good. Dakota liked the settled, happy feeling that came from an act of service.

The only time Rose allowed that was when her kids' rabbit died. It had been a beautiful lop-eared bunny named Lollipop. She told him how the kids would sit on the couch after a day of overstimulation at their day care and pet the bunny to calm their bodies and help them settle down for their night routine. When the bunny died, Rose, even though she was a nurse, couldn't make herself reach into the cage and take out the dead rabbit. She called him, sobbing into the phone. He'd had to wait long minutes while she just cried before she could explain the situation and ask if he could get rid of the dead bunny before the kids came back from their dad's house.

Dakota had been out training with Tank, and they were miles from the car. The window to get in and out without the kids seeing him was tight. To Tank's delight, they'd sprinted the whole way back to the parking lot.

It was the first time Rose had asked him for something; there was no way he'd let her down.

And apparently, it was also the last time she'd ask.

Dakota was genuinely hopeful for her. She had those two little kids, and if she loved their dad and wanted to work on that, more power to them.

But now he had a fist full of flowers, and he was on his way to the airport.

A taxi turned the corner, and Dakota lifted his free hand to signal it.

As the cab pulled up to the open space on the curb, Dakota put his hand on the back handle. Movement in his peripheral caught his attention.

A woman sprang through the doors at the medical building. The wind whipped her long brown hair across her face.

Her body language was pure fury.

As she pulled the hair from her eyes, she spotted the taxi and jogged forward, her eye on the driver. It seemed she missed Dakota standing there holding the door handle.

The taxi driver shifted his glance from the woman to him, looking like he didn't want a fight. Dakota sent him a wink to let him know it was okay. This woman obviously was going through something, and she'd just run out of a medical building. She could have just received a terrible diagnosis.

Dakota pulled the door open for her.

"Here you go," he managed. It was *her*, the woman from the race. Different clothes, Makeup today. But he'd recognize her anywhere. It was her. How crazy was that?

Dakota's face flamed red, and his body did that same odd atomic particle dance it had at the finish line of the mud race.

He really couldn't say that his body was reacting to the stranger.

Correlation was not causation, after all.

He mentioned the doctor to Benny that morning, but maybe he was the one who needed a once-over. What the hell was wrong with him?

As she climbed into the cab, her eyes changed from anger to fatigue in a flash. "I'm sorry. Were you … That was … I didn't …"

He sent her a warm smile. "You're fine."

She pursed her lips and nodded. It looked like she was struggling, and Dakota took the gesture as a thank-you.

Dakota bent, handed the woman his flowers, and shut the door.

He watched her until the cab disappeared in the traffic.

He was a controlled, steady man. And he wasn't down with these wild sensations that made him feel disorganized on a cellular level. Yeah, he needed to pull himself back together.

And just as suddenly as the sensation came on, Dakota felt normal again.

His recovery this time was much faster than last time.

Still, it was such a crazy, disorienting sensation that he stood there waiting for his brain to kick in and tell him what to do next.

There was no next. Not with this brown-haired lady anyway.

The goal, he reminded himself, was to get to the airport in time to test Tank's sniffer as the Colombian flight disembarked.

This could go badly if, search warrant in hand, they found nothing or worse, a false positive, on the folks coming through.

Then it would be back to the drawing board, training Tank.

Maybe it was anxiety that made him buzz like that.

Yeah, maybe that was it.

Dakota's hand shot up to signal for a different cab.

6

———

Monday

Four years ago, Dakota made a life-changing visit to see a military buddy, Joe, who retired from service to put his decades of K9 handling to good use at his own dog-training facility. Joe had a stellar breeding pair of working-line German shepherds that he'd found at two different rescue shelters before their vets could get in there and clip them.

Were they pedigree paper-holding pups?

No.

And that was good for Dakota's wallet.

A military working dog, bought from a breeder and trained, was worth upward of $100,000. But a pup from two rescues, Dakota could manage even on his government salary.

The training? Joe would talk Dakota through it via video mentorship for a nominal fee.

And with that understanding, Dakota had told his friend he wanted dibs on a male from the next litter.

When Dakota went to make his selection from amongst seven litter mates, it was a done deal once he locked eyes with the furball in the purple collar. It was love at first sight, completely unconditional. What a sensation to look into Tank's eyes and feel their connection right from the first.

Curious and intelligent, Dakota found out right away that if he wanted to keep Tank's puppy teeth from destroying everything in his home, he'd need to teach Tank self-control. They both loved the tactical training that built Tank's body and mind. They worked together every morning and evening when Dakota was in Virginia.

Joe boarded Tank at his training facility when Dakota was off on an assignment.

Tank was spot on with the kinds of tactical skills they trained. Practical-tactical was how Dakota labeled it. Dakota wasn't jumping out of a helicopter into a hot zone. That was his last life.

Take-downs, alerts, and sniffer training were Tank's bread and butter.

Yeah, he was good at that work, passing all of his certifications with flying colors.

He just wasn't Cerberus good, and that was the gold standard.

Tank was Dakota's family, his partner, and in the field, he'd be his weapon. Dakota absolutely needed Tank to have every advantage so they could both come home safe at the end of the day.

And here they were at the end of a long road, ready to

test his skills in the field. It was up to Dakota to do his job as a handler precisely.

And the sooner Tank tested out of the certification program, the sooner he would leave Cerberus Kennels and come back home. For now, Dakota was like a parent with visitation rights.

That's how he felt as he stood at the back of his vehicle, giving Reaper space to unload Tank.

Magnificent was the word that came to Dakota's mind every time he saw Tank's regal posture.

"Hey buddy, look at you all fresh and clean after your mud bath yesterday. You good?" Dakota scrubbed his hands over Tank's thick fur. "You're so soft. They must have given you the spa treatment, huh, bud? Did they put on some conditioner to make you pretty?"

Dakota stuck his hand out. "Good to see you again, Reaper. I read in the paper that yesterday was a blockbuster day for the children's hospital."

"They got what they needed. As soon as the spring rains let up, they'll be building the inclusive playground and the trail for the kiddos. Appreciate you playing along."

"An honor, any time." Dakota folded his arms over his chest and rocked back on his heels. "Let me bring you up to speed. My department has a search warrant for passengers on a direct flight from Colombia, looking for counterfeit money. There are a hundred plus on today's flight, and we don't want to search every single passenger. Our reason for pulling someone aside will be Tank's alert." Dakota checked his watch. "Their plane was delayed, so we're still good with time. Kumar texted they're a red light away."

"All right, how do you want to play this?"

"My colleague Kumar Singh will instruct the passengers about their conduct. If they participate, that's good. If they don't, we have the search warrant. There will be an airport guard to support this effort. Jasper and Benny will stand off to the side to gather people who have been identified by Tank."

"Do you expect more than one?"

"I have no expectations at all. I was called in and contacted you. Thanks for making yourself available at the last minute."

"That's what we do," Reaper said.

"You could, maybe, observe my performance, standing near Jasper. We'll have the passengers walk by Tank and see if he shows any interest. If so, my colleagues will escort those passengers to a room for a search of their belongings. We have a holding room and a search room set aside for our operation. Next, Tank and I will position ourselves at the suitcase chute. If he's interested in anything there, we'll pull the bags."

"You do expect something today, correct?"

"There's a possibility that there is nothing there. Kumar noticed a pattern of counterfeit bills that he was interested in pursuing, and my department knew that I was looking for a field opportunity to test Tank. This is really a fishing expedition."

"Sounds good. I knew you'd be in a suit with a badge on your hip. I hope you appreciate that I left my tactical at home."

"You clean up good. Did Kate pick out the tie?"

Reaper adjusted his charcoal gray tie. "Yeah, she said the blaze orange one I got for Christmas was a joke."

"Kate's good?" Dakota asked. "The kids?"

"I'm living the life." Reaper lifted his chin to indicate Jasper pulling into the lot, with Kumar riding shotgun.

The men parked and walked over. "Ready?" Kumar called.

"Where's Benny?" Dakota asked as he whistled Tank back to his side.

"He stayed back at the office. He had some things to finish up. I told him to take off early. He's really not looking good."

"Time, gentlemen," Kumar said.

They took Reaper's vehicle. If there were any arrests, he'd bring Jasper back to pick up his car.

Walking into the terminal—four men in suits, glorious Tank in his tactical vest with "Working Do Not Distract" patches—turned heads and made worried eyes search the area. Surely these vacation-goers didn't want to be caught up in an arrest situation.

By the time they had badged through security and taken the tram to the right gate, the plane had landed.

Airport security had moved retractable belt stanchions into place to herd passengers forward.

And here they came, business class first.

Dakota showed Tank his tug towel and then said, "Work time. Scent chemicals."

Kumar directed the passengers to walk forward one at a time, stand for the count of three, then move on to baggage claim and customs.

Dakota stood to the side with Tank on a loose lead, watching people trickle by.

Tank's nose was chuffing the air, looking for the scent that would get him play time with his favorite toy.

It was the typical medium-sized plane that brought people up from Colombia. There were a hundred and fifty-two on this flight. A group in red-and-white uniforms from WorldCares was coming through the door. This was the group that Kumar had targeted, and it was up to Dakota not to signal that information to Tank in any way. Dakota eased his body, maintained his breath, and started reciting soccer stats, focusing on forming a mental image of the numbers.

The group moving past looked exhausted.

One. Two passed.

Then, sure enough, Tank sat.

Jasper walked the man to the side.

Dakota reset Tank to continue his task. There would be no tug-of-war until Dakota was sure that there was coun-terfeit money present. Tank knew this. He was right back to work.

Four people walked by.

Tank sat again.

There was consternation in the group as they gathered against the opposite wall out of the way.

"What's happening here?" the man asked as he was sent to stand near Jasper.

"We'll explain in a minute," Jasper said. "Raisin?"

Dakota redirected Tank to his task, and one more person from WorldCares was a hit.

The rest of the plane was clean.

Without speaking to his team, Dakota signaled to the

airport security officer that he was ready. The officer escorted Dakota and Tank straight to the proper baggage belt.

Reaper trailed behind.

The moving bags really jazzed Tank, but he didn't pick out a single scent. The group pulled their detained friends' gear off, and the security officer went over to ask for those bags, since they could only pass through security with their own belongings.

One of the people, obviously in distress, was on the phone explaining with broad gestures what had happened to them.

Dakota's phone pinged, and he followed the map to meet up with his colleagues.

Reaper was watching his every move as they stopped in the doorway to assess before entering. The three World-Cares responders sat on metal seats. On the table were two bands of hundred-dollar bills, and some loose hundreds spread out along the edge.

"Scent chemical," Dakota commanded and walked Tank into the room. Tank indicated on both banded stacks of bills and four of the single hundred-dollar bills.

Jasper put one through the identification machine, and it lit up as a counterfeit.

Dakota took Tank into the hall before they played their reward game of tug, with scritches and high-pitched praise.

"I'm interested to know why you didn't give Tank an immediate reward once you saw the machine light," Reaper said, his shoulder pressed to the wall.

From his crouch on the floor, rubbing Tank's belly, Dakota looked over his shoulder. "Did you see their faces? I wasn't doing a victory dance in front of those men. Is it wrong to ask Tank to wait thirty seconds when we're not in training to show some humanity?" Dakota heard how that sounded, so he added, "Serious question here, Reaper. I don't want to mess up Tank's training."

7

Rylee
Monday

Rylee tapped on the office door next to hers, then stuck her head in to see if Neesa, her co-director of operations here at WorldCares and, more importantly, her very dear friend, was up for an interruption.

Neesa spun her chair toward Rylee. "Hey, good you're back." She pushed her laptop to the side. "That took a while. I figure that's a good sign?"

Rylee sauntered in and flopped into one of the guest armchairs. "I should track my period, take up yoga, and put an app on my phone so I can learn to breathe deeply."

Neesa laced her hands and stretched them across her forehead, tipping her head back. "Shit. Again?"

"Yup."

She brought herself upright and focused on Rylee's

bouquet. "Beautiful flowers. Did you buy them to cheer yourself up? I love the colors."

"Amazing, aren't they?" Rylee turned them for Neesa to see. "I thought you might have a spare vase in your credenza that I could borrow."

"This is the only one." Neesa stood to pick up a vase on the edge of her desk, then, holding it over the trash can, picked out the wilting flower bouquet and dropped it into the garbage. "I got the flowers with the nice sentiment written on the card, then the guy ghosts me." She walked over to Rylee and held the vase out with two hands. "I don't need to sit here staring at the flowers, wondering if he's dead in a ditch or just dead to me."

"Morbid." Rylee glanced at the water in the cut glass crystal vase. Since it looked like it was freshly changed, she plunked her own flowers in.

Neesa turned and put the vase on the edge of her desk, then made her way back to her chair.

"So this is what I can tell you about the flower story," Rylee started.

"It's a story?"

"Yup, a whole story, might as well get comfortable," Rylee said, slipping her feet out of her shoes. "I was on the top floor of the stupid medical building, and since I was snorting mad like an angry bull, I figured I should take the stairs rather than be near people."

"Wise."

"The sound of me slamming my feet against the steps echoed so loudly, I bet the people in the halls thought there was some kind of emergency evacuation drill going on."

"Understandable." Neesa laced her hands in her lap as she leaned forward.

"It makes me question my mental health, Neesa. Maybe I *am* just anxious."

"You're the least anxious person I know. Go on. Flowers?"

"I'm pounding down the stairs, thinking that my dad and my great uncle, in separate states mind you, went to the doctor and on the first office visit, the very first one, both were sent on for further testing, both got their diagnoses in short order, and then were put on medication to help stop disease progression, which everyone knows, when it comes to MS, the sooner the medical intervention the better."

"Exactly," Neesa nodded.

"And so I wait for a doctor who will diagnose me. And while I wait, I research. I'm looking for experimental drug trials to help my dad and uncle, and possibly—probably—me. One comes up, I offer to help Dad, and Uncle Wilf throw their names in the hat. Nope, neither is interested in being a guinea pig. I," Rylee pressed her hands to her chest, "would make an excellent guinea pig."

Neesa nodded. "Agreed. Phenomenal guinea pig."

"Right! And then I find a doctor friend of mine from Afghanistan is doing a research study on an IV drip medication that they believe stops the progression of MS in its tracks."

"Here in the U.S.?" Neesa asked.

"London. He's British. Anyway, I reached out to him and sent him my labs and so forth, and he said that he would get me into that study as soon as I have a diagnosis. He *promised* me. And he owes me. I didn't save his life or anything, but I did introduce him to his wife, and he's still very much in love with her. They have a baby on the way."

"Aww." Neesa smiled.

"I know. Wonderful. I'm so happy for them. But here I am with no diagnosis but a lovely offer of anxiety pills and an admonishment that I really should sign up for a yoga class. Neither of which is getting me any closer to the bliss of sitting in a London hospital with a needle shoved in my vein."

"Which does sound amazing," Neesa said. "Flowers?"

"Yes, well, by the time I got to the lobby, I had burned off maybe half my fury."

Neesa nodded.

"I plowed out the front door, thinking cold air was going to serve me well. And by that point, I'd decided to go see the name on the sticky note rather than call and leave a message."

"Lost me." Neesa leaned back in her captain's chair.

Rylee looped her finger in the air. "I'll circle back."

"Thank you."

"I burst out of the building like my hair was on fire."

"You'd stop, drop, and roll."

"Seriously, Neesa?"

"Sorry." She pointed at Rylee, "Continue."

"Okay, so I burst out the front door like … like something—"

"Angry," Neesa offered. "I get it. I don't need a simile."

"Thank you. I'm out on the street, and I see a cab just sitting there. I make eye contact with the driver. He knows I've claimed the cab. I reached for the door handle, and the door was pulled open for me by this guy."

"A helpful guy, hanging out on the sidewalk, opening cab doors?"

"I wasn't thinking straight. As I replayed it all in my mind, I realized he was getting into the cab when I burst onto the scene."

"Good use of burst that time," Neesa said. "And you stole his cab."

"Seems so."

Rylee thought back. She was so in her head that she was sort of moving forward using muscle memory. Then she was in the cab. She had flowers in her lap. She had the guy's laughing eyes and his nice smile in her awareness. Then the taxi was moving, and the cabbie asked where to go. Rylee had nothing. So she thrust Rose's blue sticky note at the guy. He looked down at the name of the medical building. "I know that one." And off they went, weaving through lunchtime traffic.

Rylee felt like she'd been rolled by a massive wave.

And when she came up sputtering, she was sitting there, clutching the bouquet, her nose buried amongst the petals, feeling them smooth out her prickly mood.

"But he was a gentleman," Neesa was asking, bringing Rylee back to the conversation, "or do you think he saw your face in full bull-mode and you frightened the poor guy?"

"Half bull-mode by that point. But one has to assume that the look on my face made him wary of fighting me over the cab. Just to be clear, I wouldn't have fought over it. I would have apologized."

"Of course. The flowers?"

"He handed me the bouquet and shut the door without saying a word."

"You're kidding." Neesa blinked. "That's got to be a hundred-dollar bouquet."

"Not kidding, and I know, right?" Rylee turned her focus toward the vase. "I wonder why he was hanging out with a spare bouquet." She sighed loudly. "I'll never know."

"Cute?"

"I think so. I—it was strange, and I got flashes of information." Rylee held her hand over her head. "He was built like a basketball player. He was wearing a suit, and it fit him well. I remember short blond-ish hair, lawyer kind of feel, maybe? He was blushing pretty hard, though, and he had an easy smile that seemed like a natural part of his face."

"Huh. So my takeaway is that your guardian angel thought you needed some flowers and provided tall-guy."

"My thoughts exactly. So," Rylee planted her feet on the chair to hug her knees, and since she was wearing the sweater dress, Rylee angled so she wasn't flashing her friend. "And that's the story of why I'm late to our meeting about attrition."

"It can wait," Neesa said. "And so, where were you all this time? Your appointment was hours ago."

Rylee did a quick recap of what had happened after the doctor left the exam room. "I went to the place on Rose's sticky note and sat my happy butt in one of their chairs and waited until the nurse friend got back from lunch and then dealt with her patients, and she finally had a moment for me to hand her the note from my nurse and to get an appointment."

"When?"

Rylee grimaced. "Eight months for an appointment."

"Eight!"

"Neurologist. It's usually longer. But they put my name in their computer as a priority for cancellations. Just a warning, if they call, I'm gone."

"I insist. Absolutely. You think the new doctor will do another brush past?" Neesa asked. "I mean, I think you should consider taking a sick day, stay home, find the top fifty people within an hour's drive, and make an appointment with every single one of them so you're not getting the 'Whiney Woman' treatment, then having to recover from the indignity and start again. Number one says anxiety, but the next week you have two other pans in the fire."

"Put it in a spreadsheet so once I was diagnosed, I could cancel the rest?"

"Exactly."

"Tempting," Rylee said. "Aggressive but tempting. And now, I would very much like to change the subject."

"Okay, attrition then. Here's our problem synthesized down to stark terms: We're losing too many of our crisis field workers."

"Turnover is too fast for the newbies to feel like they have mastery before those who have the skills down and have figured out the ins and outs leave," Rylee said. "That overwhelm leads to anxiety. Anxiety leads to dissatisfaction. Dissatisfaction leads to attrition."

"I looked at the stats and exit reports," Neesa countered. "They're leaving for good reasons: injuries and health issues, pregnancy or young children, spouses moving out of our area." Neesa ticked off on her fingers.

"Some of it, yes. I think they're being nice to us. I know

they are because Baji all but said so. He wanted to make sure that in his exit, he didn't say anything that would make it seem as if we were responsible for his decision to leave and become a paramedic. The exit interviews are polite and encouraging, but they aren't getting at the meat of the issue."

"Ideas?" Neesa asked.

"I had one. But after today, I'm rethinking it."

"Tell me anyway."

"So your background is numbers, and my background is boots on the ground. Being in the Navy but working on the green side as a Marine medic gave me the hands-on field experience we need, particularly for our fast-action responders. I'd like to focus on that team first. My work for the Navy was gratifying, and serving is my calling in life. Having said that, there were a lot of pieces that made my military career shorter than I had anticipated, and they might apply here."

"Give me two off the top of your head," Neesa said.

"For women, there are safety issues and sanitary issues not faced by men."

"Right." Neesa leaned forward and picked up her pen.

"There are normal health issues and personal injuries. For our people, I think we need to consider morale issues as our people deal with the psychological effects of seeing how devastating Mother Nature can be. PTSD. Our people aren't dealing with war. War is a government choice. The events our fast-action crew deploys to internationally are out of the blue. Male and Female, newborn and frail with age, all impacted in the middle of living life, suddenly having all their resources destroyed. It takes a toll on those in the field.

Then there's the idea that you have to jump off at any minute, right? That's not something we did in the military. Maybe for a special forces group, they might get a call, and snap, they're gone. We had time to plan and wind things up."

"But our people get the call out, and whatever was happening—tickets to the big game, dad in the hospital, wife in her ninth month of pregnancy—they have to grab their jump bag, race to the plane, and fly to somewhere in the world for some amount of time."

"Exactly," Rylee said. "Mail, plants, pets, clothes at the dry cleaner, you have to have that all planned for in advance, all the time."

Neesa laid her pen back on the desk. "It's a particular type of person we're looking for. Someone who's down with all that."

"A very small population. And we want them for us. Other groups want that unique demographic for themselves. So there's a competition for that small field. The more we form a cohesive, supportive family, the better. But a questionnaire won't do it. It's standing shoulder to shoulder that will get us our answers." Rylee reached up and scratched her scalp. "So I had two ideas. One was to talk to Hailey Stapleton, sorry, Sterling now. Hailey Sterling. Since she left us to work for Iniquus Logistics, she told me they have a whole program to support families when their Iniquus operator gets called out. These support workers go in and fill the need. I'll give you a for instance: When Hailey's husband is out of town, her yard work is done, her car is cleaned and repaired, if she's sick, someone's there cooking and cleaning and tending her, this group picks up the day-to-day load that Ares would shoulder if he were around. Does it replace Ares? Absolutely not. But it doesn't force his family labor onto her shoulders. That helps Hailey, and Ares is content knowing that his wife is being cared for by the Iniquus family. ISO, she calls it, an Iniquus Support Officer."

"Honestly," Neesa said, "I'd much rather allocate money to help keep our people than spend it on recruiting and training while we watch the rotating door spin."

"We don't know those needs, and we don't know if that would move the needle. So I was going to propose that I train with a few of the Fast Response folks and deploy with them—not to do their job but to observe and ask questions about their experience. I don't want to be what we call in the military a 'good idea fairy,' someone who sits in the office and thinks they know better than boots on the ground."

Neesa pursed her lips. "I don't think your deployment is a good idea. Not with your health issues."

"Tingling fingers and toes. It's not advancing past that yet. I'm good."

"Are you?" Neesa canted her head. "Seriously, Rylee, are you?"

"Today, yes. Tomorrow?" She shrugged. "But I could always start and see. I can pull myself out if necessary. This isn't a vanity project. I'm not going to endanger anyone, let alone myself. By the way, our team that was down in Colombia is coming in. I told them to rest and catch up with their personal lives, and we'd see them Monday for a debrief. But I already reached out to Lima Team, and tomorrow I'll join their evolution, fast roping out of a helicopter."

"Rylee, no."

"I know how. I did it for years, remember?"

"That's—"

An urgent knock sounded at the door before it cracked open for Sun Yu to stick his head in.

"We have a problem." The lawyer said, sliding his slight frame into the room, shut the door, and leaned against it like he was holding back a gale.

Both Rylee and Neesa dropped their feet to the floor, put their shoes back on, and shifted into professional postures.

"Murphy, the leader of the team coming in from Colombia, called from the airport. The Secret Service has detained three people from that team."

"No shit?" Neesa gasped. "Secret Service? But why?"

"They had a counterfeit scent K9 sniffing people as they got off the plane. Three of our team had counterfeit money on their persons."

"That doesn't make them counterfeiters," Rylee said. "That means they were the victims of a counterfeiter."

"The Secret Service agrees. They aren't accusing our people of anything."

"So what's the problem?" Neesa asked. "Give the special agents the fake money and be done with it."

"Apparently, it's more complex than that. The Secret Service is requesting a meeting. I had the CEO and CFO on a conference call with Kumar Singh, one of the Secret Service special agents on this case. We all agreed that their team should come here and meet with you tomorrow morning at nine o'clock."

"Who is the 'you' in that sentence?" Rylee asked. "Both of us?"

"The CEO said Neesa, since she's the money side of the shared operations directorship."

"Good, because I'm going to be jumping out of helicopters." She sent a searching glance toward Neesa.

Neesa caught Rylee's gaze, then turned to Sun. "Yeah, that's fine. Anyway, I can help, I'm glad to. I'll catch Rylee up after her evolution."

"Hey, Sun, was this fake money on their persons?" Rylee asked.

"It was mixed in with WorldCares cash straps. The three had the banded money in their carry-ons and said they were never out of sight, per our rules."

"Mixed in with, like in our bands?" Rylee asked.

"That's my understanding." Sun hadn't moved further into the office but stayed there pressed to the door. "The Secret Service wants to bring their K9 tomorrow to sniff through our vaults to see if this has happened in the past. It's possible that we might have sent the teams out with the fake currency. Somehow, we might be the distributors rather than the recipients."

"*Mixed* in the straps?" Neesa said. "I certainly don't break the band and look at each bill when I inventory them back in the vault."

"I'm trying to wrap my head around this one. You said the Secret Service detained them?" Rylee asked.

"They are detained," Sun said.

"Do we have someone over there supporting them?" Rylee asked.

Sun shoved his hands deep into his trouser pockets. "We sent counsel."

"No criminal charges, though. Right?" Neesa asked.

"Right now, our people are in full cooperation with the Secret Service. They're showing documentation: the money they were given, the money they spent, and the money that's coming back. Unfortunately, we send them out with hundred-dollar bills."

"Hundred-dollar bills are what we always send," Neesa said.

"Hundred-dollar bills," Sun nodded, "are the denomination of U.S. notes that are the most popular for counterfeiting in the world."

Rylee leaned forward. "And a *dog* smelled this? The dog is the one saying these bills are counterfeit."

"That's right," Sun said.

"Did anyone follow up on what the dog alerted to? I mean, were they counterfeit?" Rylee pushed despite Neesa's scowl. "I'm serious. What if our people just had bacon grease on their hands, and that's what Fido was sniffing? This could be a nothing burger."

"It's a something burger," Sun said.

Rylee lifted her eyebrows. "Because?"

Sun shifted off the door and grabbed the knob. "Because the Secret Service said it's a deluxe burger with all the fixings." And he walked out.

RYLEE

Monday

NEESA KNOCKED on Rylee's open office door. "Hey, quitting time."

Rylee rested her fingers on the keyboard and swiveled her focus away from the screen.

"I'm taking the Metro up to McPherson Square to meet some friends for dinner," Neesa dropped her purse to the ground and shoved her hand into her coat sleeve. "You should come."

"I don't think so, Neesy. It's been a long day." Rylee reached out and closed her laptop. "I think I'm just going to head home."

"No, you're not." Neesa shrugged her coat into place. "You'll just relive today, get angry, and not be able to sleep." Threading the zipper together, she yanked it up. "Then you'll try to jump out of the helicopter tomorrow and break your leg because you're tired. I'm not having it." She bent to scoop up her purse strap.

"Fast rope, not jump."

"Come out." Neesa reached for Rylee's coat and held it out to her. "Put good conversations into your brain, laugh a little."

"Do I know anyone?"

"Other than me? No." Neesa said. "But they're welcoming people. This isn't a clique I'm throwing you into."

Rylee was vacillating. She'd envisioned a hot bath, a glass of wine, and some ridiculous romcom that could never happen in real life. But Neesa was wise. And maybe it was better that she was distracted from today's disappointment. "What kind of restaurant?"

"Soul food. Mom and pop place. You can suffocate your angst in a bowl of mac and cheese and a side of collard greens."

Since it was her belief that humanity should support each other through the tough times and rejoice together at the good, this might be the perfect antidote to her present funk.

Rylee turned her attention to the vase filled with bright flowers and recalled the befuddled smile on the stranger's face. He wasn't angry with her at all; he just handed her the flowers, and off she drove.

Strangers could be generous and kind.

Rylee hoped that guy knew that he made an indelible memory for her.

Clutching those flowers while she waited for Rose's

nurse-friend to make eye-to-eye contact with her was like holding a psychological buoy to Rylee.

And here was Neesa, offering another help line.

Why wouldn't she allow that?

"Yeah," Rylee stood and stretched her hand out for her coat. "Why not?"

The two women took the elevator down to the ground floor and out into the night air. The sidewalks bustled with people leaving, their minds elsewhere—what to cook for dinner, how to get the kids through their homework and into bed, would the boss be mad that they left without finishing the report?

They walked the short distance to the Metro station in companionable silence.

As they started down the stairs, Neesa said, "So here's what I learned today—"

Rylee turned her head to catch Neesa's bemused expression.

"Titivate doesn't at all mean what I thought it does."

"Titivate?" Rylee repeated.

"Yeah, do you know what it means?"

Rylee wanted to reach for the railing as she moved with the after-work crowd down the stairs, but the germ count was too high. "I think I've seen it written before. Titivate? No, I don't know."

"Titivate," Neesa glanced up at Rylee, "just hearing it, what do you think it means?"

"Sexual tingling?" Rylee offered. "Getting someone aroused? His intelligent conversation titivated me."

Neesa quirked a brow. "Intelligent conversation is what does it for you?"

"Absolutely," Rylee said. "Every time. Give me a reading, thinking man, and I'm in a swoon." She pulled her Metro card from the back of her phone and pushed through the barrier, then waited for Neesa to join her. "So what does it mean?"

"To tidy." Neesa threw her hands in the air. "Titivate means to tidy things up or do a little something to improve them, like gargling with mouthwash. 'She titivated her hair.'"

"Disappointing."

"I know, right?" Neesa checked the Metro map, then pointed out the correct platform. They started down the stairs, and Neesa lifted her voice to be heard above the crush of commuters. "So titivate is not in the same word family as titillate."

"You know it's been a while since I found a nice nerd boy to titivate me or to titillate me," Rylee sighed.

Neesa laughed. "You and me b—What the?"

Instead of standing in knots of folks who knew each other or packed into efficient lines down the platform, people had formed into what Rylee called the "death ring." It was the circle people formed when they watched a crisis unfold.

It happened the same way all over the world.

It was the unmistakable and very human reaction that was like a great big crisis bullseye that had drawn Rylee into many a lifesaving effort.

Sometimes the rescues were successful; often, the situations were doomed from the start, which was why Rylee named them "the death ring."

Adrenaline kicked her senses into high drive as Rylee caught Neesa's hand, holding her back.

Rule number one of rescue: Don't become part of the problem.

First step of rescue: Take in the lay of the land, assess the dangers.

From the stairs, they could see a man, clutching his chest, contorting his face with agony. No one had entered the ring of observers to help. That usually meant no one had the necessary skills or the confidence to try.

That crush was surely taking up the guy's available oxygen.

Neesa and Rylee came to the same conclusion at the same moment—this emergency was limited to a single subject's medical situation—not a fight, not a contaminant.

Rylee commanded, "Back. Back. Back," as she raced down the stairs, shoving people out of the way.

Neesa, her elbows bent and held high, plowed forward. "Clear the way. Move!"

By the time they reached the center platform, the man had one knee on the ground and was hovering over his bent leg, using it to support himself on his elbow as he clutched his heart.

Rylee quickly shucked her coat and laid it on the ground behind the man, then put her hands on his shoulders. "Sir, I'm a trained ex-Marine medic. May I help you?"

The man nodded without looking up. His breath came in quick, shallow puffs.

Rylee pointed at a sturdy-looking, gray-haired woman with the stoic face of a bean counter. She was dependable. "Ma'am, do you have a phone with bars?"

She pulled her phone from her pocket, looked down, "Yes. Yes, I do."

"You're in charge of communications. Call 911 and give them this location. Answer their questions. Stay on the line."

Rylee angled down so she and the man were face-to-face. "Sir, my name is Rylee, and my friend is Neesa. We're getting you help, and we're not going to leave you. Right now, I'm going to sit behind you and bend my legs to make a backrest. I want you in a semi-sitting position. Neesa down there is going to bend your legs and help you hold them in place so we can take the strain off your heart as much as possible." Rylee lifted her chin to Neesa.

Neesa had steadied the man in the W configuration to wait for EMT help.

"And we're focusing on our breath," Rylee told the man. "We're slowing the inhale. We're exhaling longer than we're inhaling, so we don't hyperventilate. We're breathing together." Rylee breathed through her mouth, exhaling onto the man's neck so he could have a focus point and so he could feel her rhythmic breathing. "In for four. You're breathing into your abdomen, not your chest. Exhale slowly for six."

His breath whooshed out.

"That's fine," Rylee soothed. "We're trying again. In two, three, four. Trying to hold for a second. Good and exhale for six."

The breath came out to the count of one.

"Sir, what's your name? Is there anyone I can call?" Rylee asked.

The man weakly lifted his arm with his cell phone aglow.

Neesa reached for the phone. "You're on the line with someone?"

"Here we go," Rylee said, "focus on my words, breathing in for four."

Neesa put the phone to her ear. "Hello?" She held. "Sir, I'm on the scene of a cardiac episode in the Metro. Can you tell me the name of the man you were speaking with?" Neesa turned to Rylee. "His name is Benjamin Burnett. Everyone calls him Benny."

"We've got you, Benny," Rylee said, snagging her own phone from her purse. "You're breathing." She opened her clock app to the stopwatch and reached for the man's wrist to count Benny's erratic pulse.

While Neesa asked the person to stay on the line so they could ask questions if necessary, she rummaged in her purse, pulled out a pen and a piece of paper, and thrust them toward Rylee.

Rylee wrote the time and Benny's pulse and breath counts. Then held the paper up so Bean Counter could see it.

Bean Counter lowered her voice and gave the 911 operator the numbers. After a moment, Bean Counter caught Rylee's eye. "The paramedics are on their way. I'm staying on the phone." She shifted her weight, seeming to plant herself on that spot.

While Rylee knew the first responders would race with screaming sirens and flashing lights, this was end-of-day Washington, D.C., so cutting a path through traffic-clogged roads was going to be a feat.

A lone Metro officer snaked her way through the crowd

and punctured through the death ring. There, she bent to see what was going on.

Rylee said, "It's inconvenient, but this is a medical emergency. You need to close the platform." As soon as the words left her mouth, a Metro train slid loudly out of the tunnel and stopped with a hiss.

"Clear this platform and shut it down." Rylee used her most commanding, military, give-me-no-shit voice, which always seemed to get results.

The woman was flustered as she talked into her radio, but she did what she could. People got off the train and were sent to the other end of the platform to exit. People got on the line and left.

Bean Counter stayed, phone shaking in her hand.

A nervous-looking guy with a fox-shaped face and a black leather briefcase stayed.

Two men built like whiskey barrels and a woman who fried her hair with a home perm, all wearing Paddy O'Donald T-shirts under black leather jackets, looked like they were heading to work but stayed to help.

Rylee turned to the bouncer-looking dudes, "Can you post at the stairs and let people know they can't access this platform?"

"We'll keep them out." Both of them looked like they'd enjoy the job. And Rylee was grateful they happened to be around. Serendipity.

"I'm going to go get barriers to put up and make an announcement." The Metro officer seemed happy to go take care of those tasks. No one was asking her to mouth-to-mouth a stranger.

Rylee thought that leaving the scene was probably

contrary to the woman's protocol, but if she was protecting this space and mobilizing help, that was a good thing.

There were now five on the platform. Benny, Neesa, Rylee, Bean Counter, and Briefcase.

The open space seemed to lower Benny's anxiety and help him cope.

Rylee imagined that there was no feeling quite so claustrophobic as not being able to get enough air and then having all those bodies looming overhead.

"Sir, I'm putting you on speaker." Neesa lay Benny's phone on the ground as she pushed Benny's sleeves up, then searched his neckline. "Do you know if Benny has a medical condition? Is he taking any medications that you know of? I'm checking for medical alert jewelry."

"No," A deep voice rumbled with concern. "Benny was complaining of indigestion earlier. He said he's felt like that for the last few days. We noticed this morning that he was a little gray and sweaty. And our colleague asked Benny if he needed to see a doctor. He said he'd go tomorrow if things hadn't improved. I'm in a ride share. I'll have them turn around."

"Sir, the paramedics are en route," Neesa told him. "Please stay on the phone for questions."

"Sir, did you say that Benny was sweating earlier?" Rylee asked.

"Yes. Not a lot. On his forehead and upper lip."

"Had he just exercised, like climbed the stairs?" Rylee asked as she felt Benny's forehead for a fever. "Or had he just eaten something spicy?"

"No. I don't know. I doubt either one. Benny takes the

elevator, and he said he'd had heartburn for a few days, so he was having antacids for lunch."

Benny was cold and clammy. Rylee locked eyes with Neesa. Obviously, this situation was dire. But anytime someone was sweating without a reasonable explanation, it was time to seek medical help. Benny should have been in the hospital hours ago.

Rylee suddenly found herself holding Benny's weight as he lost consciousness, going slack in her arms.

Shifting out from under his back, Rylee lay Benny flat on her coat. As she scrambled to get around to Benny's side, Neesa was pointing at the briefcase guy, "Find the AED machine now. It's hanging on a wall, probably somewhere near the tickets. Use your voice, call out to get everyone looking. Run there. Run back. *Safely* run back."

Rylee didn't see what happened next. Adrenaline shrank her world to only the information that would help her save this man. On the battlefield, with her injured Marines, it cancelled out the sights and sounds around her, to her benefit and detriment. It was indeed a double-edged sword. She didn't hear the bombs whistle, or the ratatat of machine gun fire. She had to act as if her own life wasn't in imminent danger as she focused on the work in front of her.

And as it was then, so it was now, tunnel vision.

Tapping hard on the man's shoulder, Rylee shouted, "Sir, can you hear me?"

Nothing.

She spat on her fingers and used that to wet her cheek as she dipped Benny's chin back and hovered over Benny's nose and mouth. There she held, counting ten. If there was even a stray wisp of breath, the moisture from her saliva would make the air movement more pronounced.

Nothing.

Rylee looked at Bean Counter. "Repeat this: He's not breathing—cardiac arrest."

Bean Counter's face burned red as she screwed her features up tightly, looking determined not to cry over the human tragedy unfolding in front of her so she could keep doing her part.

Rylee loosened the man's tie and reached into the opening between the buttons on his blue and white pin-striped shirt. Grasping either side, she pulled her elbow up and out in one swift move, ripping the shirt open.

Tiny buttons pinged across the platform.

Sweat formed in Rylee's pits, and her shoes had somehow come off her feet. She flipped to a four-by-four combat breath.

Rylee had performed life-or-death interventions in the battlefield with bullets whizzing over her head, a bullet-resistant vest strapped around her torso, and a metal helmet cooking her brain under the desert sun. She could certainly deal with this. "Neesa, start CPR with me. I'll take compressions first. There's a vapor barrier on the keychain in my coat pocket."

Rylee knelt beside the man, using her fingers to trace down his sternum to find the end of the ribs so she could stay clear of the tiny triangular bone that could wreak havoc if it was dislodged. One hand stacked on top of the other, lacing her fingers, locking her elbows, and placing the heels of her hand about halfway down his breastbone and in between his nipples, she thrust downward.

Rylee was back on the battlefield, where she set all emotion aside to focus; she'd deal with the human side of all this later, in the quiet and dark of night. Now, she used her body weight to increase the pressure, her hands buried in a thick carpet of chest hair. When the AED got there, they'd have to shave patches on Benny's chest to get the pads to stick.

"He's lying on your coat." Neesa was reaching under Benny as she fished around and drew out Rylee's keys.

"Neesa, put music on."

Lunging forward, Neesa grabbed Rylee's phone, held it in front of Rylee's face to open the security, and pulled up the music playlist they'd created at work for CPR training.

Each song ranged from 100 to 120 beats per second. The variety of music helped the teams from zoning out on the counts.

"Twenty. Twenty-one. Twenty-two," Rylee huffed as she felt her hands descend violently into Benny's rib cage. *Two inches, two inches, or you're just wasting your effort. Dig deep. Push hard.*

Neesa was scrambling around, pulling the barrier from its little blue keychain packet, unfolding it with uncooperative fingers, then laying it on Benny's face.

Just as Rylee huffed, "Thirty," and sat back on her heels to catch her breath, Neesa bent to fill Benny's lungs.

"Another breath, Neesa," Rylee said, scanning for anyone else who might have arrived who could take turns with the compressions. She was a machine that was running out of gas. As she emerged from the adrenaline-induced focus, she was surprised that no other helpers had arrived on the scene. There was Neesa and the Bean Counter.

The Bean Counter was gripping her phone in both hands, looking traumatized but steadfast.

As Neesa lifted, Rylee went back to her counting.

Five rounds of thirty thrusts—her turn complete, Rylee changed positions with Neesa.

When Rylee took up the kneeling position alongside Benny's head, she was gasping for air.

Poor Neesa was a lighter, shorter woman than Rylee, and so it took a great deal more effort. Rylee watched to make sure Neesa was getting the required depth.

When Neesa, sweat dripping from her forehead, gasped out, "Thirty," it was Rylee's turn to tip Benny's head back, lift his chin, and form a seal over the plastic sheet that hopefully kept possibly dangerous germs and vomit out of her mouth.

Not her first time, probably not her last. This was all muscle memory and determination.

The friends had traded places five times—ten long minutes—when they heard a commotion on the stairs.

Briefcase came flying down the steps with an AED in hand.

"Rylee, can you keep compressing while I set up the AED?" Neesa asked.

"Wilco," Will comply. Short, sweet, and zero energy to get it out.

Neesa opened the AED lid, pressed the machine on, and pulled out the pads.

"Razor," Rylee said as she counted aloud. Beside her was Benny's phone, and she knew the friend was listening to all of this because she could hear the guy calling, "Come on, Benny, you've got this. You've got it. Hang in there."

Rylee thought that there was probably some part of Benny that was aware and could receive those messages of encouragement from a friend rather than two strangers on the Metro platform.

Neesa worked fluidly, shaving and placing the pads on the upper right chest, then the left at armpit level. With hands trembling from adrenaline, Neesa connected the pads to the AED.

As soon as the machine said, "Stop compressions. Analyzing," both women pulled their bodies away from Benny.

A quick scan of the area said they had Bean Counter and Briefcase helping. Rylee wondered why the D.C. police hadn't swarmed down the stairs. Sure, they could be running full-out to get there, or there might have been a communications breakdown. But at least the Metro train whizzed on by without stopping or letting anyone off.

Snatching up Benny's phone during the momentary respite, Rylee moved it next to the man's ear, a safe distance from any interference with the AED, and called down. "Benny's friend, you're on speaker phone. Keep it up. Keep encouraging him."

"Yes. Yes. Benny, man. I texted Martha. Think of your wife and kids. They need you. You can do this for them, right?"

A robotic female voice came through the AED speakers, "Shock advised."

"Clear," Neesa and Rylee said together, holding their hands in the air to visually confirm that no one was touching Benny.

Then, Rylee reached out and pressed the shock button.

She'd seen the process on videos in training, and she knew what to expect, but she'd never been around when an AED was used on a person in front of her.

It was violent, and Rylee's own heart slammed into her rib cage.

"Resume compressions," the AED advised. And Rylee went right back to work, turning her head to see the brief-case guy. "Can you do this?"

"Touch him?" Briefcase took a step backward.

"Compressions," Neesa said, as Rylee counted toward thirty. "We're tired."

"Yeah. No. No, I can't," he stammered. "I can run errands for you, though. Should I go find other people who can do this?"

"Yes," Neesa said, moving back to Benny's head, ready to administer artificial breath. "Get a bunch, not just one."

As Rylee said, "Thirty," Neesa pinched Benny's nose as she leaned low.

The two-minute mark was timed by the machine: "Analysis complete." "Shock advised."

Benny's body arched backward as he was jolted into the air.

Where was help?

Neesa took over the compressions as Rylee caught her breath.

"Benny? Benny? Hey man, I'm here with you, brother. You're going to get through this. Hang in there, man." The voice on the phone was solid and focused. Rylee used the man's cheerleading to bolster her own morale.

Bean Counter leaned in, "The 911 operator said the paramedics are on location."

Two minutes flew by, and the AED was in charge. "Stop compressions. Analyzing."

Another shock.

The man's friend was clearly traumatized by the sounds. There was a swallowed sob in his voice as he switched from cheerleading to "remember when" stories, making plans to go fishing, and talking about the games of poker yet to be played.

"Resume compressions," the AED advised.

Rylee thought about the man beneath her palms, the mentioned wife and children. She dug deep into her personal resolve, using all of her weight and will to make her thrusts go deep enough.

Clattering on the stairs came a moment later.

The chaos of uniforms and equipment was welcomed.

Rylee picked up the phones, then scooted on her butt over the filth of the platform to the wall and out of the way. It stank of stale urine, but her limbs were jelly, and she couldn't stand. Once home, she'd wash under scalding water until the tank ran cold.

Blouse damp and clingy from exertion sweat, Neesa came to collapse against her, hugging tightly as the friends caught their breath. Hearing the paramedics' radio communications, Rylee lifted Benny's phone to her mouth. "Sir, you can probably hear the paramedics are here and took over Benny's care," she panted. "They're taking Benny to the level one trauma hospital on Georgia Avenue."

"Georgia Avenue. My god. Thank you. Thank you so much."

"I'm sending the phone on with Benny."

"Yes, thank you. I'll stay on the line, though, talking with him. Is that okay? Who am I talking to? Who is this?"

Rylee had already handed the phone to one of the paramedics. "This is Benny's phone, and his friend is on the line. He can describe Benny earlier in the day, signs and symptoms, and family contact information."

The paramedic accepted the phone, and Rylee went to stand out of the way so she could eventually retrieve her coat, which had, if nothing else, kept Benny off the freezing platform during his ordeal.

Neesa turned toward Rylee and weakly lifted her hand for a high five. "Damn, girl."

Rylee laced her fingers into Neesa's and closed her eyes.

Life was fragile.

9

———————

Tuesday

WHEN RYLEE WALKED into Neesa's office the next morning, Neesa was sitting in one of her side chairs by the window. Her legs were draped over the arm, and she was cradling a mug of steaming coffee. She looked a little bleary. "Did you sleep last night?" she asked.

"Nope." Rylee headed over to Neesa's coffee pot and poured herself a mug of her own. "Thick. You made it high test." She made her way over behind Neesa's desk, flung herself into the captain's chair, and kicked her feet onto the desk surface with a groan.

"Yeah, that's how it feels. My whole body aches. All of it. Every tiny little forgotten muscle." Neesa sipped her coffee. "Want to hear the crazy shit that was circulating through my head at three in the morning?"

"I'm afraid," Rylee said. "Do I want your middle-of-the-night crazy thoughts in my head? I mean, I have my own." She reached for her mug and wrapped her hands around the warmth. "This about Benny?"

"I just kept wondering if he would make it, and then I was lying there talking to the ceiling, asking his wife to forgive us because she wasn't the last woman to kiss her husband."

Rylee blinked in bewilderment. "Wait, Neesa, you were kissing him?"

"You get what I mean. Put my lips on his lips. It feels sacrilegious that he should go out with another woman's lips on his and not his wife's."

"Okay, that's dark, and I didn't see it coming. I will remind you that he had the pressure of your lips on his, but you were using a shield. Also, we'd only be the last if he died before his wife could get to the hospital. And I refuse to believe that happened."

"The only way we'll ever know is if it ends up in the news, which it won't because there was no one around to film it and put the images out on social media." Neesa pulled in a deep breath and exhaled it toward the ceiling. "I'm imagining he lived. In my mind, he got to the hospital, and they had to do some tests, some interventions. We cracked some ribs, he's sore but grateful and wondering who the hell it was kissing him back to life like some gender-bending Snow White tale."

"Girlfriend," Rylee said with a shake of her head, "you need some sleep." She took a sip of coffee. "This tastes terrible." She took a second sip. "It's my observation that when you're in a life-or-death situation, working for survival, relationships are cemented. We will think about Benny for the rest of our lives. He and Briefcase and Bean Counter."

"Bean Counter was on the phone with 911?" Neesa paused. "Bean Counter, okay, at least she has a name since she's cemented to me."

"I swear I can feel the tug of my Neanderthal roots," Rylee said.

"See? I'm not the only one who's sleep-deprived and filled with odd thoughts. Neanderthal?" Neesa asked.

"What I'm saying is that it's got to be written in our DNA that in a situation that intense, irrefutable bonds are forged." Rylee sniffed the bitter coffee. "I wish I knew who everyone was," Rylee said. "It would be nice to raise a toast together to acknowledge our forever connection and then send Christmas cards each year with an update. I can't tell you how many Marines—just kids, really—I patched up on the battlefield. In my mind, they're all my brothers and sisters. I declare—because I want it to be so—that they are all healed and living wonderful lives. They visit me in my dreams. I think of them and float good thoughts their way."

"You don't see them in real life, though?" Neesa asked. "None of them?"

"Another day, another battle. I choose to think about it like a mother who can't leave Ireland during the Potato Famine because her roots are set too deep, but her children sail across the ocean to Canada, where they're filling their bellies and thriving. My love flows to them on the wind."

"Poetic."

"Don't be that way. I'm a little bit serious here." Rylee closed her tired eyes.

"What did you name them, Bean Counter and Briefcase?" Neesa asked rhetorically. "Them, Benny, and weirdly the friend on the phone with his steady beat of support and love for this guy, you're right, I'll never forget them."

"Yup, there was Phone-a-friend and, of course, me," Rylee said.

"Girlfriend, you've been my ride or die for over a decade. These people are newly cemented."

Rylee lifted her mug. "May our newly cemented find peace."

Neesa lifted hers in response, and then the women sat in exhausted silence.

Rylee peeked at the clock on the wall. "What time is the lawyer getting here?"

A knock sounded at the door.

"Now." Neesa pulled herself around, so she was sitting professionally, but Rylee did not.

"Come in." Neesa waited for Sun to snick the door shut before offering, "Find a chair. Tell us what you know."

"Hello." He followed Neesa's finger to the empty chair and went to sit down. "The Secret Service will be here in about twenty minutes. They're bringing their K9 with them," he said, facing Rylee.

"I'm out on a training evolution. Neesa will be handling all that."

Sun swiveled toward Neesa. "Our plan is to bend over backward to be helpful."

"So you're suggesting we stretch before they get here?" As soon as she said it, Neesa held up her hand and shook her head. "Coffee hasn't kicked in yet. I'm 100% taking this seriously. The special agents are going to brief us, right?"

Neesa asked. "We don't know what we don't know. This is the first time anything like this has come up. We have a lot to learn from this, so we can prevent it from happening again."

"This is the third time," Sun said quietly.

"What?" the women said simultaneously.

"Two other times, fast response team members brought counterfeit U.S. dollars to foreign banks, attempting to convert the money to local currency. At that point, they discovered that it was counterfeit. The embassy and the local government got involved. I think if they weren't associated with a group bringing them disaster relief, that it would have been a bigger stink."

"And you didn't tell us?" Rylee swung her feet off the desk and planted them solidly on the floor. "This wasn't in any of their reports. No one brought it to my attention." Rylee turned to catch Neesa's gaze to check in.

And Neesa shook her head.

"In this case, our legal team was apprised, and we were allowed to bring the CEO and CFO into the circle. But the Secret Service asked that it be kept to counsel and heads of our organization while they investigated the situation. I will add that other international charities working in disaster response were impacted as well."

"Not just us, then," Rylee said.

"Also, the two previous incidents involved twenty-dollar bills and not hundred-dollar bills from our bands."

"This happened in two completely different countries?" Neesa asked. "But you don't bite the hand that feeds you. That must mean that someone in the disaster community was involved. Could it be like domestic violence, you test the waters to see what you can get away with, then up your crimes?" Neesa scowled. "Twenties went okay, so now they're trying for hundred-dollar bills?"

Sun leaned in. "Yes, they could have been stress testing their process. Those first two incidents were a year ago, give or take."

"Were the three incidents all from the same team? This is Oscar, who deployed to Colombia." Rylee asked.

"Different teams," Sun said. "But all three were rapid response teams. Oscar, today, before that, November, and Papa. Tell me, this team that was down in Colombia, were they training?"

"Does this matter?" Rylee asked.

"Yes," Sun clasped his hands and dropped them between his knees. "I wish to understand the circumstances."

Neesa bent over to grab her laptop, tapped, then spun the screen around to show Sun a map. "Here in the north-western region, there was a series of landslides. That area included the city of Bello, which is right here." Neesa picked up a pen from the side table and pointed to a spot on the map. "There was unusually heavy rainfall that created mudslides, with a significant number of the population either dead or missing."

"We sent in Oscar Team after coordinating with Italy," Rylee said. "We've trained together, and we have a good working relationship. Italy sent in their search K9s, so we sent in Oscar. Oscar focuses their training on finding people in shifting terrains, extracting people from debris, and dealing with crush injuries. To do that, they figure out where they think the person was positioned before the event, then feed that information into their physics model to predict where the person might have ended up. There are a lot of variables that make this prediction unreliable, but in a river of mud and building materials, it's a starting point."

"Did they find everyone?" Sun asked.

"Their last report said fifteen known missing," Rylee said. "At this point, it's a recovery effort, and that's not our team's training, so we brought them home, and Greece is sending in their team to help find the deceased."

"And when the teams are called out for a mission, they carry bands of U.S. hundred-dollar bills. Why would that be the case?" Sun asked.

"In an emergency, cash is king," Neesa said. "But all over the world, when markets are rocky, the U.S. dollar in cash is pope,"

Sun scowled.

"It's because everyone puts their faith in it," Rylee clarified. "I can give you a non-mission example of why we send them into a situation with U.S. dollars," Rylee said. "Following President Milei's inauguration in 2023, Argentina's government carried out a sharp devaluation plan on its pesos. One day, a tourist could exchange a dollar for so many pesos, and the next day, they could get twice as many pesos. I had a friend who was driving in Argentina on that fateful day, and he was in a car crash." She skated a hand out. "He's fine, barely a scratch. The car was not. But he had failed to get car insurance. With a totaled car that he'd have to pay for out of pocket, at least he had the luck of the US currency doubling in buying power from the day prior. U.S. money is stable in a world of chaos. And that's why U.S. currency is so important on rescue missions all over the world. As a matter of fact, most of the international NGOs that we work with have the same game plan as we do. They carry U.S. currency."

"Sometimes, when things are bleak, and resources for a given tragedy are thin," Neesa said, "for better or for worse, having American dollars in one's pocket makes all the difference."

"All right." Sun sighed and leaned back in his chair. "Okay, this is what we're going to do." He drummed his fingers on his knee. "Yes. These are your people who are, we assume, innocently involved. Still, they are your responsibility. I think a good solution is that Rylee works with various teams out on rapid response team missions, and that way, Rylee, you can monitor everything until the Secret Service can get this figured out."

Rylee pulled her chin back and blinked.

"You have these skills, I think? Sun asked. "You just need to pull them out of your closet and brush them off, right?" Sun shifted in his chair. "Why are you blinking at me like that. You stay in shape."

"I stay in shape, so I lower my risk of heart attack and dementia and hopefully keep myself as free from disability as I can for as long as I can, especially given my genetics. I don't stay in shape to do tactical insertions and hike mountain passes with my bodyweight in a pack on my back."

"Hopefully it won't come to that," Sun said. "Hopefully, it's a catastrophe somewhere that you can get to with an off-road vehicle. Until then, you could double your protein and start taking creatine to bulk up your muscles. Maybe get a trainer to work with you. I was thinking this through last night. And I came to this conclusion because the Secret

Service doesn't want anyone to know about their investigation. So it has to be a known face."

"I already doubled my protein and creatine," Rylee said dryly. "I'm just not in my twenties anymore. You're a known face, Sun. You go."

"She's teasing, Sun," Neesa said. "She was already going to train with the fast response groups and head out into the field. Just so you know, we're both sleep-deprived and in physical pain from an emergency yesterday."

"Sorry, Sun," Rylee said, "it's been a weird twenty-four hours, but I shouldn't be giving you a hard time."

"Okay. So you will go and investigate. You *are* up to it."

"I'll have to feel my way through situation by situation. I was being serious when I said I'm not in my twenties anymore, and my body doesn't just bounce back after injuries the way it used to." Rylee turned to Neesa. "Saying that out loud gives me insight into what our teams are thinking as they're aging in our ranks."

"We'll need to work with our people, so they aren't on a merry-go-round that doesn't stop."

"I'll talk to them about what they think might help," Rylee said. "In the meantime, counterfeit is dangerous not just to derailing our missions when they're functioning on foreign soil with foreign laws and foreign prisons, but also to their health and well-being if locals think that World-Cares is a scam. In a disaster, when survival isn't guaranteed, emotions run hot."

Neesa focused on Sun, "Did they put our people in jail?"

"They were asked questions at the airport," he said. "The counterfeit currency was confiscated, and everyone went home."

Rylee's phone alarm sounded. "That's my signal that it's time to skedaddle. I have to dress out and head to the training ground. Today, Sun, per your good counsel, I will start training with Lima Team on how to leap out of a hovering helicopter."

10

——————

Tuesday

THE WALK from his office to the WorldCares Operations building was only about fifteen minutes.

He wore his urban male uniform: a medium-shade blue suit, brown hard-soled shoes, and a tie. Dakota hated the tie; he'd never get comfortable wearing a tie. Especially now as it flapped around in the wind. He kept tucking it back into his suit jacket, putting "tie clip" on his mental shopping list.

Last night on the way home from work, Benny had a heart attack, and Dakota had joined Jasper up at the hospital supporting Martha until her family could get there. Worried for his friend, Dakota had taken Tank for a good, long run that morning to shake off any prickly energy that might interfere with today's mission.

It was still good to fast-pace their walk, settling any

nerves either of them might have going into a new experience: their first real-world solo sniff test.

He'd have to ask permission to use his video camera during the part of this meeting where Tank was deploying his sniffer. He could imagine that it wouldn't normally be allowed for security reasons. But Reaper wanted to see how they did when he wasn't around to keep fine-tuning the team's approach.

When Dakota was with the Navy on the swift boat team, it was all about honing skills, building best-practice muscle memories, and consistency so that missions flowed like water. Dakota and Tank could never let up on their daily training.

Just as Dakota put his foot on the bottom stair of the WorldCares Operations building, the right-side door swung open. A brown-haired woman in a black trench coat stepped out onto the stoop, angling her head toward the sky to check the weather, then turning her attention to her phone before raising her hand in the air to signal someone. She hustled away from him, down the stairs toward the cross street.

Yeah, it was *her*.

A moment later, she disappeared from view.

Dakota would have liked better reflexes and a quicker brain at that moment, then he'd have jogged around the corner to see if he could introduce himself.

Yeah, definitely *her*.

It wasn't just the brown hair; it was how she moved with the fluidity of an athlete and an aura of confidence, even when she was storming out of a medical building seething with anger.

She was the same woman he'd seen Sunday at the races, too, because Tank knew her.

Tank leaped forward like he had at the mud race, hellbent on getting over to her this time.

Dakota had to lift Tank off his feet by the handle of his work vest to maintain control.

That was no small feat, since Dakota's body flew apart into those particles like some kind of sci-fi film character. His gray matter wasn't firing on all cylinders.

Luckily, he pieced himself back together much faster than the first time it happened at the race, where he blamed the sensation on depleted electrolytes.

And yesterday, the same damned sensation when he turned suddenly at the taxi to see her coming out of the medical building. It had dissipated a bit faster.

If this sensation was a reaction to that woman, he was slowly acclimating to her strange effect on his circuitry. He felt whole again much faster. The zap of energy left him feeling powerful and clear-minded, like a shot of adrenaline when he was deep in the fight. It was the side of effervescent tingle that felt strange.

Correlation isn't causation, Dakota reminded himself.

One of his Swift Water brothers had developed something called Bow Hunter's Syndrome that stemmed from his years on the football field and on the battlefield, which created lasting neurological trauma that made him pass out with sudden twists of his head.

Dakota swung his head quickly side to side just to see, and it changed nothing.

After yesterday with Benny's heart attack, this sensation Dakota had experienced three days in a row was catching his attention, especially given his own traumatic injury list.

Dakota asked Benny if he needed a doctor; Benny said he'd go the next day. That decision on Benny's part almost cost him his life.

Was Dakota being a coward for not stopping by some walk-in clinic to at least run these sensations by a doc? What would Dakota even say? "Listen, I think something's been shaken out of whack from all the times I crouched too close to a blast radius back in my days in the sandbox. Maybe something finally came loose."

That seemed a reasonable way to start.

More reasonable than that, he had developed some weird reaction to a brown-haired woman who was about five feet eight and had the build of a tennis player. Suddenly, he was spotting her all over Washington, D.C., and every time he did, he fragmented.

Dakota set Tank back on the ground. "What say you, Tank? Have you got it together?"

Tank's body had stiffened with concentration. His nose was chuffing the air. Then he sat and looked up for his next instruction.

She must be gone.

Signaled to walk by his side, Tank plastered his body to Dakota's thigh, but his tongue hung long, drooling with hyped nerves. Dakota decided to take a couple of minutes to circle the block so that when they were inside and hopefully, given permission to search any cash reserves as a team, they were squared away.

When Dakota and Tank were back to even keel, Dakota

went through the door to the security desk and showed his credentials.

Tank's nose was chuffing the air, and the guard lifted off the seat and leaned over the desk to get a look. "That's a magnificent dog," he said as he sat back down. "Straight through to the elevator bank, then up to the fifth floor. Out of the elevator, take a right, then another right, and you'll come to the director's PA's desk. I'll let her know you're on your way up."

Tank's feet were wide, and his nose was on the ground as he followed a scent. Either someone had dribbled steak juice, or they were following the brown-haired woman's trail. For a flash, Dakota thought it would be interesting to just let Tank do his thing, trace the scent to its source, and maybe learn the woman's name.

But then, what would she think of that? "Stalker material, buddy. How about you stop that? Let's give the woman some privacy." Dakota signaled "leave it" to Tank, who then swiveled and plastered himself to Dakota's side.

Up they went. Following the directions from security, the team landed at the PA's desk. Stepping back to wait patiently for her to finish up her phone call, Tank focused on the open door of an empty office and stomped his foot.

And there it was, a vase of distinctive tropical flowers.

Very distinctive. Very tropical.

Dakota reached down and scritched the top of Tank's head. "Got it."

"Sir, may I help you?"

"Yes, ma'am—"

"Erica." She smiled.

"Yes, thank you, Erica. I'm Special Agent Dakota Kayne

with the Secret Service." He held up his badge. "I have an appointment with Neesa Meesang this morning."

"She's on a call and will be just a minute. May I offer you a cup of coffee or a bottle of water?"

"No, thank you, ma'am. But could you tell me whose office this is?" He pointed toward the open door.

"Rylee Jones? She's co-director of operations along with Neesa."

Tank leaned into his leg and looked up at him.

"It's Rylee," Dakota told him as a diminutive woman with long black hair leaned around the door, one office down. Her wide-legged pants and tunic seemed like an effective executive style for an NGO. Her look said clean and precise, but also comfortable and welcoming. "Hey, you must be Dakota Kayne and Tank." She focused on Tank, "You are magnificent. Wow." She looked up at Dakota. "Huge."

"Yes, ma'am, thank you. Jasper Lee texted me that he's running five minutes late. My apologies. We usually run a tight ship, but last night our colleague ended up in the hospital with a life-threatening condition, and Jasper wanted to stop by this morning to check on the family."

"Of course."

Neesa flicked a hand toward Rylee's office. "This is Sun Yu with legal."

Dakota bobbed his head in greeting without walking Tank farther into the room. Some folks were intimidated by Tank's size; better to hang out by the door and give everyone the necessary space.

With a hand signal, Tank lay neatly at Dakota's feet, pillowing his chin on his paws and closing his eyes.

"My co-director is involved in a training evolution this

morning. I'll do my best to answer all your questions, and I'll note the ones that need more research or Rylee's input. I expect her later today." She turned to the PA. "Erica, we're expecting one more. Just show him in when he gets here."

"I understand from Sun that three of our teams have caught your attention." She picked up a pen and held it with both hands. "I wish I had known right away, so we could try new security protocols to protect our people."

"Not a team," Sun clarified, "in the first two incidents, the concern centered around a single individual. In this latest incident, three of our team members carried the unused cash back to the United States. All three teams involved were our fast-reaction teams."

"How many teams do you have?" Dakota asked.

"Twenty disaster teams, their size depends on their mission focus. Seven of those are the fast reaction teams, Kilo through Quebec. They can either work together, each performing their specialty at a site, or they can break off and work alone. Each team develops different skill sets. For example, we have an avalanche team. They train out of Newfoundland, so they can drop down into the Arctic region quickly. They develop mainly European language skills, which are becoming less relevant as most people under 35 speak amazing English. Our teams work with older generations, too, so part of our training protocol includes survival language skills of the more populous language groups, so we don't always have to rely on a translation app. Which becomes clunky in an emergency. Oscar had the right skills and languages for Colombia."

"Out of curiosity, how do you handle it if your teams don't have the language for the deployment?" Dakota hoped that some banter and curiosity would ease WorldCares into a comfortable relationship with Jasper and him. They weren't here as adversaries. Quite the opposite.

"There are locations that aren't on our language list, so on the way over, you'll find our group sitting on the airplane learning basics: stop, go, come, water, food, shelter. Simple-simple, there's only so much you can learn in a few hours. And for much of their travel time, they prioritize sleep. Sleep becomes a precious commodity once they're boots on the ground."

Erica showed up at the door, showing Jasper in.

It was interesting to see him stall out when he met Neesa.

She stood and walked from behind her desk, extending her hand. "Neesa Meesang and you're Jasper Lee? I'm so glad to meet you."

The handshake hadn't ended.

"Yes, Jasper. I'm sorry to be late."

Still, the handshake hadn't ended.

"Traffic in this part of town is difficult," Jasper explained.

Erica came back to the room, pushing a rolling chair.

"Right here," Neesa said, gesturing to the open space by her desk. "Thank you." She turned to Jasper and ended the handshake with a gesture toward the chair.

Interesting.

Dakota introduced Sun and gave Jasper a quick summary of what had been said.

Jasper unbuttoned his suit jacket. "At the airport yesterday, we were surprised at how much cash your people were carrying."

"Which they declared at customs after your interrogation, correct?" Sun asked.

Neesa looked at Sun, then turned to Jasper. "I imagine you have access to the border records, and you'll see this is the norm for our organization. If you need them, I can provide you with our records. Everything is accounted for."

"Yes, thank you," Jasper said. "The thing I'm trying to understand here is why there is so much cash flowing over the borders with your organization."

Dakota noticed that Jasper had pitched his voice lower and smoother than usual. Dakota tucked that away so he could ride Jasper about it after they left.

"That cash is kept here on site or in a bank?" Dakota asked.

"Here we have a walk-in safe and a security guard," Neesa said. "Tank is the dog that smelled the fake money on my team?"

"Yes, ma'am." This might be sticky, and it could go either way if Neesa got protective of her staff.

"Thank you. It's important that we figure this out to protect my teams from even the shadow of any illegality. So we need to get to the bottom of this." Neesa pointed toward Tank. "He came today to see if we had any more counterfeit money in our safe?"

"All the money coming into the United States with your teams is stored there?" Jasper asked.

"The money that's associated with WorldCares, yes. But we don't regulate in any way the personal money of our responders."

"Can you explain why you deal with so much cash?" Jasper asked.

"Oh, for a lot of reasons. We can't always pack in everything we need, so we either buy from other NGOs or from locals, including cases of water, food, fuel, medicine, and medical equipment. If our people can buy locally, it is preferred because it helps to strengthen the local base economy. Sometimes, we hand out cash to affected people so they have the resources to leave the area and go stay with friends and family somewhere that wasn't experiencing the disaster. That helps remove some of the population from areas with the greatest need and the least resources. Many foreign groups bring in U.S. dollars because it is widely recognized and flows freely and with trust from hand to hand in the local economy. Of course, if you're thinking about inserting counterfeit dollars, that would be an easy way to do it. The local people have probably never handled U.S. dollars in person, because why would they? So how would they know they were being swindled? It's immoral."

"The money that your team brought in was in hundred-dollar denominations," Jasper said.

"Otherwise, the money would need its own suitcase. Hundreds are easy enough."

"How do you protect that?" Dakota asked. "People in dangerous situations and dire straits can do things that are normally outside of their morals and ethics."

"Agreed," Neesa said. "Of course they do. This is especially true when it comes to food. Everything and anything becomes precious under such circumstances. How do we protect it? It starts here with recording all the serial numbers and banding the stacks using the tracking system. That's monitored. We keep the money in a location where a team member is always present. They don't leave it, even to go to the latrine. They develop a duty roster when they get boots on the ground. Someone has to be awake with the equipment; they take turns."

Neesa stopped and swiveled toward Jasper, sitting very still with a frown pulling at the corners of her mouth.

"I'm worried about what you're going to find in the vault," she said. "I was thinking about it all night."

"What did you come up with?" Dakota asked.

"That if it were me in the field trying to pull a fast one, I'd put a real bill on top and bottom. In the movies, they just fan through it." Neesa said. "So people would only see the top and the bottom if they were handling a stack."

"That's ten thousand, do you hand out a stack like that?" Dakota asked.

"Absolutely. The price-gauging in these situations is high. Here in the United States, if there's a hurricane coming through, greedy people jack up the costs of gas, hotels, food, and tarps. If it's a survival item and there's a limited supply, the price flies sky high. Same around the world. It's a get-while-the-getting's-good mentality. That doesn't mean we'd be in a position to go without. We pay what we need to pay in order to get the job done. That job is saving lives." Neesa turned her focus back to Jasper. "There's the personality of the thief to consider. Who the hell steals from a charity that's saving people in dire straits?" She pushed back into her chair. "They're going to hell."

Sun's eyebrows shot up to his hairline when she said 'hell.'

Neesa slapped her palms onto her desk. "But we can't wait around for karma to kick in. We need to protect WorldCares. So this is where I want to start: I need permission from you to talk to our CEO about getting a public relations crisis team involved here." She swept her hand through the air. "I want to make a full disclosure of what's happened. Talk about our commitment to integrity, not just the rule of law, but the rule of doing what's right for the best for those I need." Neesa's voice grew louder as righteous anger rose in her chest.

"Yes, ma'am," Jasper said. "That's a strategy. One we'd rather not act on immediately."

"Kumar Singh, he was at the airport, but he's not here today," Sun said. "How does he fit into this picture?"

"Kumar is on our team," Dakota said. "He's been developing this case. We're joining in now that he believes this is a single actor who is working for personal gain, taking advantage of all the aspects of targeting groups such as yours, which move from country to country with unusual but legitimate amounts of cash."

"You're just going to go through our safe and remove any counterfeit bills, so we don't do anything illegal, right?" Neesa asked.

"Yes, ma'am, that's correct," Jasper said.

"You don't have to ma'am me. I feel like we're all in this together, and saying ma'am kind of makes me an outsider."

"Thank you," Jasper said with a smile.

"Can your dog detect all counterfeit money?" Sun asked.

"Tank was trained to find the money that is generated from two different countries," Dakota said, putting a hand on Tank's head as he roused after hearing his name.

"From Peru and Colombia?" Neesa asked Jasper.

He didn't respond.

"I looked up the countries where most of the counterfeit

money comes from, and of course, my team was coming from Colombia. We also sent in teams to the recent flooding in Peru. That was team November." She nodded toward the lawyer. "Sun told me how we had team members stopped at the bank there. Someone really should have told me immediately."

"Neesa, I didn't submit for a search warrant for today," Jasper said. "Sun indicated that your organization wanted to be cooperative."

"Absolutely," Neesa stood. "I'm not putting our teams in danger by accidentally sending them out with fake currency. I'm appreciative that you're here."

As the men stood, Dakota said, "We'll use Tank to help us out. But Jasper also has a machine with us to test the bills, should Tank indicate on any of them."

Neesa was tense as she stood up from her desk and passed through the door. "Okay, the vault is on this level, just around the corner."

Jasper went out first, walking beside Neesa, followed by Dakota and Tank.

Sun came up behind them.

"We keep our cash in a safe cabinet on one side of the secured room. In that area, we also keep medications. Some of them are controlled substances." She rounded the corner. "Our fast-response teams are all trained in advanced trauma, but we don't have doctors on board. Setting up the field hospitals is something we leave to specialized organizations." She turned the second corner. "We do pack in what our own people might need should they sustain an injury and evacuation is delayed. It's prescribed via communications with an on-call doctor who is always on duty here at WorldCares."

Tank knew that he was about to play one of his favorite games of sniff and find. His whole body was alert and ready.

They moved to a security gate. "Hi, Stew," Neesa greeted the guard. "You're expecting us this morning."

Jasper and Dakota pulled out their badge wallets and lifted them. "Secret Service," Jasper announced.

Stew took another look at Neesa, then over to Sun to see if there were any signals or signs of distress before he unlocked the gate from his side.

"Do you keep a lot of money on hand?" Jasper asked, eyeing the security structure.

Stew shut and locked the gate behind them, moving them to the biometrics box, where Neesa looked into a black screen as she laid her hand on a pad.

"A necessary amount," Neesa said as she heard the whir and click that meant the computer had properly identified her and processed the lock. "Remember, we have twenty teams. It's often the case that they are fanned around the world. Much like a street fight, a disaster in one part of the world doesn't mean another one isn't revving up in another part of the world."

They walked into the room, neat as a pin, with shelves of medications in careful rows and two refrigerators. "O negative blood and saline," she said, "for our most remote ventures. That requires quite a bit of cross-border paperwork, so it's ready for exceptional circumstances." She pulled one side of a shelving unit, which swung away from the wall, revealing a hidden security door. There, Neesa typed in a code and tugged it wide.

"So here it is." Neesa gestured to what looked like perhaps a hundred banded stacks of bills.

A quick calculation meant that they kept approximately a million dollars in cash on hand.

Neesa seemed to read his mind. "Twenty teams with fifty thousand each. Yes, it's a lot. But we are ready for extremes. What if there's a collapse of a market? A run on a bank? An EMP or a hacker? Illiquidity risks lives. And cash and carry is always a lower price."

Fifty thousand per team, trying to buy equipment and supplies in-country for an undetermined amount of time? Yes, that was more than reasonable.

"Each time a group goes out, we record the tracking band. If you were to find more counterfeit bills, we can trace that down to all the locations where that band of money was taken."

Jasper turned to Dakota. "You're ready to go in?"

Dakota, in turn, turned to Neesa. "Is it okay if I video record with camera and mic to share with Tank's trainer?"

Neesa shifted uncomfortably, but Sun said, "Of course, anything you need."

Dakota handed his messenger bag to Jasper, taking a moment to attach a camera to a chest harness. Then he reached back into his bag and pulled out a rolled-up towel.

Holding it under Tank's nose, Dakota signaled it was go time.

11

———

RYLEE

Tuesday

NEESA PUSHED BACK from her desk. "How was the helicopter jumping, bonding experience?"

"Well, if everything hurt this morning," Rylee said, easing herself into the guest chair.

"This afternoon, it's worse." She dropped her backpack to the floor. "I forgot just how strenuous that crap is. But I gritted my teeth and tried to make it look like a smile so everyone would think I was Miss Mary Sunshine and wouldn't bitch when I told them I was going on the Fast Reaction Roster to head out with the next team." She reached behind her head and started pulling bobby pins from her bun. "So that's me, what happened here?"

Rylee listened carefully as Neesa walked her through her meeting with Jasper, Dakota, and Tank. "Gorgeous dog."

"Accurate, though?"

"They had a machine, and when Tank alerted, they tested the notes. So I don't know if he found them all, but I do know that every alert was accurate."

"We need everything in the safe to go through a machine to be tested, though, don't we? To be extra sure?"

"We do. Since the Secret Service found evidence, they're sending someone over tomorrow with a faster machine. Their special agent will be in the vault with Erica. We have the video recording anyway, but she'll monitor everything. After that's done, Erica will make sure we have all the serial numbers properly documented, counted, and banded. They were surprised that we kept that much cash in our vault and wondered why we had so much cash on hand."

"You explained the number of our teams, that we serve all over the world, and the length of time they're often on site without a banking system, with major expenses?"

"I did."

"All right. I'm going back to my office to look over our cash protocols and see if I can't find some glaring hole that this bugger is sneaking into. I mean, we video-record every aspect of our missions. Did you mention to them that we have storage tent surveillance and body cam from all the missions on file?"

"It didn't occur to me since I'm the numbers side of things." Neesa scooped up her phone. "Can you sit for a second while I try to get Jasper on the line before he leaves for the day?"

Rylee slid down in the seat until the back cradled her neck, pressing into the space that was starting to feel like a headache.

"Jasper? Neesa Meesang here. I'd like to put you on speaker phone. I have my co-director with me, and she mentioned a resource that I hadn't considered."

After a moment of silence, with permission, Neesa tapped the speaker feature and laid her phone on the desk.

"Rylee Jones, Jasper Lee." Neesa introduced the two.

"Glad to meet you," Jasper said. "So what have you got?"

"Rylee here. On missions, we use videotapes for security surveillance, and our responders wear bodycams. We maintain a library of the footage for ten years."

"Interesting." Jasper's cogs were obviously whirring. "This is for security reasons?"

"Rylee. For many reasons, including the risk of being sued. We need to be good stewards of the money people donate and not hand out millions in legal battles. Equally importantly, responders are hard-driven men and women. They will run themselves into the ground trying to save lives unless we, by directive, tell them to stand down for eight hours of sleep and two hours of rest during the day. So movement is clocked. It seems a bit 'big brother,' but it has turned out to be necessary."

"Neesa here. We have footage of everyone who would have contacted our teams and all movement in our storage area, which is usually on site."

"A tent of some sort?" Jasper asked.

"Neesa. Yes, a refugee tent."

"The tape is interesting," Jasper said, "but we simply don't have the manpower to go through that volume of data. By telling me about this, I'm assuming you believe there might be a common face that needs to be identified?"

"Rylee here. In my mind, it would have to be a known

person. Someone that one of our people would say, 'Hey, can you sit here with the packs for ten minutes so I can go find the latrine. Or even take over a stint. So, for example, if they set up their area next to ours, they could say, 'I'll watch both if you want to get going.' It's the only thing I can think of."

"Hailey Sterling and Iniquus," Rylee whispered toward Neesa.

Neesa stilled and then nodded. "Neesa here. I can't offer this as a solution, but I can reach out and ask." She tapped the desk in thought. "I don't know how big of an ask this is." She looked out the window, obviously processing her thoughts. "It would mean widening the circle of your investigation. Surely, you know of the security company called Iniquus?"

"I do," Jasper said.

"They have a supercomputer that isn't connected to outside sources. This means that all the data was entered into their system purposefully, therefore it is trustworthy and uncorrupted."

"Interesting." Jasper's voice told Rylee he wasn't sure where Neesa was going with this.

"Neesa here. The WorldCares family and the Iniquus family have, since Iniquus's inception, worked at many of the same mission sites. Two of those events led to marriages between our specialists and Iniquus operatives. We're a family of sorts. So, with your okay, I thought I might reach out to one of our alums who now works over there and see if Iniquus would be willing to process the footage."

"I don't see that as a problem. We'd appreciate any data that narrows the playing field."

"Alright. There are just a few more minutes in the workday, so let me reach out now. I'll let the special agent we're expecting tomorrow know what comes of this idea."

"Or," he paused. "Or you could call me directly. Thanks so much to both of you. Neesa, I'll speak with you tomorrow?" Jasper's voice was warm and soothing, what Rylee would deem a "boyfriend voice." Why would he be talking to Neesa like that?

But then Rylee saw Neesa's face, Rylee realized, yep, she was bitten by a love bug.

When Neesa ended the call, Rylee lifted her brows high, waiting for the scoop.

Instead, Neesa got right on the phone with Hailey, and Rylee wandered back to her office to take a pain pill.

The buzzing in her hands and feet had kept her awake for the last few nights, and this week had been physically taxing.

She really should think twice before she flew off with one of the fast-reaction teams into the desperate circumstances of a mass disaster, where sanitation was at a premium and exhaustion was a given.

Should she be putting her body under undue stress? Or was there someone else who could fill that role?

And with that thought, Rylee stared out her window, her mind a complete blank until Neesa barged in with a grin on her face. "The videos, that was a clever thought. Kudos."

"What did Iniquus say?"

"Hailey got me on a call with General Elliot and, since we already had Jasper's blessings—"

Rylee quirked a brow.

"What?"

Rylee grinned. "Just the way you said Jasper."

Neesa stopped and lifted her chin. "How'd I say it?"

Rylee lifted a coy shoulder and, batting eyelashes, purred, "Jasper."

"I did not." Neesa objected. "Did I?"

"We can talk about this Jasper guy later. What did General Elliot say?"

"I explained the situation and the ramifications to the integrity of our organization. Something the general well understood," Neesa said. "He thanked me for the heads up because, like most groups going into disaster zones, Iniquus uses a cash economy, too. They're putting their bills through the machine to check for authenticity. But yes, they're sending an operator team over to collect the video data in the morning."

"Did you consider, Casey Andrews?" Rylee asked. "His face is going to be all over those tapes."

"Oh, shit." Neesa froze. "I did not."

CIA Case Officer Casey Andrews, at Langley's request, often deployed alongside the WorldCares Rapid Response Teams to monitor issues arising from mass disasters. Things that WorldCares wanted protection from: terrorism, governmental instability and regime change, human trafficking, and other forms of exploitation. Andrews let WorldCares know when there was a threat and scooted them out of the area before they became victims, and in return, Andrews got to show up in parts of the world where he might stick out like a sore thumb if he wasn't attached to a logo-wearing group.

"Okay. I'll call Langley in the morning and let them

know that Andrews might end up as a data point. And until given approval, I won't mention Andrews to Jasper."

"Jasper," Rylee sing-songed. "Okay, tell me, what's he like?"

"Smart, not too tall, which is good for someone of my stature. He just seemed really kind. Capable. Unflappable."

"You could use those things in your life. Is he single?" Rylee asked.

Neesa dropped her purse on Rylee's desk. "No ring. But what does that mean?" She pulled her coat on. "Speaking of Jasper. You done for the day?"

"Yeah. I think anything else can wait until morning."

"There's a bar up the street called Macadoo's." Neesa walked toward Rylee's coat hook. "How about we go get a drink to unwind?"

"Suspicious," Rylee said, tipping her head back. "We don't go out for after-work drinks as a rule. Spill."

Neesa lifted Rylee's trench coat and held it to her chest. "On his way out, I heard Jasper saying on his phone that they were leaving here to go to the hospital. But they'd still be on time at Macadoo's for their weekly meet-up."

"It's not at all suspect that you know they'll be there?"

"No," Neesa walked to the hook where Rylee kept her coat, "because I was slinking from potted plant to potted plant so I could eavesdrop."

"Stop."

"I'm kidding. I was walking to the ladies' room when he was making the plans on the phone. All is fair in love and war." She handed Rylee her coat.

Rylee pulled her hair over her shoulder out of the way before slinging her coat on. "And which is this?"

"The war would be against corruption. Love on the other hand?" She shrugged. "Wouldn't that be nice? How about we go have a beer and leave?"

"I don't see why not. Let's get Erica to come with us. Two can look desperate—which we are not—and three looks like a girl group."

Neesa pulled her phone from her pocket and sent a text. "Erica's in the vault. I asked her to join us so I could buy her a beer."

The phone dinged.

"She says she's game, and she'll meet us there. She's just helping Stew close up."

The sidewalk was busy with people moving from their work-a-day life toward their evening obligations.

It was only a ten-minute walk to get to the bar.

Rylee could tell by Neesa's shortened pace that Neesa was getting anxious. Neesa wasn't a jittery kind of person. She was mostly Zen about life. The rare exception was Neesa's nervous reaction around men she found attractive. This was a big tell about how much she liked Jasper, so it was Rylee's duty as the wingman in this situation to change the energy. "You've got that look on your face," Rylee said.

Neesa raised her face with her eyes held unblinking. "What look?"

"Sour. Tense." Rylee pushed her hands in her coat pockets as the night turned cool. "The look you get when you haven't been laid in a while."

Neesa pressed her lips together.

"Jasper's going to pick up on it, and you're going to scare him off," Rylee said. "I'm serious."

"I don't want anything serious. I'm at full capacity right now."

"I disagree," Rylee shifted gears again as Neesa's pace slowed. "If the right guy walked into the picture, you'd make space and time for him. But you interrupted. I'm *serious* that if you can't find Mr. Right, at least for now, you should find a man equally uncommitted to a future, and you can call each other to burn off some steam."

Neesa considered that. "He'd have to be good."

"Agreed, someone who has excellent sack skills and no desire to talk to you."

"Isn't that the dream?" Neesa laughed. "If only such a man existed. It's the sack skills that are missing. There are plenty of men who don't want to talk to me."

"Why do you think that is?" Rylee wasn't sure if Neesa was going along with the riff or if she meant that.

"I don't know." They came to the corner and stopped, waiting to cross. "I don't give off the approachable vibe. Like that woman over there."

Rylee looked across to a woman in a soft pink sweater and comfortable jeans. Her hair was long and glossy, and she was holding her Maltese doggo in her arms. She did indeed look like she'd smile and welcome any conversation, especially one that praised her dog. "Very approachable," Rylee agreed. "Well, you could try a wardrobe change for a bit and see if you can't lure in what you're looking for. You'd have to invest in a dog, though. I think that's her schtick."

"I don't want a dog. I want a booty call—wasn't that popular around the time we were born?" Neesa asked.

When there was a break in the traffic, Rylee bumped

Neesa's arm, and they trotted across the street. "I don't know why that had to fade away as a popular thing. At the same time, I don't like you putting those two ideas together."

"Why's that?" Neesa asked as they stepped over the curb and turned toward the shops.

"Women were getting their needs met with booty calls, and we happened to be born about that time."

"Neither of us is the product of a booty call gone bad," Neesa scoffed. "Your mom was married, and I'm sure she got it when she wanted it without making a call. My mom's a lesbian who picked my dad from a catalog at the sperm bank. Stop." She grabbed Rylee's sleeve. "Look, they're coming up the sidewalk. Stand by this tree."

"What is this, seventh grade?" Rylee found this incredibly funny. She'd never seen Neesa so worked up over a guy.

"Yeah, well, you know, I might be having a good old middle-school girl crush on Jasper. It's been a while since I felt the zing. Can you give me this without handing me a hard time?

"I think that's what you want Jasper to hand you," Rylee whispered.

"Stop," Neesa said, striking a casual pose under the tree. "See? That's what I mean. Don't make this a joke."

"Okay. Turn around. Stand here and look in the shop window with me. We can watch them walk up in the reflection. So Jasper, which one is he?"

"The short one in the middle."

"Who are the other ones with him?" Rylee asked.

"The couple I don't know," Neesa said. "The tall one is the Secret Service dog guy. His name is Dakota Kayne."

"Hmm, he looks familiar to me, but he's also a little warped looking in this window."

The two women waited outside the bar for Erica to show up until a text came through saying she had to take a phone call and was just leaving work. It would be about ten minutes to go in before it got too crowded and snag a stool for her.

She had a point. It looked like everyone had had a shit day, and they were making a beeline for libations.

Inside, Rylee and Neesa snagged the last three stools that were together, and the friends draped their coats over the center stool for Erica before ordering beers.

Neesa stood on her toes. "They're in the very back, in the corner."

"Go let them know you're here."

"We'll both go," Neesa said.

"I'm going to wait for Erica and guard our beers when they're served. Besides, I'm your wingman. You keep me a secret until you need a way to duck out gracefully, then you nod my way and say, 'Oh, look, there's Rylee. Nice to see you. Cheers.' And make your way back to me."

"You think I'll want to flee?"

"No, but you just want to let Jasper see you out of the work sphere as a normal human, and then you leave him wanting more."

Neesa looked their way, then back at her friend. "You okay here by yourself?"

"Yeah, I'm fine. There's a bro who's trying to catch my attention from the other side of the bar, hopefully Erica will get here before he finishes his glass of liquid bravery and comes over here." As Rylee said that, the man sent her a smile, picked up his glass, and stood. "Shit, too late. Here he comes."

"I should stay then," Neesa said.

"I've got it handled." Rylee flapped her hands, shooing Neesa away. "No worries. Go. Go enjoy."

12

Dakota

Tuesday

So apparently, Dakota didn't need to see Rylee to feel that odd sensation.

When they found a table at the back of Macadoo's, there it was, the now familiar buzz. Boom experiment complete. *No Rylee in sight, and my circuitry is going nuts.*

But before he could take that thought to its next rational step of medical intervention, Jasper said. "I think that's Neesa at the bar. She's here with another woman."

Dakota turned and looked across to the front. "Rylee Jones, Neesa's co-director." This time, Dakota managed to keep his atoms mostly stitched together, but she definitely gave him butterflies. Wasn't it interesting that he hadn't seen her when his nervous system first reacted?

"Rylee? I've only spoken to her by phone. You already met her?" Jasper asked.

"Never," Dakota said. "I think we've crossed paths three times this week; this might be number four." He stood to the side and let Veer slide down the booth seat.

"Seems significant," Veer said, adjusting herself into the curve of Kumar's arm. "Maybe your guardian angel is trying his best, but you're not cooperating."

"Either that," Kumar said, "or *her* guardian angel keeps seeing Dakota and is steering her in the other direction."

"In that case, you should probably leave the poor girl alone," Veer said.

"Three times? Where was this?" Jasper asked.

"First time at that charity race on Sunday. She was at the finish line. The second time, she was the woman I handed my flowers to when she got in a cab. Third time, I passed her running out of the WorldCares Operations offices."

"The woman in the taxi could have been anyone, right?" Jasper asked. "A doppelganger?"

"I don't think so." No, Dakota was absolutely sure it was the same woman for no other reason than how his body reacted when she was around.

"Wait," Kumar leaned forward, "You thrust a bunch of flowers at a strange woman?"

"She didn't deck you and run away screaming?" Veer asked.

"It's not like that," Dakota told Veer. "I had just bought some flowers. Then Jasper rerouted me, and I was suddenly heading to the airport. I had the flowers in my hand. She looked stressed out. I didn't really think about it. It all just happened." Dakota beat "She got into the cab, I gave her the flowers, shut the door, the taxi drove off. So yeah, that's about how it went down."

"And you know her name because?" Jasper asked.

"When we went to WorldCares, I first saw her coming out of the building. Then I saw the bouquet on the desk in the office next to Neesa's. When I asked whose office it was, Erica said it was the co-director, Rylee Jones's, office. It was Sherlock Holmes 101."

"Must have been a very distinctive bouquet," Kumar said.

"It was."

"So, no room for a mistake?" Jasper asked, taking off his coat and draping it on the back of his chair. He seemed to be slow-rolling, settling in his seat, perhaps to give Neesa time to see him and come over.

And maybe that was why Dakota was standing there, too. "I'd say not, especially with Neesa sitting right next to her at the bar right up the street from their office."

"Look at Jasper grinning away. I do believe our Jasper is smitten." Veer grinned up at him. "Both of them," she told Kumar, "are smitten kittens."

"Go invite them over, Jasper," Kumar said, "for your sake, but also so Dakota can finally meet his future wife."

"Stop." Dakota pulled out a chair and forced himself into it.

Jasper turned and looked Neesa's way. "Yeah, I'll be right back." As he started toward the front of the bar, Neesa took a step his way. Jasper raised his arm and flagged her over.

The crowd was growing thicker as people left work and came for a drink to unwind.

Neesa was making her way over, but much to Dakota's disappointment, Rylee stayed at the bar. Dakota smiled, stood, and gestured for her to take his seat. "Neesa, good to see you outside of the office."

Neesa's face pinked. "Yes, it's a nice little place here, very convenient to my work, and, I guess, yours too."

Jasper introduced her to Veer and Kumar.

"Should we invite your friend over?" Veer asked, sending an evil grin in Dakota's direction.

Neesa turned to look Rylee's way. "She's waiting for Erica to get here."

As Dakota went to a nearby table to ask if they could spare one of their chairs, Jasper's phone pinged.

Focusing on the screen, Jasper said, "Hey, Benny's out of surgery. All's good."

A sigh of relief made its way around the table.

Dakota put the chair at the far side of the table and sat down across from Neesa. "Our friend had a heart attack going home on the Metro yesterday."

"What now?" Neesa went blank-faced, her lids blinking in a steady tempo.

"I was on the phone with him when it happened," Jasper said. "The people around him were rock stars. They saved his life."

"Goose flesh," Neesa whispered as she rubbed a hand up and down her arm.

"How's that?" Veer asked

"Balding head, blue pin-striped shirt, wife named Martha?"

"That's right," Jasper said with a scowl.

"That was me. Rylee and I did CPR on a man at the L'Enfant Plaza Station right after leaving work on our way to go meet friends for dinner last night."

The table stilled until Veer whispered, "Me too. Goose flesh." She leaned toward Dakota and lifted her brows.

"Many people believe there's no such thing as a coincidence. And if you don't believe in one set of odd circumstances, certainly you can't ignore an entire string of coincidences," she whispered, then raised her voice, "Dakota, go invite Rylee over. We need to thank these wonderful women and toast Benny's successful surgery."

Veer was right about coincidences. It all seemed very neatly woven. Enough so that it was throwing him off.

"How's Benny doing?" Neesa asked. "He's out of surgery, but do they have a handle on things?"

"Good," Jasper said. "Well, not good. He's had better days. But alive. He's on the right road to get him to recovery." He swiveled closer to Neesa. "I'm so glad I found you. Benny wanted to thank someone, but of course, the police don't give out information." He nodded toward Dakota. "Dakota was telling Benny he looked bad and to go to the doctor the morning of his heart attack."

"In my experience," Veer shot a glare in Kumar's direction, "men don't like to know their vulnerabilities, so they rarely go."

"Well, they're rewarded when they do show up. Doctors take men seriously, and they diagnose them with great efficiency," Neesa said. "Their medications are correct and appropriate, and they're very much cared for."

Dakota thought there was a bite of bitterness in her tone.

"It's a little in my face right now, through a colleague," Neesa said, "that women's interactions with the medical establishment are vastly different."

"Really?" Kumar took a moment to shoot a glance back at Veer. Obviously, this was an ongoing point of tension for them. But his expression was neutral when he asked Neesa, "How did you arrive at that conclusion?"

"In every way you can imagine. Mostly, they never really studied the female body until the nineteen nineties. Even things as simple as the BMI. Most people know their BMI, and doctors use it to tell women about their body composition, but it was invented by a Belgian statistician in the eighteen thirties who studied—ready for this? European men. So, white men two centuries ago created the framework for what is a mathematical, not medical metric, that we're judged by at the doctor's. There was no diversity in his work. Women just need to conform to the male scale."

"Huh," Jasper scowled with a hand to his chest. "So not black men or men of Indian descent," he raised his chin toward Kumar.

"And certainly not me," Veer said. "I have two strikes—female and Punjabi, so to hell with the BMI, I'm going to eat what I want." She turned to Kumar, who smiled at her, then leaned in for a kiss.

"Be right back." Dakota stood and wended his way toward the front of the bar. From his height, he could see over everyone's heads. His height was good for that. It was bad when he was trying to blend; his head and shoulders rose above everyone else's like a whack-a-mole, stuck in the upright position, making it easy to bonk.

As Dakota bladed his body to move sideways through the crowd, he could make out a man talking to Rylee and Rylee sending out visible barbs to ward him off.

The bell on the front door continuously jingled with every newcomer. And with each sound of bells, Rylee was checking the door. Her face brightened with a smile as

Erica, her PA, pushed through the door, swinging her head to find her friends.

A group doing a round of hugs and birthday wishes stalled Dakota's progress.

Rylee took Erica's hands in hers and was making a kind of barricade with their bodies to wall out that bar leech.

The guy wasn't letting off.

Yeah, Dakota was aware of the protective growl that rumbled in his chest as he moved more aggressively through the tightly knotted klatches. Dakota got pinned by the corner of the bar, still an arm's length away from throttling the guy.

Suddenly, there were bobbing heads, a gasp of bystanders, and the crowd spread to make a ring around the man who was face down, his hand bent backward, locked in Rylee's arm bar, and Erica dropped to kneel on the man's lower back.

"Security!" A woman called out, holding her phone out, recording the scene.

As always in these types of situations, the crowd surged to make a ring around the action. The crowd was three people deep, and Dakota would have to muscle in. Rylee didn't know him, Dakota reasoned. Didn't know he was on her side. He'd just be another man pushing into the space that she controlled with mastery. The only reason for him to drop in on her then would be ego.

Rylee looked unhurt, or there would be zero hesitation from him.

"I have 911 on the line. They have a car coming," called out another woman.

Dakota decided to hold there until something changed. He could be at Rylee's side in a flash.

When Dakota felt a hand encircle his arm, he looked down to find Neesa looking worried. "Hey, Neesa, Rylee, and Erica look like they had to put some guy on the ground."

"They must be okay, or you wouldn't be standing here."

"They have it handled. But I've got their backs."

"Thank you," Neesa said. "Any chance you can help me get over to them?"

It was a gift. Now, Dakota was the white knight escorting the friend, instead of being a Tasmanian devil hell-bent on shredding the man.

He reached for Neesa's hands and pulled her around behind him, placing her hands on his hips. "Don't let go." Blading his shoulder and lifting his hands to gently move people to the side, he started forward. "Excuse me, we're friends of theirs. Excuse me."

And in that way, they made it through the crush to the inner circle when the cops pushed through the door and pressed everyone back. "Go on and enjoy your evening, folks. Let's keep this doorway clear."

"Did you see what happened?" Neesa asked Dakota.

Dakota recognized Rylee's expression from his days on the battlefield: fierce, stoic, unyielding. "It was fast. Was Rylee in the military?"

"Navy," Neesa said, "but worked green-side."

"She hung out with Marines? That makes all the sense in the world."

Since the cops blocked his view of the man, Dakota held his phone overhead, took a picture, and brought it down for

Neesa to see. "She's got him pinned. When you got to me, he was in an armbar. Now, she has him restrained. See this? By crossing his legs and pushing them toward his butt like that, there's nothing he could do to get free."

"What happened here?" a cop asked. That's what Dakota wanted to know. What the hell happened in the blink of an eye that she was rebuffing the guy one second and she had him in a face plant the next?

And he was so close. So close.

Another couple of seconds, and he could have saved Rylee the effort, or maybe eliminated any threat by showing up and escorting the women away.

"I have video of it." It was the lady who said she called 911. "You can see plainly. I started taping because that woman was saying 'no' on repeat and the guy wouldn't let up."

"Thank you for that," Rylee said, standing and brushing off after the cop got the handcuffs on the assailant. She leaned in to watch the video with the officer. "Yes, see that? He grabbed my boob, and I'm pressing sexual assault charges."

Violence rippled through Dakota's body, and Neesa must have felt it because she petted a soothing hand down his arm and then held him a little tighter as the cop brought the groper to his feet.

"That woman is nuts," the groper spat. "She's crazy. I asked if I could buy her a drink, and she turned rabid on me. If I touched her, it was because the bar is crowded, and I got jostled into her." As the man focused on Rylee, Neesa tightened both hands around Dakota's arm.

Dakota had his focus on the man's posture; the groper

was still within kicking and head-butting range of Rylee, and Dakota was ready to snatch the groper's soul straight out of his body with one wrong twitch.

"Look, lady," the guy gasped, "you need to take your medicine on the daily. You're obviously out of control."

Rylee's face was emotionless as she turned toward the cop jotting notes. "Let me give you my contact information, so I know when to go to court."

Another woman standing there waved her hand. "I'm a witness. You should take my information, too. I'll go to court. He approached her, she told him no, and he got verbally aggressive. I didn't see his hands, but I did hear her say she didn't want his attention."

"Exactly," the woman with the video said. "I saw the expression on his face and started videoing right from the start. The man wanted a fight, and it looks like he got more than he bargained for." The woman turned to Rylee. "Good for you."

Once the officers wrote down Rylee's details, she said, "If you don't need anything else from me, I'm leaving." To Dakota, Rylee was taking care of business. She seemed completely unruffled. Coming out of Rose's building the other day, Rylee looked much more perturbed, and he wondered, as attractive as she was, how often Rylee had to put up with crap like this.

With a nod from the police, Rylee stepped over by the door, where she pulled out her phone to text, Erica at her heels.

"Hey, you forgot your beer," a man at the bar called.

Erica looked over her shoulder. "I don't trust it."

The cop had started the groper's Miranda statement when Neesa's phone pinged.

Rylee: **Sorry, I'm going home. Erica is heading back toward your table. See you tomorrow.**

"Should we go after her?" Dakota hoped Neesa would say yes. "If you introduced us, I could see her safely to where she wants to go."

The door opened, and Rylee left.

Neesa raised her hand and waved it overhead. "Erica!"

Erica scooted around the cops and came to stand near them.

Dakota offered again, "If you introduce me to Rylee, I'm happy to see her safely to where she wants to go. That was a lot." He had an overwhelming need to be with Rylee to see if she was really okay, to possibly comfort and protect her. Of course, his needs had to take a backseat to Rylee's sense of safety. Without an introduction, he would do nothing.

"Rylee?" Erica asked. "No, she says she's fine. The Metro's only a block away. And there are plenty of people on the street."

Dakota walked the women back to their table, and for the rest of the night, he wondered whether what Veer and Kumar had said was true: his guardian angel desperately wanted to put Dakota and Rylee together, while her guardian angel was steadfastly steering Rylee in a different direction.

13

———

Wednesday

"Why are you dressed like that?" Neesa asked as she walked into Rylee's office.

Rylee looked down at her yoga pants and hoodie. "In just a minute, I'm going over to the warehouse to put together my jump bag, so I'm ready to rocket out of here when there's a new call out. Then, I'm going rock climbing with Papa Team."

Neesa shut the door gently before turning to ask, "I'm not inside your body, Rylee, so I can't tell. Are you up for a deployment?"

"If I'm not, I'll pull myself off the roster." She closed the lid on her computer. "I'm not going to endanger anyone."

Neesa got a wicked grin on her face. "I'm going to sit for a second and spill some tea while you sip your coffee."

Rylee picked up her cup, cradling it between both hands, and leaned back. "Tea? Yes, please."

Neesa moved over to the guest chair and sat. "Before I get to my news, are you okay from last night?"

Rylee sighed. "Fine. Just another night at the bar. How about you and Dapper Jasper? I didn't abandon you. You had Erica, right?"

"I had a good time. I really like him." Neesa's face pinked. "I'm glad I went, though, I'm sorry that you had a shitty time of it."

"Meh. One more guy removed from polite society." She took a sip, then set her mug back on the coaster. "The dude is getting his comeuppance. I checked the court website. He was arraigned, and he posted bail. I used his name to find his socials. He's asking for lawyer recommendations and bitching to his bros about how women in his father's day enjoyed being beautiful creatures for men to enjoy. He's got a lot of videos up about the kind of women he laments are not in his life."

"He needs a mommy cooking for him and cleaning the house?" Neesa asked.

"And who takes care of his natural male needs on demand. No means yes is his philosophy."

"You did womankind a favor," Neesa said. "But you did give your PO box and your burner phone number to the police, right?"

"Yup, and my initials. The groper would have trouble pinpointing me as RR Jones. There are about two hundred in the area, mostly men."

"RR? Do I know your middle name?" Neesa asked.

"Rose."

"Rylee Rose, that's pretty. I've never seen your whole name written out. Rose, I heard that name recently."

"From me. The nurse who gave me the blue sticky note that got me to the new neurologist's office is Rose."

"Serendipity," Neesa leaned forward. "Also, not the only alignment of fates that's happened in the last few days."

"This is the tea?" Rylee took a sip from her mug. "Spill."

"Benny Burnett is with the Secret Service."

"Our cemented-for-all-time Benny? Get out. Are you sure?"

"He's Jasper's colleague. And when I picked up the phone in the Metro and put it on speaker?"

Rylee stopped breathing. "Yeah?"

"That was Jasper on the line."

"Oh my god, Neesa. Argh, that just hurts my nerves. That's racing through my entire body like a sizzle. That's insane."

"I know, right?"

As the sensation faded, Rylee thought about the shifter romance she'd just finished and the wonderful sense of certainty that came when characters were fated. Oh, to know you were with the right person at the right time and that all the world aligned to allow it. "So when do you and Jasper get married?" Rylee grinned. "I mean, that's the next step in this story, right?"

Neesa rolled her lips in as if trying to contain her joy. "Jasper called to make sure I got home okay last night. He said he was sorry that things turned out the way they did. He's taking me out for lunch today, and he stressed just the two of us."

"There you go. Lunch. See? That's serious."

And maybe this was all *too* romantic and *too* close to the fantasy fed to women from birth. From childhood books and adult romances, women learned that love was a quest filled with dragons and magic. Only once they found their prince could a woman start her happily ever after.

And yet, that was not the lived experience of any woman that Rylee knew.

"Listen, Neesa, you're lonely for male companionship that's meaningful and not … not what either of us has been dealing with lately. We talk about how low the bar has been set on the dating circuit. I think a little bit of caution is important here. I can see you're walking on a cloud over Jasper. And that's a great feeling, but the Secret Service has a reputation for not following the rules of monogamy. And that is your deal breaker, right? I mean, they look squeaky clean but—"

"But what?" Worry darkened Neesa's eyes.

"They're in the news every few years for doing scandalous things on foreign soil. Back when I was with the Navy, I remember they had a whole prostitution scandal. About a dozen Secret Service men, many of them married, paid prostitutes in Cartagena, Colombia, when Obama was down there for some summit. And most of those men lost their jobs because their behavior was so egregious and brought so much scrutiny and shame to the Secret Service."

"Obama was a while ago. Institutions can retrain and make things better," Neesa whispered.

"Off the top of my head, I remember reading about them drunk in hotels in Amsterdam, drunk driving and hitting the barricade at the White House, Pence's security was suspended for meeting up with a prostitute at a Maryland hotel."

"Maybe he wasn't in a relationship," Neesa countered. "I don't think sex work is criminal."

"But he was security for the Vice President. Breaking the law like that could easily compromise the guy. He could be fired. He could be outed to his wife. Can you imagine what a foreign government could do? 'So we just need you to tell us X or do Y.' Neesa, I'm just suggesting you exercise caution. They have a culture of recurring misconduct that includes alcohol and inappropriate relationships with women. You can't think that their shiny badge makes them shiny people. I'm asking you to tread carefully and not ignore red flags."

"But those are special agents that are on close protection duty, right?" Neesa's brows pulled lines across her forehead. "Does that extend to counterfeiting?"

"I don't know. I've just read about their douchey behavior, and if that's what the bro club is about, it's not for me. They do hard things, but their behavior isn't what I want in my life."

"You seem to be keeping a list."

"I guess they stick with me because it's so antithetical to what I expect, you know? It's like the SEALs acting shitty. It's so unexpected. And sad. I'd never date a SEAL."

"Just SEALs?" Neesa asked. "Or are others in the group?"

"Other special operations forces? I don't know. SEALs are the only ones I've heard about in the news. You said that like a leading question. Why?" Rylee asked.

"Oh, Jasper and the guy who handles the dog, Dakota,

were with the Navy doing a thing I've never heard of before, saltwater combat crew?"

"Swift Water Combatant-Crew, SWCC?" Rylee asked. "Really?"

"Yeah. I didn't know that existed. I had to look it up on my phone. And here I thought it was the SEALs who did the badassery."

"Yeah, those are the guys who use high-speed stealth boats to do the SEALs insertion and extraction. They're the ones responsible for getting the SEALs where they need to go and get them back out successfully."

"Jasper and Dakota were in selection at Coronado at the same time. Anyway, you, Dakota, and Jasper have the Navy in common. We should all go out one night, double date."

Rylee wrinkled her nose.

"Dakota's cute."

Rylee pulled her lips into a thin smile and lifted her brows.

"You're in a dry spell."

"Well, there is that." Rylee stood and walked to her coat hook. "When do we think we'll hear from Iniquus about the list of people that our teams interacted with on missions? You told them not to document the locals, right? Just the foreigners there to provide relief?"

"I did. I'm not sure how long it will take," Neesa said. "General Elliot mentioned something about prioritizing it in the queue. They must have some kind of triage system. They're concerned they have counterfeit bills in their safe as well, and they're contacting Jasper and Dakota about it. Ironically, Hailey says Cerberus Tactical is doing Tank's training."

"Iniquus is in the same boat as we are," Rylee said. "Their reputation allows them to operate. I think that's motivation to find out who's doing this and deal with them. I'm glad we have tapes to maybe help figure it out. You contacted Casey Andrews?"

"I left a message to get back with me, and that it was urgent. If I don't hear from him within the hour, I'll reach out to Langley and give them a heads up."

. "Okay, well, I'm off to figure out how to make life better for a group of very important people, and I'm doing it by dangling off the side of a climbing wall."

"Enjoy." Neesa started out the door when Rylee's phone sounded with a new ringtone—an obnoxious, braying alarm clock.

Rylee snatched her cell phone from her thigh pocket, looked at the number, then shook the phone victoriously at Neesa. With a grin, she brought the phone to her ear. "Rylee Jones, speaking."

"Ms. Jones. This is the scheduling desk at Browning Neurological Group."

"Yes, thank you for calling me." Rylee held up crossed fingers.

"You're on our expedited list, and we have a cancellation spot this morning for a full workup if you can get here in the next thirty minutes. You will need several hours to move through the process."

"I'm on it. I'm coming. Hold my spot." Rylee's hands were shaking as she tapped her app to get a car headed in her direction. "Change of plans." She looked up to catch Neesa's gaze. "There's an opening at that doctor's if I go now."

Neesa stood up and pointed toward the door. "Why aren't you downstairs already? Go. Go. Go."

Rylee raced down the corridor and stabbed her finger into the elevator button.

By the time Rylee reached the front, her car was waiting.

She was whisked magically from green light to green light, making almost magical time as she sped through the city to the Browning Neurological Group.

Multiple Sclerosis was a chronic autoimmune disease that affected the central nervous system by breaking down the myelin sheath—the fatty protective layer that wraps the nerves like the jacket around the wires that run through her house. If you strip a wire and expose it to the air, it can shock and spark, short-circuiting the system. Same with the nerve bundles in the body.

The trigger wasn't known. Possibly a virus like Epstein Barr set it off, sometimes it was a lack of Vitamin D. Though, from her own time in the war out under the hot desert sun, Rylee figured she'd banked enough Vitamin D for two lifetimes.

And she trained hard as a triathlete, so the D was a constant.

The training was supposed to help her build a vital force against viruses. She covered her bases as best she could.

But today was a full work-up, a *full* work-up.

When Rylee had planted herself in the waiting room to look Rose's friend in the eye and personally hand over the blue sticky note, the nurse said they had their own team that included advanced imaging and blood tests. Rylee wouldn't be sent from place to place as they assessed her symptoms. And the nurse emphasized that it allowed them to take a team approach, sharing expertise in meetings and developing a comprehensive plan that included nutrition, exercise, and the potential to work with experimental treatments.

Rylee had left her spreadsheet, which included her preferred clinical trials, the one she'd worked up with her friend John Madoc, who was now doing research on the use of CAR T-cell therapy to treat autoimmune conditions like MS.

And now this was it. She was about to get answers.

Upstairs, she gave her name, and the nurse whisked Rylee straight into a well-oiled machine that moved her smoothly and thoroughly through weight and height, blood draws, and on to an eye doctor checking for changes in eyesight and eye tracking.

She had to put on a shirt, button it, and unbutton it. They tested her strength, her ability to balance on toes and heels. They hammered her knees and had her close her eyes to feel the vibration from a tuning fork. And of course, they checked her short-term memory.

The nurse who took her through these steps was Rose's friend from nursing school.

Rylee wondered if Rose had seen in Rylee's file that they shared a name, and for a fellow Rose, Nurse Rose was willing to take extra steps to help.

Rylee liked that idea: the Sisterhood of the Thorns and Roses.

So named in her imagination because, very obviously, they both lead prickly lives.

Now, Rylee shivered in her blue hospital gown, sitting on the edge of the MRI table, part nerves, part freezing temperatures that made her skin white and her goose-fleshed.

The superconducting magnets needed to be kept cold. This was a necessary cold, unlike the frigid temperatures at Rose's doctor's office that just felt punitive.

The tech was having some difficulties with the computer in her little glass booth. The first glitch of the day. She was dressed in scrubs with a thick fleece sweatshirt over top, a hat, and fingerless gloves. It must be like working in a fridge all day.

Rylee knew her symptoms in general weren't caused by anxiety.

But today, she was anxious.

This test was a big deal, and the results could change the trajectory of her life.

The ease of this day was throwing Rylee.

No man would understand the gaslighting that females go through. Not even Rylee's dad, though he'd listened to her complain for years.

When her dad went to the doctor, he told them about his family history and explained his symptoms. It was Bing. Bang. Boom. Done. One doctor. One visit. And straight through to diagnosis and treatment.

Rylee tried not to seethe. It would make lying still in the MRI machine that much harder.

Getting to this point had been a marathon.

A marathon in someone else's shoes that pinched her toes numb while wearing a fifty-pound pack. It had been all uphill, and no one, until this last stretch, had offered her a banana or a bottle of water.

She was at the finish line.

She'd cross through and either get the diagnosis or get the reprieve.

Yeah, Rylee knew it was going to be an MS diagnosis. And she was ready for it. She'd already decided on three different medical trials she'd throw her hat into, starting with John's. It was like being a kind of explorer, heading out into the wild unknown. She was up for that.

Rylee could do hard things.

She had broken molds, had faced down death, and had been brave in her career.

Something about the way the medical world treated her —women in general—had worn her down, made her wonder about her mental health. Self-doubt, now that was a hell of a cudgel. Bring on life-or-death scenarios where she trained to be a force of good. But going to war for basic care, to have her self-advocacy be dismissed with the shake of a head, to have WW written in her chart—whiney woman—over and over.

It took something from her.

"All right, Ms. Jones, you can lie back now on the platform."

Rylee scooted back, feeling a bit cottony and off-kilter. She arranged herself in a way that she thought she could maintain for the duration.

Then the table slid into the machine.

The attendant read the instructions over the loud-speaker.

The lights dimmed.

And the jackhammer banging of the MRI machine began.

14

Rylee

Thursday

Rylee got out of the taxi at WorldCares and slugged her way to the elevator. Her hand hovered over the button, and she was too emotionally wiped to push it.

That medical appointment had been the miracle that she had prayed for. The thing she'd plotted for. Hoped for. Worked for.

And now it was over.

And on the other end would be a phone call. A diagnosis. Answers were hard. Even when they were the things that she wanted most.

Someone else pushed the button, and the car arrived. "Are you going to your office, Ms. Jones?"

Rylee's "Yes, thank you" felt burdensome to say.

As soon as Erica greeted her, it signaled Neesa that she was back.

Neesa read her mood instantly and shut the door softly. "We can talk about what happened later," she said. "What do you need right now?"

"I don't know," Rylee said, plopping into her chair and turning toward the window. "I just want clear answers. No more running around. I hope it's not ..." She licked her lips and turned to see her friend's worried face. "I hope it's nothing worse."

"It's something, though. Yoga isn't the fix. Baby steps."

"It is something. And as I was lying there in the MRI with its ratatat that put me right back on the battlefield with all the images dancing through my head—" she stopped to close her eyes. "I might be wrong. I might see my family and hear how they describe the sensations and say, 'Oh yeah, that's got to be it.' But in the tube, with memories of war, now, I'm thinking brain cancer or issues I developed from my time in the military. I mean, I could smell the burn pit at night. I'm not immune."

"What do you need to cope?" Neesa asked. "Something in nature. It's a surprisingly sunny day. How about water? On the way in this morning, I saw that guy Jesus setting up his kayak rental booth. Why don't we put on our drysuits and take a paddle in the river?"

"It's chilly yet to be on the water," Rylee said.

"Just what you need. A bite of cold, the feel of the waves. No wind, so it shouldn't be too bad, and I've got some travel mugs, I'll fill them with piping hot tea for when we get to the shore."

For sure, sitting here in the office, swiveling her chair back and forth until quitting time, simmering in a broth of apprehension wasn't a good way to cope. "Okay, yeah, that sounds good. I have my gym bag, so I'll put a swimsuit on under my sweats."

They walked to the park right outside the Bureau of Engraving and Printing, where Jasper had his office. It was also where they came often on days when the weather helped them cope with the enormity of the global crises their organization helped address daily.

Neesa was right, sometimes, a little sun could bolster morale better than anything else.

The kayak guy, Jesus, recognized them and showed off a picture of his new baby girl. They were his first customers of the new year. Jesus said it was lucky for all three of them.

That was nice. Rylee felt like she could use some luck.

She pulled off her sweats and put on her dry suit and swim shoes. Then, packing up her dry bag, she pulled the straps over the turquoise life vest Jesus had lent her.

Off they shoved into the water, with the setting sun splashing gold across the Potomac's cyan waters. Birds flew low, gliding peacefully on the still air. Rylee had exerted enough energy in her paddle toward the center that she felt the stress lifting from her body.

Neesa was right; this was exactly what Rylee needed. It was wonderful to have a friend who knew her so well.

Rylee pulled the paddle across her lap, letting her body rise and fall with the current. As she dipped the paddle back into the water, she looked down.

And that's when she saw a hand reaching upward.

It was shocking.

And Rylee's brain stuttered as she stared at it.

White and swollen by the water, the fingers were about eight inches under the surface.

Dead. Obviously dead.

She should reach in and grasp that hand.

Someone loved the person beneath the water, and they were tormented because they didn't know what had happened to their family member.

In all the disasters where WorldCares was present, the rescue teams knew there would be no peace for the survivors until they found their loved ones.

Reach for it, Rylee told herself. But she didn't move.

On land, Rylee was very used to handling something like this. She'd given artificial breath so many times, pressed her hand into gaping wounds so many times. She'd seen people with their limbs melted away, the stumps burned black. And one woman with her eyeball dangling from the connective tissues, resting in her hand.

Rylee had dampened a cloth and draped it over the eye. Dampened another and lightly pressed it into the socket just to keep things moist, but careful not to stop the flow of whatever was flowing in her veins. Hopefully flowing. That woman was triaged as walking wounded, not one of the ones in the worst shape. So she had held her eyeball and waited for more medical help.

That one still gave Rylee nightmares.

And yes, Rylee had been around dead bodies. More than her share.

But bodies in the water?

Rylee only knew what Ed had told her when they dated last year.

Ed worked for the D.C.P.D. and trained with their swift water search-and-rescue team, so he could dive into the Potomac looking for evidence that had been tossed in.

And of course, that meant bodies too.

Ed had described the terrible conditions of those dives. The deeper he went, the colder it got. With zero visibility, he inched forward, feeling around with his hands, learning to identify items by touch through his dive gloves.

There were all kinds of dangers on the bottom: sharp objects, trees, rocks, and debris that could entangle and entrap him.

He said that bodies don't behave the way they're portrayed in movies. They didn't lie flat on the floor of the waterway. The upper half suspends at an angle buoyed by air trapped in the body. So if he was looking for a newly deceased body, he was feeling around in the water quite a bit above the floor, and he usually found the corpse when his fingers pushed into an eye socket.

After about seven days, depending on the temperature of the water, the body fills with decomp gases and floats to the surface.

Once it reached the surface, fish and birds looking for food punctured the skin, released the gas, and the body sank back down.

A floating hand, that could be on the way up or the way down, Rylee reasoned.

The water was cold but not that cold. The thermometer Jesus put in the water to warn people about how long they could safely stay out said the river was fifty degrees that day.

But still, if she was right about the float and descent, this was someone who had been in the water for ten to twenty days.

And her second guess was that the corpse would lead

with the gaseous pocket, so abdomen first on the way up and lightest last on the way down.

If she was right, this body was on its way back to the bottom.

She should call the police.

If she lost sight of the hand and the team came out, Ed would be there for sure.

Rylee remembered asking him how he coped with reaching around in pitch black, *hoping* to put his hand into decaying flesh. He said he sang opera the whole time he was under. It took up a lot of the air in his tank, but singing at the top of his lungs kept him sane.

That, and the extra bubbles, meant his team would notice if he became entangled and needed an assist.

Rylee pulled out her phone and, through the protective plastic case, tapped the Maps app, got her exact location, and took a screenshot.

The family. All Rylee could think of was the family.

Should she call Ed? He was still in her contacts. They'd parted on friendly footing.

Rylee could call the D.C.P.D.'s non-emergency number.

Her instincts told her not to. She had no idea why.

Perhaps they would want her to stay with the body, and it might take them hours for a call-out to spool up—grabbing gear and getting on site. There was no way Rylee could handle this cold for that long. And she wasn't willing to paddle away lest the body be lost forever, and the family have no closure.

If she reached for the wrist, would it detach from the rest of the body like chicken bones in a soup pot? Rylee wished she hadn't made that simile. That one would stick with her. She was probably off chicken soup for the rest of her life.

If she reached and pulled, and she ended up holding the dead person's hand, would the rest of the body sink away?

What if it were only the hand that came up? Wasn't that better than nothing? There would be DNA at least.

And what if it was a whole body? What if she pulled the hand and Uncle Jim, in his blue jeans and National's jacket, came gliding into sight?

That would be hard, but better.

At least she could take pictures. A visible tattoo or piercing, the color and length of hair, and possibly clothing might help identify the person. That was really what a family wanted: to know what happened to their loved one. Though those kinds of pictures wouldn't be something to share beyond the forensic team.

She was done thinking.

Oh, she didn't want to do this.

But she was going to do this.

"What's going on?" Neesa called, letting the wind sweep her voice down the twenty yards of river that separated them.

Rylee didn't look up.

I have to do this quickly before the remains get swept away by the current. Do it. Just do it.

Rylee tugged the sleeve of her dry suit down, covering as much of her hand as she could.

Her gut clenched. Her ribs tightened down to cage her breath.

With chattering teeth, she bladed her hand and tried to shoot it down into the water.

Her whole body flinched with heebie-jeebies.

She'd deal with a patient on the battlefield any day of the week. This was a level of gruesome that Rylee wasn't prepared for. She imagined a lifetime of nightmares in front of her, then replaced that thought with a grieving family finding solace.

Too bad Rylee didn't know opera like Ed did. The only song she could think of was Baby Shark and that seemed wholly inappropriate.

Do it!

Do. It.

Rylee looked up at the swirl of gray clouds.

"I'm coming over to you," Neesa called, slicing into the water.

Yeah. Rylee probably looked like she was having an existential crisis, and Neesa would be worried that Rylee would freak the hell out on the water in her kayak. And that was no bueno.

Do it before Neesa gets here or even close enough to see.

You can do it to protect your friend. No need for her to have these images.

"Do it!" She hissed at herself, and she bladed her hand and lifted her elbow toward her ear. "Do it!" She spat through gritted teeth.

And with that, Rylee squeezed her lids tight and shoved her hand into the water, felt something other than water, and closed her grip on it as she pulled her elbow back up.

What happened next could only be described as a moment of brain warp.

Part of her mind wanted to tell her that she'd pulled the skin from a hand.

The rational part of her brain correctly identified the object as a surgical glove that, full of water, had been floating, hand-shaped and fingers up, eight inches beneath the surface.

Rylee began to laugh hysterically.

It was the culmination of everything that had been going on in her life, and she just let it flow from her chest—crazy and unfiltered.

"Crap, Rylee, what's happening to you? I mean, we came out to the river for it to be cathartic – are you catharting? Is that a word?"

Rylee waved her hand through the air, then dropped it to her lap and lifted the surgical glove.

"What are you doing? Don't touch that. You have no idea where it's been."

"It's been in the water," Rylee said, the bubble of anxiety burst, and she told the story to Neesa's horror faces.

"That was so brave," Neesa said. "I mean, you don't know what you're pulling up when you reach in the water. The hand could have pulled away from the arm bones like a chicken in the stock pot. Cripes, I shouldn't have said that. I'm going to remember that image every time I try to make someone chicken soup."

"I had the exact same chicken thought," Rylee said.

"That's why we're friends. Birds of a feather as well as dead birds in a pot with no feathers. I'm freaking out. I don't want to be on the river right now."

Rylee put her paddle in the water. "It was bad."

"We have to change this mood because I am all kinds of wigged out." Neesa searched along the surface of the water. "Okay. I propose that we go home, take scalding hot showers, and put on some nice, comfy clothes, get some fast food, and go to the movies for something loud and violently therapeutic." Neesa waited for Rylee to thumbs-up the idea. "And we're going to be grateful for all the things we have to be grateful for. And one of them is that you didn't fish a corpse from the river with the skin peeling off."

Rylee slapped her paddle in the water to splash Neesa.

Neesa laughed and yelled out, "Come on, I'll race you back to shore."

15

———

Dakota

  Thursday

Dressed in running gear, Tank patiently waiting at his side, Dakota looked up the staircase when the echo of footsteps hustled his way. "You ready?" he called up to Jasper.

"What are you thinking, twice around the Tidal Basin?" Jasper asked as they pushed through the back door.

Working at the 14th Street office had its perks.

Right out the back door was a green space around a wide pool of water that connected to the Potomac. Typically, D.C. had about a week of spring weather that showed up between winter cold and summer heat. Dakota liked to take advantage of it by taking a picnic out on the grass to watch the crews scull up the Potomac. In the summer evenings, it was usually a good place to run.

Today, the weather had rolled the dice, and they were back to the pleasant weather they'd had on Sunday.

Tank was sniffing the air which today held the promise of green shoots and cherry blossoms.

Dakota patted Tank's side. "Iniquus has been working on Tank's physical and mental stamina, and I need to keep that up. If you need to peel off after two laps, we may keep going."

The three took off at a slow trot for the warm-up, then increased their speed to a good clip. The push felt good in Dakota's body as he fell into a well-practiced rhythm. Running was meditative for him; he could pound stress into the pavement and clear his mind.

As they ran, they could see vendors parked along the street with water bottles, winter hats, and tourist souvenirs.

Rounding toward the inlet that connected to the Potomac, Tank started pulling hard. "Yo! Tank. Hey. This isn't the charity race, you're not on a bungee," Dakota called.

Tank looked back tongue long, panting hard, sending Dakota the signal that he should pick up the pace.

Dakota scanned for something that would have excited Tank, maybe some birds gliding low over the path.

The only thing of interest Dakota could spot was the two women, one in a yellow kayak and one in a red kayak, paddling to shore. The air filled with their laughter as they stepped out in water shoes, with dry-bag packs on their backs over bright turquoise life vests.

And that's when Dakota felt the zap that floated distance between his atoms.

That was Rylee Jones. It had to be.

At the same time, Jasper backslapped Dakota. "That's Neesa Meesang. Come on."

Rylee held something up in the air, and Neesa fell against her friend, laughing.

Tank barked a look-at-me bark that pulled the women's attention around.

"Tank!" Neesa called out, squatting with her arms wide.

When Dakota dropped the lead and signaled a release, Tank shot off like a rocket toward the women as the men jogged to catch up.

It was interesting that Tank briefly greeted Neesa, whom he knew from the search the other day, but he was full-body wiggling and whining as he circled, greeting Rylee.

As they closed the distance, Dakota's heart pounded in his chest, and butterflies rioted in his stomach.

"Hey!" Neesa called. "Fancy seeing you here."

"This is right outside my office," Jasper pointed behind them, then brought his hands to his hips. "Beautiful spot."

Both men were breathing heavily from the sprint, catching up to Tank.

Tank was fine. Tank was standing there with his eyes half-shut as both women massaged and patted and scritched his fur.

Ah, the life of a dog.

"Hi, I'm Dakota Kayne," Dakota said as he reached out a hand to Rylee.

Dakota was expecting an electrical shock, but it was quite the opposite sensation. Despite being wet from the river, her hand was delicate and warm in his. There was strength and certainty in her grip. But he read confusion in her eyes.

"This is Tank," he said.

"Tank, the amazing sniffer." Rylee had a warm, inviting smile that brightened her face. Her intelligence shone in the depth of her chocolate brown eyes.

For a moment, Dakota forgot to breathe.

He hadn't released her hand.

"And this is Jasper Lee."

Rylee nodded his way with "Jasper," as a greeting, then she tightened her hand on Dakota's. "Dakota, we know each other, don't we?" She squinted her eyes and tipped her head, taking a step closer to him. "You are so familiar to me."

She let her hand drop.

Neesa turned and, with a flourish like she was presenting a work of art at an auction house, said, "Gentlemen, this is Rylee Jones. You all keep missing each other, but now you finally meet."

"Rylee Jones," Jasper said, "we are indebted. I'm sorry things turned shitty last night. We wanted to invite you for a drink to toast your heroism."

Rylee suddenly stumbled forward into Dakota. With Dakota steadying her by her elbows, she spun to see that Tank had pushed her forward. When she pulled back, she swiped her hands over his chest, where her life vest had left two wet splotches in his T-shirt. "I am so sorry."

"Tank's fault. He's excited to see you again." Dakota was going to reward Tank with a game of tug later. He was a hell of a wingman.

"Wait." Rylee tapped a finger on his chest. "I'm placing you now. You were the lovely man who gave me your taxi and the flowers."

"That was me," Dakota confirmed.

"It was a bad day, and that gesture made all the difference. Thank you. But I don't remember Tank being there."

"That was the second time we almost met. Were you at the Children's Hospital mud run?"

"As a matter of fact, yes. My father's foster child is in and out of the hospital, and we think it would be an amazing thing for the kids to get a park. Were you running?"

"With Cerberus. Your dad and the child were in wheelchairs?"

"That's right." She tipped her head. "But there were thousands of people there."

"Pompoms at the finish line. And your bright smile." He said that without thinking. What a cheesy thing to say. "Something about you caught Tank's attention. The pompoms, maybe? He wanted to join your family. But we were both covered in clay."

"Oh!" She pulled the lanyard that attached her phone to its waterproof sleeve, then scrolled through her photo album. "Ta da!" She turned it around. "Is that you in the war paint?"

"Team colors."

She'd taken a picture of him. He was in her photo album. He shouldn't feel this satisfied with the most tenuous of connections. Yet there it was.

"You all looked like something out of, I don't know, Braveheart. Which was perfect. The kids are surely in a battle, and it's great to have warriors showing up for them. But you're not Cerberus, right?" She raised a questioning brow toward Neesa.

"Secret Service," Neesa said.

"Tank is training with them. They use a dog-to-dog

mentorship model, so Tank was invited to run with the pack." A grin pulled across Dakota's face. "Tank decided to drag me along, quite literally."

Rylee handed her phone to Neesa. "You can see he's being modest. The group came thundering over that hill, first the Malinois, then the shepherds. Everyone looked like they were having a great time. There was one guy who came in just after, let me …" She pulled up another picture. "Look at this mastiff trotting along like he was Ferdinand the Bull. And his guy there looked like he wished they could run faster."

"That's Nutsbe Crushed, Panther Force."

"Bilateral amputee," Neesa said. "My goodness, he looks like he could be in the Paralympics."

"He's competing in Track and Field at the Invictus games this year," Dakota said. He pointed at the picture of Nutsbe running near the crowd. "That's his girlfriend, Olivia, standing next to you."

"Invictus, that's impressive." Rylee accepted her phone back. "Henry, my foster nephew, was thrilled to cheer him on. Nutsbe you said?"

"Call sign from the Air Force," Dakota said, reaching out to stop Tank from giving Rylee another nudge into him. "I don't know his given name."

"Ah, well, Nutsbe inspired Henry, and now Henry wants to start training to be a hero too."

"A hero." Dakota chuckled. "I'll pass that along. It'll make Nutsbe's day."

Jasper nodded toward Rylee's hand. "What's with the glove?"

"Rylee plucked it from the river." Neesa gave a whole-body shiver. "Apparently, when it's filled with water and floating fingers up, it looks like a cadaver hand."

Jasper scowled. "And you reached in to grab it, thinking it was a dead body floating in the Potomac."

Rylee grimaced.

"That could have been a life trauma. And you reached for it?" Jasper sound bewildered.

"Someone's family needs to know what happened to their loved one," Rylee said. "Closure."

"Selfless." Dakota bladed his hands on his hips. "Guts of steel. Not many people would have done it."

"I wouldn't," Neesa said with revulsion painted across her face.

"You would," Rylee challenged her.

Neesa turned toward Rylee. "Nope. I would have called you over."

"Neesa." Rylee laughed.

"Serious. I would have called you over. And if I were out on the water and you weren't there, then I would have gotten the GPS numbers and called 911. I might have babysat the hand while it was in the water, but that's all I'd do." Neesa turned to Jasper. "You should have seen her face. It was sheer panicked horror. She scared me just looking at her."

"The professionals could do a proper extraction, and I considered that. But can you imagine if I hadn't reached in?" Rylee asked, slipping the glove into the mesh pocket on the side of her pack.

"And you got a dive team in the water to pull out a glove?" Neesa laughed. "Yeah, good call."

"Hey, Rylee," Dakota said, "you didn't get to stick around

for a drink last night when we figured out that it was you and Neesa who saved Benny. I want to thank you. I know Benny and his family want to meet you if you're up for that."

"I was glad to hear that he's getting the help he needs." Rylee brushed away the gratitude.

"You know it's lucky that Benny was a guy when he went down," Neesa said.

"A guy versus being a woman?" Dakota watched Tank circle, then lay down between him and Rylee, putting a paw on each of their feet, like they were all holding hands. "Why's that?"

"Well, Neesa and I would have helped regardless," Rylee said, "but women don't have the same presentation as men. It was easy to see what was happening to Benny. On women, it's not very obvious. And once it is obvious, ladies are twenty-five percent less likely to get CPR than men. A woman would have likely died had she been in Benny's straits."

Dakota scowled. "Are you serious about that?"

"She is." Neesa gestured toward her chest. "Boobs."

"Which *can* be intimidating," Dakota offered up a half smile.

"Life-threatening under such circumstances, unfortunately," Neesa said.

"Would you have ripped her shirt open and given compressions?" Rylee asked Dakota. "Of course, you would. You're the Secret Service." Rylee reached out and laid her hand on his arm. "Also, I assume you're a good human being."

I try to be." Her fingers were cold on his skin. The

women were wet and standing still. "Are these your kayaks, or do they need to be returned over there?" Dakota asked.

"Returned," Neesa said, bending to lift hers. "Jasper, would you get the other one, so we don't disturb Tank?"

"I—" Dakota started.

Neesa put a stop hand up by her face. "Nope. I insist."

Rylee dropped her pack to the ground and unbuckled her life vest. "Neesa, here," she extended it out.

As Neesa and Jasper trudged off, carrying the kayaks, Rylee unzipped her dry suit. "I've only met one other Dakota in my life, but she's a girl." She peeled a sleeve off. "She's a chonky chocolate lab that likes to lie belly up in a sunbeam and not move except to chase balls rolled across the living room." She peeled the other arm of her suit off to reveal a bright pink bikini top. "She wags her tail with her whole body as if she's just too full of happiness to contain. And that energy is contagious. I'm always in a good mood after a visit with her."

It took the fortitude of a Swiftwater Crewman for Dakota to keep his gaze locked with hers and not focus down on her bikini.

"Dakota, are you from that part of the country?"

"My mom gave me that name because of a trip she took to North Dakota in college. She thought the land had stories to tell. She wanted that for me, a life filled with stories to warm my heart on cold nights."

"Very nice." She pushed her dry suit to her ankles. "So how did Tank get his name?"

"It's really Brunhilde Von Panzer Tank."

"I see. And how many beers were you into the night when you gave him all those names?"

"Zero. My nephew Bo named him."

"And Bo didn't realize Brunhilde is the warrior maiden —female—who guides heroes to Valhalla?"

"He heard it in one of the books my sister was reading to him, and he liked the sound of it. I tried to convince him that he meant Hildebrand for battle sword, but he said that a Panzer Tank was more powerful than a little sword."

Rylee pulled a towel from her bag and sat on it. "I remember that the UK had an online thing going on to name their new ship that was doing polar exploration. As a group, they named it Boaty McBoatface. So I feel like you dodged a bullet with Brunhilde Von Panzer Tank."

"I knew the risk. I think I got out of it with something useful. And Tank's girlfriend doesn't seem to mind."

Dry suit cleared from her feet, shivering in the skimpy pink bikini, Dakota shifted his attention safely to Tank. "Tank is in love with the poodle next door, Fifi La Cute."

"He is not." She laughed as she pulled a hoodie over her head. "There's no such neighbor dog."

"I promise you." Dakota pulled out his cell phone and showed Rylee a picture of the two dogs lying belly up, side by side. Heads pressed together, looking very content.

He accepted the phone back and swiped right. "Fifi's mom is planning a wedding. This is Fifi's mom." Dakota handed his phone back to Rylee with a picture of an elder woman knitting a cupcake hat. "Swipe to the next picture." Tank and Fifi posed with matching cupcake hats.

"You can see the indignity in Tank's eyes, poor guy." She handed the phone back. "What a man won't do for the woman he loves?"

"Everything in his power, every time," Dakota said as their gazes caught.

She released the phone and reached for her sweatpants. "About Tank's name, that I can understand. My niece named my parents' dog Sir Reginald Barks-a-lot."

"It's a mouthful."

She pulled her pants up her thighs and reached for her socks and tennis shoes. "We called him Roofy for short or Roof for shorter. He was a Newfoundland. Such a glorious goofball. When Roof wanted sympathy, which was quite often, he would lift a paw and walk with a whine that was pure pain. 'I love you, and I'm coming, but it's so terrible!'"

"And you're sure it was affected?" Dakota asked.

"My parents spent a couple of grand trying to figure out how to make Sir Barks-a-lot better, and the vet couldn't find anything. But if my folks said, 'Roof, let's go get an ice cream, the paw went down, and he would bolt over to the car and sit at the door with a wagging tail. I'm telling you this dog gave an Emmy-worthy performance."

She was tying a bow on her shoe when Tank wriggled around to put his nose on her knee and sighed contentedly.

Dakota had never seen his dog so obviously in love with a woman before.

"Tank, you have beautiful eyes. I hope you have a wonderful wedding and many happy days to come with Fifi." She kissed him on the head, then gently stood.

Neesa and Jasper were walking shoulder to shoulder as they made it back over.

"Temps are dropping, how about a hot chocolate?" Rylee asked.

"I have to get back to the office," Jasper said. "I'm

expecting a call from the West Coast." He looked down at Neesa, "I'll pick you up for dinner around seven?"

"Looking forward to it." Neesa smiled.

"Nice meeting you, Rylee." Jasper gave Dakota a nod, then raised his hand and loped back toward his office.

"How about you, Neesa?" Rylee asked. "Hot chocolate?"

Neesa looked at Dakota, then back to Rylee. "You know, I forgot a thing."

"A thing?" Rylee asked.

"Yeah, I've got to do a thing," Neesa said as Rylee bent over, collecting her belongings back in her bag.

Dakota was just going to venture forward. "I'm starved. Would you be interested in grabbing a bite, Rylee? I have my car at the parking lot about a block away."

"Yes," Neesa sent Rylee the wicked grin. "Rylee's starving. She was just talking about chicken soup." She moved Rylee over next to Dakota, scritched Tank's ears, then took a step away from them. "You three enjoy."

16

RYLEE

Thursday

As RYLEE SET off next to Dakota, he reached for her bag and slung it over his shoulder. She noticed right off that he took her elbow and steered her to his left side so that he walked closest to the street.

She wanted to reach her hand into the crook of his arm or hold his hand.

But that would be weird, right? She reproved herself. After all, they'd met like ten seconds before.

And yet, it was so nice to be walking with him, like this.

Calming.

"Tank always walks to my left." Dakota's voice was deep and resonant, and it rumbled through her body, shaking away the sticky parts of her day, letting them waft away in the breeze that was kicking up now that twilight was descending. "I'm sorry if he's bumping you."

"No worries," Rylee said.

"We just met, and I don't know if you're comfortable driving with a virtual stranger. I'm not offended in the least if that's the case. Up the street, there's a guy who does really delicious Mediterranean out of a food truck, and there are benches nearby. Or two blocks around the corner, there's a place that has a bit of everything on its menu. They have outdoor seating and heat posts. I can't go into a restaurant with Tank."

"I'm okay getting in a car with you." Rylee liked the way he was handling this. No pressure. No agenda. "Neesa knows where I am, and Jasper would kick your ass if anything happened to me, so I'm not worried."

"I was at the bar and saw the outcome of your skills last night. You would kick my ass. Jasper needn't be involved."

That was laughable. If Dakota were a bad guy, she'd have zero shot at self-protection.

But Rylee felt not even the slightest pang, didn't see even the tiniest red flag.

Quite the opposite. Rylee was so comfortable with Dakota that she'd better watch her Ps and Qs. They were, as he pointed out, strangers. And the warmth she sensed between them was collegial.

Tank pranced along between them, his head lifted and his snoot sniffing. Rylee thought she could smell it, too, the hope that rides the air just before the leaves unravel their bright spring green.

"Neesa said you were with the Navy?" Dakota asked.

"Marine medic."

"On the battlefield, huh? No wonder the shithead in the bar didn't phase you." She felt his gaze on her and looked up to find worry in his eyes. "Let me amend that. From the outside, it looked annoying, but you handled it, and it didn't mess you up. But that might have been your public face, and you might well have felt something different. Are you okay?"

"I am. You read it right. I'm glad to bring accountability to public gropers. And at the same time, I would rather not have to deal with it. I went home because I wasn't in the mood for a crowd. I had only planned to have a beer and leave. He didn't run me out or ruin my evening."

They came to a stop at the corner, waiting for the light to turn green.

"You're craving chicken soup?" Dakota asked.

"Absolutely not," Rylee laughed. "That is the last thing I would want to eat tonight. Neesa was giving me a hard time about finding a surgical glove."

He lifted his elbow, an offer to lean on him for stability as they stepped off the curb; it was smooth and gentlemanly. Not the look-at-me kind of gentlemanly that expected some type of reward for the performance, but an easy, natural gesture that was an invitation, not a demand.

In fact, Rylee was a little stunned by the whole Dakota Kayne thing going on.

Rylee slid her hand into place; his skin was warm against her tingling, chilly fingers. He covered them over with his hand. "I'll get the heat going as soon as we get to my car. You're braver than I am, paddling this early in the season."

Which was ridiculous. The man spent days lying in the pounding surf on Coronado Beach, proving that he'd never give up.

"Chicken soup." Dakota chuckled as they walked along.

"I think I got the imagery. If you were pulling a hand out of the water. Yeah," he shook his head, still laughing, "that's dark humor there."

"Gallows."

"You do what you have to do to stay sane, right?" he asked.

They stepped up onto the next sidewalk, but Dakota was still warming her hand with his, and Rylee didn't pull away.

Yes, non-performative gentlemanliness, his behavior seemed so gracefully normal that it was a bit shocking to Rylee's system because it wasn't the norm she'd encountered at all.

It should be, though.

Of late, she'd run up against a lot of guys who believed they were the "good guy."

But they were good only as a tool. As soon as they realized they weren't getting what they wanted, the good veneer pulled away, and the angry, entitled guy showed his true nature.

On one of her last dates, she took out her credit card to pay her share. She'd already decided that she'd never see this guy again after he insisted he order for her. And he didn't even ask what she wanted to eat or if she had any allergies. She drank her water and left the food on the plate. He didn't notice. He did put his whole attention on the credit card in her hand, though. The guy was livid that she had been emasculating all evening, opening the door on her own and trying to pay. How dare she embarrass him that way?

Rylee excused herself to go to the restroom.

On the way out, she found her server, explained the situation, paid her share, gave the woman a generous tip, because she assumed bro wouldn't leave anything for the woman after he realized Rylee had slipped out the back door, hailed a cab, and left his sorry ass at the table by himself to seethe.

The dating pool that she tried to navigate seemed to be getting worse and worse. Though, honestly, it might just be that as Rylee got older, she developed a hair-trigger on her bullshit meter. And frankly, she was burned out.

Sometimes she lamented that she hadn't been born a lesbian.

This was not one of those times.

Dakota fobbed the back gate open and dropped Tank's lead. "Tank, load," he said.

And as Tank settled in his crate, Dakota smiled at Rylee.

It was an easy smile, and Rylee remembered telling Neesa that one of the things she remembered about the man who gave her the flowers was that his smile seemed to come easily and sat naturally on his face.

"Dinner. It's a little bit complicated because I have Tank. Since he's a cross-trained tactical K9, he can't be left unattended." Dakota side-stepped between the two parked vehicles, opened the passenger side door, and placed her bag on the floorboard.

"Lest someone see how beautiful Tank is and think they wanted to steal him?" Rylee asked. "I can't imagine that going well."

"That's exactly the scenario." Dakota moved to the side and extended his hand to help her as if she were in a ball gown and heels. "Hold that thought. I want to get the heat on for you." He shut her door, jogged around the front of the vehicle, climbed in, and got the engine going. "Ideas about dinner?" he asked. "Specific cravings?"

"What were your plans for tonight?" Rylee asked. If he was going to order a pizza, she had a place with outdoor seating and warming posts.

"I was cooking shrimp scampi at home, salad, and garlic bread. There's plenty if you'd like to join me for that."

He was inviting her to his home. She'd known this guy for less than an hour. She kept trying to convince herself that, in such circumstances, out of self-preservation, a woman should say, "No, thank you."

Rylee couldn't raise a single molecule of concern. A lot of that probably had to do with the way Tank looked adoringly at Dakota. True love and partnership were so evident between the two. Rylee had read a scientific study that said a dog can smell a bad guy.

Tank trusted Dakota.

Rylee, for whatever reason, trusted Tank.

She *also* trusted Dakota. That was a revelation.

"I would. Thank you."

"You're okay with that?" He did a double check in.

And Rylee decided to be honest. "I've had a rough couple of days; my nerves have been a little raw. Quiet sounds really nice."

Dakota threw his vehicle into reverse. "I've been a shadowy quasi-witness to some of your week. I've seen you wearing a lot of different emotions on your face."

"Yeah, that's right, you have."

.   .   .

"Counterfeiters, heart attack victims, gropers, then you decided to shake hands with the creature from the Black Lagoon." He sent her a broad grin.

"Ha. Yeah. That was pretty awful, and probably the whole scenario came about because my nerves are shot and my brain was glitching. So it's interesting to me that all the frenetic energy I've been wearing seemed to just flow away on our walk to the car. The calm I feel around you and Tank is really nice. Thank you. But to answer your question: yes, I'm completely comfortable having dinner with you tonight. If you can say scampi instead of chili, then you probably know your way around the kitchen, and I'm not in danger of food poisoning."

Dakota eased into the bumper-to-bumper traffic.

"So what's worrying you most?" Dakota asked.

"One of my biggest concerns right now is that we've had three deployments, and three times we were hit with counterfeit money," Rylee said. "The damaging effects to the morale of our teams as they find out about this new danger are going to be something WorldCares needs to navigate. If I can tell the teams that you caught the bad guy, it will help. You are going to catch the bad guy, right?"

"I'm going to do my darndest."

"Did Jasper mention surveillance tapes to you?" Rylee asked.

"Last night he said that you had the tapes and offered to let us put them through an AI system, and we wouldn't do that."

Rylee twisted in her seat, adjusting her belt across her chest. "Do you mind my asking why?"

"The computers that could scan through the data, cull

the static images, and make a nice neat binder of names and faces are all privately owned. We could contract to use them. That is possible. The problem is that then the data would be added to the AI database. Since that database is privately owned, we would no longer have control over who sees that data and how it's used."

Rylee instantly thought of Casey Andrews and how much danger it would mean to him to be out in the field when some rogue actor paid a fee to name him as a CIA field officer.

"So, for example, the bad guy could ask for instances when his face was searched and who had that information?" Rylee asked, her face flaming red with warning.

Langley told Neesa that Iniquus was safe. Thank goodness they hadn't risked Casey's image in a private security supercomputer.

"Exactly." Dakota flipped on his turn signal and moved onto the on-ramp toward the highway. "I live in Alexandria."

"Me, too. That's nice." She waited until he'd navigated past the accident on the right before she spoke. "This counterfeiting mess is potentially devastating to our organization and can have international ramifications. We serve over a hundred thousand people every year. People who are in the worst circumstances of their lives when money and prestige are meaningless as they deal with what is thrust upon them, volcanic eruptions, fires, droughts, deluges, all manner of catastrophe. If the public didn't trust us with the stewardship of their donations, thinking we were a con, the funding would go away, and our expertise would no longer be available to the world.

Thousands, even tens of thousands of people could potentially die."

He turned to catch her eye, then focused back on the road.

From the way he held his face stoic and thoughtful, Rylee knew he was taking this in and fully understood the seriousness of the situation.

"Right now, there are charities that function the way we do with our specialties. We're unique in the world because of our scope. We have one of the best records for the percentage of donations that go directly to those in need, versus big salaries and schmoozing. Believe me, as co-director of operations, I have a comfortable—not exorbitant—salary, and I'm not required to do any schmoozing." She looked out the passenger-side window, with a sorrowful shake of her head, and whispered, "This is incredibly dangerous."

"Rylee," Dakota said, his voice pulling her focus to him. "We'll do everything in our power to keep the circle tight to protect your reputation. But you'll agree that the sooner the counterfeiter is identified and caught, the better. Working hand in hand with me—with us, I mean—will make for a better explanation afterward. You say something like, 'It came to our attention, and we worked very closely with the Secret Service.'"

"Yes, of course. I'm not saying that we don't trust you to help us navigate our proximity to these crimes. Our CEO said to go ahead and do whatever is needed to rectify this. And *this* falls under Neesa's and my jurisdiction. We don't have a lot to offer. So I'm very hopeful for the data that we can get from those videos."

"Iniquus is doing it for you, right?"

"Fortunately, yes," Rylee said. "We have a good working relationship. Often show up at the same emergency events. After their team saves their contracted protectees, they often stay to lend a hand. But also, one of our best logisticians, Hailey Sterling, moved to Iniquus when she married a Cerberus Bravo operator. After speaking with Jasper yesterday, Neesa reached out to Hailey to see whether Iniquus could help us. It's a bit of a long shot that we'll get anything, but their commander gave his thumbs up. Actually, they were grateful to learn about this issue because Iniquus, like us, uses the same cash system, and they're worried, like we are, that their reputation will be tarnished if they inadvertently spread counterfeit money." Riley shifted in her seat to face Dakota. "Neesa said she couldn't tell the correct bill from the fake when you were looking through our safe, that the bills were that good." She wrapped her hands around her knee. "I know we're trying to help by allowing the Secret Service to find the guy. I'm wondering if, in helping you, we're ultimately hurting ourselves. I wonder if we should just come clean on the news, tell people what's going on, and what we're doing to thwart it. Maybe by bringing in a little sunlight, it will disinfect the situation."

Dakota didn't answer, didn't try to dissuade her, didn't work to convince her that their way was the right way.

Rylee honestly didn't know how to navigate this.

It was a chess game with an unknown opponent.

Dakota pulled into the driveway of a neat, mid-century modern with a flat roof and wide chimneys. The bushes out front were neatly trimmed to mimic the house's geometric symmetry. The glow of the lights through the plate-glass windows was inviting.

She'd been expecting a condo or townhouse.

"Nice," she said.

Dakota pulled to a stop so that when she exited, her feet would be on the sidewalk.

She unbuckled then reached down for her bag. When she was upright again, Dakota was already at her door, opening it and extending his hand to assist her out.

Only then did he round to the back to release Tank.

"Go potty," Dakota commanded, and Tank trotted over to a three-sided space with a substrate different from the lawn. As Tank did his business, Dakota shut the hatch. "Iniquus taught him how to use a toilet, and he seems to prefer that. But he still has to practice his outdoor skills. I can't let him get prim about these things." He whistled. "Come on, Tank, dinner time."

Tank raced to the door, plopped his butt down, and waited.

After tapping in a lock code, Dakota opened the door wide for Rylee. She walked into an open floor plan with natural elements of slate and wood. The colors were neutral with splashes of bright contrast. Elements here and there brought welcome moments of surprise to the geometric serenity.

"Did you design this?" she asked, wandering over to the bookcase, taking in the titles that ranged from history to philosophy to finance and government. There was a good number of fiction that were heavy on the classics with mysteries and thrillers thrown in for good measure.

"My little sister did it as her senior interior design project at the uni."

Dakota steered toward the kitchen, where he washed his hands, then pulled out the ingredients for dinner.

"Can I help?" Rylee asked.

"How about you sit at the counter and have a drink? Wine, cider, beer, water, soda."

"Cider would be nice. I was in Normandy on vacation last year, and I became a big fan."

"Co-director of operations for a major NGO, tell me a bit about that job." Dakota popped the top off the cider. "Bottle or glass."

"Bottle, please."

He set the bottle in front of her as he began prepping the food with a deftness that said he was comfortable in the kitchen and cooked well.

"My role is to deal with operational challenges both in logistics and personnel. We run into a lot of issues when we put teams into play. I coordinate not just with my team but also with local governments and other international NGOs to ensure the right team shows up and that we aren't duplicating efforts while other aspects are overlooked. The same kinds of things that happen in the military. Critical infrastructure is often damaged, making on-site arrival difficult, especially in remote areas where access is already limited. The supply chain is a challenge, and one of the reasons we take stacks of cash into an area. And, of course, we need to be sensitive to and work within the local population's framework. So that means developing meaningful relationships with local leaders, listening to their priorities, and explaining possible roadmaps we can support. But yeah,

I'm responsible for the training and management of all the personnel in the field and the success of their operations."

"Big job," Dakota said as he moved the ingredients to the stove. "This is one of my quick-fix meals. I'll have it on the table in a few minutes." He opened the fridge. "While the pasta is cooking, I'll do a salad. If you see anything I'm pulling out that's an allergy or a dislike, please tell me."

"Yes, thank you." Rylee took a sip of cider and felt the alcohol ease into her bloodstream.

"I imagine you run into issues with politics and security," he said as he washed the vegetables.

"Yeah, I like that least. My people face armed groups and sudden conflict over limited resources."

"And they're not armed, right?"

"We have no weapons. On occasion, we might hire local groups to protect us, but we don't get involved in physical conflicts. Where the local government sends us is often political rather than strategic to the disaster. It's important that we remain neutral in everyone's eyes. Right now, we're facing significant issues with attrition. Globally, attacks on aid workers are on the rise. Especially for women, it's a risk. Kidnappings are up, weapons attacks, and harassment. It's my job to figure out our policy to keep everything running smoothly so those swept up in the disasters are safe and well cared for."

"What's the plan?"

"I've started participating in training evolutions with our fast response teams. I'll go on their next call-out to get my own boots-on-the-ground, first-hand view of what we're asking our people to do. I'll engage them in conversations about what changes can be made to help them do their job."

Tank wandered over and sniffed her, then lay at her feet. And that just felt nice, welcoming.

Rylee didn't want to talk about or think about work. "I get a free question."

"Okay," Dakota said without hesitation.

"Anything?" She took another swig of cider.

He looked over his shoulder at her and sent her an easy smile. "You can ask anything. Now, whether I'll answer or not … Kidding. I'm brave. Go."

"How did you make it through Coronado?"

"Easy enough." He poured oil and vinegar into a small bowl and whisked them together as the base for a dressing. "I got out there, and I thought they weren't there to hurt me. They were there to apply a test to me. It was the same test that everyone who wanted the job that I wanted went through before they were hired. The problem was that it was fucking hard." He caught her eye. "Sorry."

"Cussing is a sign of intelligence. There are lots of scientific studies supporting that assertion. It was fucking hard?" She raised her brows, so he would continue.

He reached into the spice cabinet and started adding a pinch of this and a pinch of that. "I mean, harder than I could ever have imagined. At some point, I thought, Hey, you know who they're trying to weed out? Men who don't make the mark. Men who shouldn't have the job. What if that's me? What if I don't measure up?" He flipped a piece of carrot in the air and caught it in his mouth. "Oh man, that switched everything in my brain, and then it was a competition." He moved over and set a little pile of sliced carrots by her bottle, calling out, "Tank," as he flipped some through the air so Tank could catch them and nibble, too.

"You're competitive, you'd have to be to streak across the finish line with the Cerberus crew."

"I'm going to draw a distinction there. There are places to be competitive—on the field of battle, in a race, coming up against a problem that requires a solution—that does indeed flip that toggle in my brain. But walking around on the day-to-day? I'm not that guy. I don't need to beat my chest and constantly prove myself." He drizzled the salad with the dressing and leaned over the stove to stir his pots before turning off the element.

"But the toggle was switched on in Coronado."

"Oh, it was on. You think you can make me cold? No way. You think I'll drop from fatigue. Psh." He pulled dishes from the cupboard and set them on the counter.

"I can see you now." She smiled, then popped a carrot into her mouth.

"My turn – how did you drop the guy in the bar?" he asked, pulling cutlery from the drawer.

"Upper cut to the diaphragm. As he collapsed forward, he grabbed me – not for the second grope but stability as his brain did a little freak out. So I used his grip hand for the arm bar. Then Erica dropped onto his back. That wasn't necessary, but a little whipped cream on the cake. He was on the ground, catching his breath. Because his biggest injury was probably his male ego—"

Dakota set the platters of food between the plates and added serving utensils. "Yeah?"

"I figure better to get his thighs apart and bend his legs, so he couldn't get up. I like that move because if there's any struggle, I can swift kick his nuts."

Dakota lifted his bottle so it clinked with hers. "Badassery."

"All day, every day." Rylee felt perfectly content in that moment, as if everything wrong with the world existed on the other side of Dakota's front door.

He sat on the stool across from her, suddenly looking serious. "Can I ask you for something?" he said softly.

Rylee stilled. She didn't want Dakota to say some shit something that would force her from this lovely cocoon.

"I feel unreasonably connected to you for having just met." He moved a hand to his heart. "I need you to promise me that, if my comfort around you makes you feel uneasy, you'll tell me so I can adjust. I would never want my sense of ease to impact you by shifting a boundary that you want in place."

"Fair enough." She exhaled.

Okay. It wasn't just Rylee then; Dakota was feeling it, too.

17

Dakota

Friday

Everything about yesterday evening was a surprise. *Everything.*

Dakota had a list of, oh, say, thirteen conversation starters that he could whip out on a first or second date to break the ice, and keep the conversation from hitting a sticky spot when attention shifted awkwardly to the weather or décor.

A lot of the questions on his list were clichés because he understood people got nervous. Dakota reasoned that pulling out a well-worn date-night question meant his companion probably had a honed reply. If that answer seemed promising and not too intrusive, Dakota could wander down the conversational path with them until another cliché question was needed to keep the momentum going.

What do you do for fun? Where have you traveled that you felt changed your perspective the most? How do you pick your next book?

It was surprising to him that his dates didn't read, didn't travel, and "just whatever" was fun.

That's why he had a baker's dozen on the tip of his tongue.

There had to be something to talk about.

Last night, over shrimp scampi, he hadn't used any of his list with Rylee.

Conversation had flowed easily and freely between them.

Rylee was quick and funny. Any topic that he brought up, she could engage in either from a base of knowledge or a fount of curiosity. Humble and kind. *Astonishing*.

Too good to be true?

While social media wanted to tell men that women only wanted to date six-foot, six-pack, six-figure men, he thought there really wasn't the same quick formula making its rounds for women.

For him, the triumvirate of winning qualities included kindness, intellectual curiosity, and natural generosity with words and actions.

He had lain in bed last night talking to Tank about what had happened on the river when Rylee was kayaking. Even knowing what she knew from dating a fast water search and rescue guy, Rylee had decided to grab the hand of a decomposing corpse to protect the hearts of a family that she had never even met.

What had it taken to reach into the water with all the ghoulish sights and sensations that could follow?

Selfless.

Brave.

Courage was damned sexy.

He loved it. Loved every second of being with her.

And he thanked the Fates that he had that last phone call with Rose, or he would have missed last night altogether. And that would have been a loss and a shame.

They ate. They cleaned up together. Rylee looked beat, so he drove her home, where he held her hand as he walked her to the door.

But that was it.

That was it because Dakota felt incredibly protective of what might be happening between them, and she was tired. He wanted to make sure that if he kissed her, she wasn't kissing him back as a way to get it over with, so she could go in and get some sleep. He'd heard one too many of his friends' stories—and honestly, one was already too many—about how exhausting it was to maintain their boundaries, especially when it came to intimacy.

He was risk-averse when it came to Rylee. He'd do nothing to endanger what he felt when he was with her.

Dakota decided that on his end, gentlemanly behavior was what he'd continue to extend, and if she wanted more, she'd let him know.

The drive back to his house was only ten minutes.

In a city where traffic could make or break a relationship, ten minutes was a good omen.

Last night, he had slept deeply and profoundly, as if his whole body could relax for the first time in a long time.

This morning, he and Tank had an extra good run. Dakota's hot shower felt amazing. He was a caricature, a comic-strip man, drawn as if he were walking on air. And he couldn't seem to drop the grin.

In the mirror, he looked like Jasper did when he was looking at Neesa.

Jasper was a good guy; it would be great if he finally found his better half.

Dakota looked outside and saw Fifi pissing on her favorite tree. "Tank," Dakota's call was answered with scrambling nails on his hardwood. "Dude, we have to head over to Iniquus. They want you to sniff around their stacks of money, okay? But I'm keeping you with me through this weekend at least, so you get a shot at a date with FiFi. I'll text her mom and see if you can't get a play date."

Tank perked up his ears and tipped his head.

"Would you like that? To see Fifi?"

Tank tipped his head the other way, then ran over to the door and sat at attention, tongue hanging long in anticipation.

As Dakota checked his watch. "Okay, five minutes until Jasper gets here." He opened the door, and Tank shot over to the fence for their ritual butt sniffing just as Dakota's phone rang.

He answered with a happy grin. "Morning, Rylee."

"Good morning. I'm here with Neesa, you're on speaker phone."

"Morning, Neesa."

"Not yet, it isn't. I'm waiting for the coffee to kick in," she grumped.

"Yeah?" Dakota was starting to get her salty humor. "Rough night's sleep?"

"Rylee seeded some vivid nightmares with her river

caper. So yeah, rough, and yeah, last night is one I never want to repeat. But we're calling with what we hope is good news."

"Hailey called from Iniquus," Rylee said. "They have our analysis done. Just so you know, we only gave her tapes from the three instances when our responders had counterfeit money with them."

"Smart to set those limits." He watched Tank and Fifi running up and down the fence line together. "That narrows the playing field. What did you find out?"

"It didn't surprise Hailey because she's been a logistician for a long time, and it didn't surprise us, but it might well surprise you to know how very small the Venn Diagram is for people who were around for the times when the counterfeit money was a known factor."

"They processed it into a report?" Dakota asked, turning toward his drive as Jasper turned in. "It's not just a raw list?"

"Neesa and I are going over in a little bit to talk to Hailey about the findings. We were wondering if anyone from your team wanted to participate in her presentation."

"Jasper just pulled up. We're on our way to Iniquus so Tank can do a walk-through of their vault. Iniquus has decided to test all of their currency, but getting a nose on it seemed like a good first step. We could meet there."

"Okay, if you're heading there now—I'm not sure how involved that search is for Tank—but we're not expected there until ten thirty," Rylee said. "So if you're done by then, maybe you two could join us?"

"Absolutely, I'll let Reaper know we need to make that meeting."

The morning unfolded much too slowly for Dakota. He

kept checking his watch, hoping for ten thirty. It was high school all over again. Jasper, too, seemed itchy. Tank hadn't wanted to leave FiFi. It was spring, and love was in the air.

He smiled at the thought, then set it aside.

One thing he'd learned in his history with women was never to get ahead of the curve.

Dakota needed to stay present and work the job at hand.

In that moment, Reaper was monitoring Dakota's ability to handle Tank on a counterfeit search.

General Elliot was on hand to watch Tank do his thing in the vault, where Tank had a hit.

The general turned his battle-hardened focus on Reaper. "Reaper, do we need a K9 trained up to police our currency?"

"No, sir. The Secret Service brought in specific scents from specific known counterfeit crews from specific countries. The only counterfeit money that Tank alerts on is narrow. If Dakota wants to use Tank in the field searching for a different criminal organization's counterfeit money, Cerberus would have to start with a known sample and train Tank to those particular scents, so my training one of our K9s isn't practical."

"All right." The general tapped a finger on Dakota's chest. "When this young man brings in a new scent for Tank. We'll do the training." He turned to Dakota. "The currency I'm concerned with is coming out of North Korea. It can fool even the currency machines. So work on getting hold of that sample, and we'll have Tank do an occasional walkthrough to pay for his bread and butter."

"Fair enough, thank you, sir." Dakota focused on Tank as he lay down and rested his chin on his front paws.

"You boys going to play in the AI games today?" the general asked. "Swiftwater Crew, weren't you both?"

"I'm not familiar with what's going on, sir," Dakota said.

The general put a hand on Reaper's shoulder. "See what you can do to get them involved. I'm curious to see how today turns out." And he walked away.

Reaper pointed down the hall where Neesa and Rylee rounded the corner with their Iniquus escort. "I'll take WorldCares," Reaper told the escort, who turned on his heels and left.

"When you're done, the general was saying that DARPA's here today." Reaper used the acronym for Defense Advanced Research Projects Agency. "They have an AI system that they want to test. It can monitor a building by watching for and signaling an advancing human. They're setting it up on the barracks wall facing the field. They want to see if anyone can get to the building without the system detecting their approach. We have a couple of Marine Raiders from Strike Force that I know are taking a turn. Cerberus Bravo will all be there—Hailey's husband, Ares, with his K9 Judge. Some others are throwing their hats in the ring. No prize, no glory, but it's a break from the norm. A good challenge."

"I haven't quite forgiven Cerberus for stealing Hailey from us," Neesa told Jasper. "She was one of our best logistical assets."

"Stealing would be a stretch." Rylee shifted back so she was walking beside Dakota with Tank between them. "She fell in love with Ares, and she's still doing her good work in the world, but now she can still be home with him. We should talk to her about that, Neesa. I bet she has some insights into our attrition issues."

"Still," Neesa said.

"I miss her too. Try not to grump," Rylee said. "It's because of Hailey that Iniquus analyzed our body cam footage."

Neesa looked up at Jasper. "Did you find any funny money in the Iniquus vault?"

"I can't say," Jasper replied.

"Is that what you call it?" Dakota laughed. "Funny money?"

"Well, no, it's not at all funny," Neesa said. "I just don't like to say counterfeit because it sounds like confetti for a celebration—funny money isn't any better. I need something that means evil."

"The Devil's Cash," Rylee said.

Neesa looked over her shoulder at Rylee. "That works."

Reaper opened a door and looked in. "Hi, Hailey, I have WorldCares and the Secret Service with me."

"Perfect."

They filed in and sat down to see a PowerPoint on the screen.

Reaper left.

"There are a lot fewer names on that list than I expected," Dakota said as he signaled Tank under the table.

Hailey clicked and brought up color-coded lists. "These are the members of the World Cares teams over three deployments. These next three are the lists of names from other International teams. WorldCares tends to match up with the same international groups," Hailey explained. "They have good communication. They know each other's strengths and weaknesses. When I was in logistics for WorldCares, we emphasized those relationships when we could." Hailey shot a glance at Rylee. "This next slide has the name of our special friend."

"Langley said to share," Rylee said.

Langley? Dakota and Jasper turned to each other, then back to the screen.

"These are the two faces that have shown up in all three of the WorldCares deployments where they had a known contact with counterfeit currency."

"Casey Andrews," Rylee said as she tapped her thigh and reached for Tank, "is a CIA field officer who has our permission to ride along with us and wear our logo at disaster sites. We do that with immense gratitude."

Under the table, Tank wriggled over to Rylee to get scritches.

"Tell me about that," Dakota said. "That is, if you're allowed to. I'd like to understand the CIA's relationship with you."

"There are very good reasons that the CIA sends intelligence to these events," Rylee explained. "From the CIA's point of view, they want to monitor how foreign governments operate under stress. How efficient they are. If there are concerning levels of unrest because of what the government did or didn't do. What fissures were there in the country, and who was trying to exploit them?"

"Hailey can tell you," Neesa said. "She saw a lot of this in her time out in the field doing prep work for an anticipated crisis."

"Exactly," Hailey agreed. "Certain manipulators wanted to shove themselves in and look like the good guys with soft diplomacy and humanitarian efforts—food and a hand-shake. That wasn't the danger. Casey was looking for dangerous alliances born out of desperation—who was there to put a foot in the door to ease their reputations as a terrorist organization and try to garner the label of a brotherhood instead. And then some groups wanted to exploit the situation. They were the ones who took control of the trucks or train cars filled with supplies. To survive, people did what they were told to do at gunpoint. Paid what they were told to pay. Even then, sometimes those supplies were just rerouted to insurgent camps to feed themselves and never reached the hungry disaster survivors."

"And, of course, there's nothing like a natural disaster to exploit for extremist recruitment," Rylee said, "undermine local authority, or simply cause chaos and panic in a group of people desperate for survival."

Dakota looked across the conference table to see Jasper purse his lips and raise his brow, conveying, "That might explain it." And Dakota knew *exactly* what Jasper was thinking.

Neesa picked up on it, too. "What's that, Jasper?"

"I'm not saying I did this or specifically know anyone who did. I'm just saying it's done. Sometimes in the field, a group comes upon something of value—diamonds, gold, bags of U.S. dollars in cash meant by the CIA to bribe some tribal head. And sometimes that thing of value is moved to a secret space. The idea is that people live dangerous lives to serve the government, and the government doesn't exactly compensate them appropriately. So they set this up as a rainy-day fund. If the team member becomes disabled or dead, the family isn't left desperate. If everyone gets home safe and sound, they have a nest egg for retirement. They figure, the thing of value would only land in the hands of a bad guy, so why not put it to good use?"

"Why not?" Rylee asked. "The ethics seem okay to me if it were an enemy, and we were at war. But if you're insinuating that Casey would endanger us, or his position, or the people in crisis by trading out US dollars for counterfeit, I'm putting my foot down. I will *not* entertain that idea. Casey Andrews is a WorldCares hero." Rylee's voice rang clear with conviction.

Hailey leaned forward, her face was a storm of emotion. "Casey's work in gathering information during a disaster has led him, on many occasions, to learn of armed dangers. He has moved our people out of harm's way, hidden us in safe spots, and helped our people escape in what seems similar to the Underground Railroad, out of the country before kidnapping raids. I agree with Rylee, having personally survived an armed attack that destroyed the village where I was working, people like Casey are the greatest of heroes. I stand staunchly with him and his integrity."

The three had women shifted to a war footing. Time to change the subject.

Dakota pointed at the list. "What about the second name, Dr. Lewis McLeod?"

Rylee shook her head and looked at Neesa.

Neesa shook her head and looked at Hailey.

"He's a professor who goes to mass disasters, especially during winter break and during the summer, to work on a photography project, taking pictures of people at their most raw moments. People in disasters," Hailey said. "I met him once. He's dedicated to his work and otherwise stays out of the way."

"You sneered," Jasper said.

"I'm not a fan. To me, it's a moral gray area," Hailey said. "Granted, he sells the photos to news outlets, and that brings emotional awareness to the situation and might boost needed donations. On his website, it says that money from his photography sales goes to affected areas. Is it true that he gives the money? He's not listed as a 501(c)(3). He said the proceeds from the book will help recruit and train disaster response workers worldwide. You can see the images on his website. They're poignant. He's good at what he does."

"And yet?" Rylee asked.

"It feels exploitative of the suffering. I'm very much conflicted by it all. WorldCares asked that we not be included in the images. He's honored that request."

"If anyone who has a signed Iniquus contract is at those disasters, Iniquus sends in a team to extract them. Are they in the photos?" Rylee asked.

"We have a computer system dedicated to protecting our client's safety from the Internet. For example, say one of our people is doxed, they scrub that data to stop such things as swatting. That ongoing search looks for any image of anyone working for Iniquus. If we were on Dr. McLeod's website, we would pay to have them removed for security reasons."

"If he knew that, he could focus all of his efforts on taking Iniquus photos."

"He could," Hailey agreed. "Surely, someone sat him down and had a conversation. We do everything necessary to keep our operators safe in a world where privacy is at a premium."

"Pretty soon, I'm going to start wearing a variety of silicone masks," Dakota said. "Or start walking around in war paint stripes, like we did at the races."

"Is that why you did that?" Rylee asked. "It looked like modern art."

"How long do you think that will hold until you can't thwart the computer with the paint?" Jasper asked. "Has Iniquus considered balaclavas? Other groups have started using them."

"We're not criminals," Hailey said. "We wouldn't want to dress the part. We'll keep working to stay a step ahead."

"How dangerous is your work, Dakota?" Rylee's mouth pulled into a frown.

Dakota's job put him in the thick of things. If he were identifiable, it would end his ability to operate.

He reached under the table to squeeze her hand, so she'd know everything was okay.

But that flash of fear for his safety, that was why he'd always promised himself, whether he was with the Navy or the Secret Service, that he'd step into a different role once he found someone who cared, something that was mostly behind a desk like Jasper and Kumar, with some field trips with Tank. Dakota had seen too many good women and loving families absolutely devastated by the constant strain. And he wasn't selfish enough about his career to make his loved ones pay the price.

Had Dakota known about Iniquus back when he left the Navy, he would have liked to throw his hat in the ring for a spot on one of their tactical teams. Back in his prime, he wouldn't have minded traipsing around the world, pulling college students and executives out of their emergencies.

He would have seen a lot of the world that he hadn't seen when he was stationed on either side of the Red Sea.

Yeah, in the military, he'd seen a lot. A lot of it he'd like to forget.

Instead, his career took him to the Secret Service, where he tried to protect the integrity of the US dollar by stopping counterfeiters. That brought him primarily to Peru and Colombia.

Once Tank held his certifications, Dakota would take up assignments closer to home.

He paused for a moment as he realized that he'd already made up his mind to talk to Jasper about a lateral move out of the field.

When had he made that decision?

It was time to make a career move—this was a huge acknowledgement of his shifting priorities—he wanted a family life.

He wanted to reach out and bring peace to someone just by sitting close and holding her hand.

Dakota liked the harmony and comfort he felt last night with Rylee, and he wanted that for himself as his constant.

Possibly, Rylee wanted that in her life.

Could things work out between them?

It was early days.

Too soon to tell.

18

THEY WERE STANDING with Hailey's husband, Ares; his dog, Judge, was at his feet.

"DARPA had been working on developing smart cameras that could differentiate between a human and anything else that might be moving through an open space," Ares explained. "It would give guards enough warning to conduct a meet-and-greet before their perimeter was breached. The goal today is to get past the camera and into the building without detection."

"You're going?" Hailey asked him.

"Judge and I are next up," he said, turning his attention to the group of Iniquus spectators standing at the start line.

"And you have a strategy?" Hailey asked.

Ares chuckled. "You'll have to wait and see."

"Broad daylight. Open field," Neesa said. "Does this seem like a waste of time?"

"Looks like they chose a bunch of Marine Raiders," Hailey said. "Deep DelToro and Gator Rochambeau from Strike Force and Creed Duchamp from Cerberus Tactical Team Charlie. You can't stop a Marine."

"Creed is going out with his puppy Rugaroo," Ares pointed out a man playing ball with a black lab. "He says he's doing a little Hoodoo he learned along the way, and they'll slip on by like mist on the water."

"Not testing the system against Combatant-craft Crewmen seems problematic," Jasper said.

"You want to take a stab at it?" Ares asked.

Dakota stepped forward. "I would."

"You need a team," Ares said. "They don't want anyone to go as individuals."

"Tank." He turned to Rylee. "You wanna play?"

"I'm game."

"I'll put your name on the list." Ares bent and kissed Hailey. "I'll see you later." He turned to their group. "Good luck. I'll leave you to strategize."

"All right," Dakota slid his hands into his pockets. "Let's get some ideas together. How would you do it, Rylee?" Dakota asked.

"Surely not somersaulting across the field like those two are doing." They all turned to look where Rylee pointed.

"Deep and Gator, Marine Raiders," Hailey said.

"Of course they are," Jasper said. "Who else would do shit like that for two hundred yards? The DARPA flag is still green, though, so the AI hasn't spotted them."

"Surely, they were spotted," Neesa said, "They just weren't identified as human."

"Yeah, that's my idea," Rylee said. "They're not looking for a dog. We should go in disguised as Tank."

Dakota turned to her. "Listening."

"There was a time or two when the only way that I could get one of my injured Marines off the battlefield was to put them on my back and slither out like a turtle. Bad simile, turtles are up on their legs. Some kind of lizard. It was on packed ground, and it was rough to do. But is there anything with that image we can work with?"

"Like Dakota's on the bottom, you're on top, Tank on top of you?" Neesa asked.

"That's about two hundred and fifty pounds on top of Dakota. I wouldn't do that. Can we use ghillie suits?" Rylee asked Hailey.

"You can only use what you find in the area," Hailey said. "Oh, look, Ares is up at the line. He's going under a cardboard box, and Judge is going under another." Hailey held her hands over her mouth as she sent a whoop! their way. "That's amazing."

The group watched as the boxes started across the open space. One of the boxes moved forward, then seemed to be redirected to join the first box.

The Marines were still somersaulting, though, it now looked a little drunken and wobbly. They had to be dizzy as hell.

"Yup, green flag is still up." Hailey pointed. "Ares and Judge's sideways, forward, and angled jerky movements are definitely not human-like."

"Disorganization seems to be key," Neesa said. "What if

you weren't putting your weight on Dakota, he was slithering like a snake, and you were crawling on top, your bodies could look like a hill? Does Tank need to be disguised? He's non-human."

"Sounds like you have a picture in your mind. Should we try it and see?" Dakota asked.

Neesa gestured at the ground. "Okay, Dakota, you lie down like you're going to crawl under the wires on an obstacle course. Okay, Rylee, now you."

"Me what?" Rylee stood next to Dakota.

"Yeah, just straddle Dakota, but get up on your hands and knees."

Rylee did her best to comply. "Like this? How would we move in unison?"

"We could tie your knees together. When he moves, you move," Neesa said.

"Okay, Neesa. I just met the man, and you want us to engage in bondage in front of an audience? Dakota, just so you know, I'm not that kind of girl."

"I'm just lying here waiting for instructions." His voice was gruff with stifled laughter.

"Try it," Neesa insisted.

It worked briefly. "I'd need knee pads, and I don't know what Dakota would need to slither all that way. This is a lot more complicated than somersaulting." Rylee stayed where she was, kneeling across Dakota, shifting this way and that to see if she could come up with a better configuration.

"Yeah, but we won't be puking for the next few hours," Jasper said. "Looks like the Marines have landed. The boxes are still moving around like a video game."

"Green flags still up," Hailey said proudly.

"Here, the best I could do was to put my knees in his armpit. I don't think we look like a hill. I'm going to scratch this one off the possibilities list." Rylee pushed herself onto her feet. "We have to come up with something that we can sustain over that long a distance."

"I like what you said about Tank being non-human," Dakota said. "Tank is the profile we want to emphasize, just a dog in the field. And I like the idea of being a natural element."

"We need to keep it simple," Rylee turned to Neesa.

"Nope," she said. "I gave you my best shot. I don't do field work."

"What if we just got some of those dead branches and made a screen?" Dakota offered. "Put Tank out in front of us, and I direct him to move like a dog to distract the computer from focusing on us—"

"This would be a lot easier if we had some idea about how the AI recognized a human approach," Rylee said.

"If you fail, you fail," Jasper said. "You're not part of Iniquus, so you won't hurt their reputation."

Hailey bladed her hand over her brows to shield her eyes from the sun. "And the boxes have migrated away from the finish line."

"They definitely don't look like they're heading in a straight human pattern," Neesa said. "So you think that just the random movements Tank makes can help you disappear?"

"I say we try that," Rylee told Dakota. "Sit down flat like this." She sat down, stretching her legs in front of her. "Then we rock thigh to thigh to move our legs slowly forward. The time and the lateral movement are both very non-human."

They constructed the screens to be low to the ground.

"How do we look, Neesa?" Rylee called from behind her fan of branches.

"Like a tree blowing in the wind. Only, there isn't any wind today."

"Hailey?"

"I don't know," Hailey said. "I can see you, but there are no obvious human parts."

Once they'd developed their strategy, Rylee, Dakota, and Tank presented themselves at the starting line.

They got their signal, and off they went at the speed of a sloth.

"Wow, this is really slow," Rylee said as Dakota sent Tank out to sniff around.

"No slower than the somersaults," Dakota said, adjusting his branches into his belt loops.

"Do you think we can make it across by dinner?"

"The boxes are still out there in the field." He reached over to adjust Rylee's branches so they were less of a burden. "Ares is either crawling or squat walking. Either one has got to be miserable."

"It's in the name of science. Look over there, the flag's still up. So far, we're evading detection."

"Rylee, we've gone all of two feet."

They were silent as they made their slow but steady way. Tank followed Dakota's instructions to the letter: lie down, run right, run left, and circle. He was having a great time sniffing all the scents, but Dakota had to keep him busy so he wouldn't run over and give Rylee kisses again.

After a while, Dakota said. "What are you thinking? You hanging in there?"

"Three things are top of mind," Rylee answered. "First, this is one hell of a workout; my abs will be wrecked for weeks. Second, I bought these leggings after I saw a woman post a five-star review saying she got scared on a cliff trail and had to go down the mountain on her butt. Afterward, the leggings were still in great condition, no worn spots or tears, and so I'm grateful for these leggings."

"And third?" Dakota asked.

"Honestly? I should have gone to the bathroom before we started. I have to pee pretty badly."

19

———

RYLEE

Friday

WHEN THE TEST ENDED, the engineers were stunned — the AI hadn't detected a single team. The system, trained on predictable human patterns, couldn't comprehend movements that were chaotic, illogical, or even as absurd as the two Marines somersaulting across the terrain.

Thwarted by creativity, the engineers would go back to the drawing board.

For now, the human brain reigned supreme.

"What are you thinking about this, Rylee?" Dakota asked.

It was the three of them in her car—Rylee, Dakota, and Tank. While Dakota changed in the Cerberus Headquarters, Neesa and Jasper decided to head off for dinner in his car. And because Neesa had given Rylee a puppy dog look, Rylee had agreed to drive Dakota and Tank home.

That was a lie.

Rylee wasn't doing her bestie a solid. Her being with Dakota was pure self-indulgence.

"I think that kind of system is too dangerous to play with." Rylee was driving, and it had been a non-issue when she fobbed her car open. With men in her past, they got a little twitchy when they weren't the ones behind the wheel and in control of the vehicle. "You've heard about that kid in Maryland who got jumped by the police for having a gun when he was eating a bag of chips? Someone's going to get killed. That's my prediction. Why? What are you thinking?"

"It was fun to thwart," Dakota said. "A chess game when you weren't sure of the rules. I mostly have questions. Who would rely on this system? If the system failed, what would the ramifications be? Something we didn't test was the breaking point. No one simply crawled forward. No one skipped, or limped, or did a squat every three paces. No one wore a balaclava or carried an umbrella. If I were designing the test, I would have said, 'Do less, okay, now do less, and once again with less.'"

Rylee gave a little finger wave as she passed by the Iniquus gate guard. "They might have already tried all that, so they needed special ops to get in there and do what wouldn't occur to their engineers."

"Possibly. We'll never know."

"Where am I driving?" Rylee asked, turning on her windshield wipers as the first blobs of rain obscured her windshield. "Do you already have plans for tonight, or would you like to hang out?"

"I'd like to hang out with you. But you're going to want to get cleaned up. You haven't seen your backside."

"You were looking?"

"I was." He chuckled. "Very nice, but also filthy."

"Okay, so obviously my place. You cooked last time. I can pull something together for dinner. I could maybe do rice and chicken for Tank?"

"Yes to your place, absolutely no to your cooking."

"Scared?"

"Terrified," he said with an easy smile. "Pizza? I do need you to run by my house so I can pick up my car. Thunderstorms are in the forecast for tonight, and I don't want you on dangerous roads alone in the dark, and it's a weekend, so it's hard to get a taxi to come out to the burbs. I'll go home, feed Tank, and pick up a couple of pizzas. I just have to know what you're in the mood for."

Rylee turned her face as if she were checking her mirror. She absolutely didn't want Dakota to see the lascivious glimmer that must be sparkling in her eyes.

What was she in the mood for?

Ever since they were rubbing thighs over two hundred yards, feeling the power of his body against hers, she knew *exactly* what she was in the mood for, and pretending otherwise only made the ache deeper. "Whatever looks good on the menu, I'm game. No pineapple or sardines, though, please."

He held out his phone, the map app open, showing the route to his house, where she left him off.

At home, she had to do a quick run-through of the rooms because she wasn't company-ready like Dakota had been.

She jumped in the shower where she did a power prep, shaving and moisturizing, swiping on deodorant, throwing her hair up into what she hoped was a sophisticated messy bun before tugging on a pair of oversized sweatpants that hung low on her hips. For her top, Rylee chose a lacy bra and a little cami. Easy access, and hopefully the only invitation Dakota would need.

Then she lit a fire and dimmed the lights. "I just have to know what you're in the mood for," he'd said.

She was in the mood for everything.

She was in the mood to talk to him. And look at him. And touch him. All of it, all at once.

"Slow your damned motor," Rylee whispered as she answered Dakota's call.

"Hey, I found a place to parallel park down the street from your townhouse. Can you open the door and call Tank so he runs to you? You don't want the smell of wet dog in your house."

Rylee grabbed a towel from the guest bath. "Ready," she called, leaning out the door.

Off in the distance, she saw Dakota open the back door, and with her call, Tank raced down the street and inside, where Rylee rubbed him dry while Dakota jogged in with the pizza protected by an extra-wide umbrella.

They decided on a picnic in front of the fire.

"Good?" he asked as she peeked into the boxes.

"Perfect." But when she said, "I'm starving," she was looking Dakota in the eye.

The blush. The smile. So damned cute.

Rylee, leaning back against a chair and crisscrossing her legs, lifted a slice to her mouth. "Thunderstorms set the stage for pillow talk." Then she took the bite.

"Yeah?" Dakota settled against the chair, facing her. "I'm game."

Tank lay on the cool slate in her foyer, where he'd been banished while they were eating.

"Why don't we catch up on all the things we would already know about each other, if we were, say, two months into a dating relationship?"

"Interesting." Dakota reached for a napkin and pulled a slice of pizza from the box.

"Isn't it?" Rylee asked. "I'll start. You were with special operations forces. Why did you choose to be a little-known Special Warfare Combatant-craft Crewman and not go for the SEAL Trident so you could have life-long bragging rights?"

"I don't know. I wanted to be on a special forces team, and I'm not great at swimming in black water. I'd rather be sitting in a boat."

Rylee leaned forward, wiggling her fingers in the air. "Something might come up and nibble your toes?"

"That's it exactly. Nightmare material. Like that hand you thought you'd be dragging from the water." He made a stink face and shook his head. "That's a nope for me."

She laughed from her belly because it was so endearingly humble.

Dakota felt so solid and dependable to Rylee. If circumstances were different, she could imagine a relationship with him rather than simply enjoying his company.

While wonderful, this was merely a moment in time. Rylee was in survival mode, and a relationship didn't make any sense.

"My turn," Dakota said. "If I had known you for two months, I would already know what you wanted in a relationship. Right now, I'm more interested in what you *don't* want from a relationship."

"Neesa and I were just talking about this. I don't know if you know this, but Neesa has a doctorate in mathematics."

"Smart cookie."

"Intimidatingly brilliant," Rylee agreed. "We were talking about game theory and how relationships can be seen through that lens."

Dakota's mouth pulled into a bemused expression.

"What? Are you telling me that your friends don't sit around discussing the application of game theory to relationship status?"

He laughed. "Okay, let's go. Are we looking back at your past relationships? Present?"

"I'm single."

"Same," he said, looking straight into her eyes.

That word flooded Rylee's system with relief. But then again, she reminded herself, she was living in the moment; her future was too tenuous. That MRI truly freaked her out. She had only put MS into her health equation. But because of her time in the sand, sniffing in the fumes from the burn pits, she was now thinking about imminent, lethal diagnoses like glioblastoma and cancer on her spine.

"Which game theory did you and Neesa apply?"

"Neesa said The Prisoner's Dilemma worked best. Originally, we were talking about it in terms of our corporate culture at WorldCares. We want to stay dynamic and growing. Our goal is to be a source of good for people outside of our organization by serving human needs in disasters, but we also want to be good to our people inside the organization. And that means we need to know that everyone's pulling their own weight over time."

"Same with my crew in the Navy," Dakota said. "You were only as good as your weakest link."

"Exactly. But humans are humans, you can't always show up with the same level of go-juice. Sometimes others need to step up and, for short periods, carry more weight. Let's say you and your crew have a log overhead, and one of the guys is low glycemic, everyone takes on an extra pound or so. But he gets some calories, he's energized and able, and now he does a little more lifting to give the guy who just ripped his rotator cuff a bit of a break."

"Show me how the Prisoner's Dilemma applies here."

"In this game, two suspects are interrogated in different rooms. If they both stay silent, they're golden. If one confesses to receive a reward, like immunity, the other will go to jail. If both of them confess to gain the reward, they both lose, and both go to jail. Both of them should choose to remain silent. But that takes an enormous amount of trust."

"I've seen this dilemma as a war game run on things like price wars and environmental agreements. I've never applied it to a love relationship," Dakota said, taking a bite of pizza and putting the slice down on the box lid.

"Neesa really liked that because it said that, sight-unseen, you needed to trust the agreements made in a rela-tionship. For her, that's not always been the case. She's had some philanderers who have made her distrustful." Yes, Rylee told Dakota that on purpose because if Jasper was a shithead, Dakota probably knew and should tell Rylee about it or risk messing up her trust in him.

Manipulative? Sure. But it was in the service of a friend.

"Principled Reciprocity was the game I thought applied best to my experiences," Rylee said.

"Oh, we are getting deep."

"I saw the philosophy books on your shelf," Rylee countered. "So they were either there to impress, or you're up to this conversation."

Dakota chuckled and took another bite.

"To make sure we have the same working definition in Principled Reciprocity, if you do a favor for me, I do a favor for you. Your kindness is returned by my kindness."

"I feed you scampi, you feed me pizza," Dakota said.

"No, you fed me scampi, and then you fed me pizza. The only tit for tat is spending an evening in your house, then one in mine."

"Fair point. But with the good stuff in Principled Reciprocity, there is also a penalty. If you do something bad to me," Dakota said, "expect the same from me. And here I can see how you and Neesa intertwined the Prisoner's Dilemma. If both do an act of kindness, both win. If someone does an act of kindness and it's met with a negative, the relationship loses."

"And it's doomed when both prisoners decide to be rats," Rylee said. "In the game of Principled Reciprocity, it's rarely an even back and forth. Sometimes you do two or three nice things in a row. Scampi and pizza."

"Keep going."

"I think that we have days of strength and days of weakness. Months of health and vigor and weeks of ill health when we need to lean more heavily."

"You can't show up with the same level of energy all the time," Dakota agreed. "It would be good if I don't feel like cooking, the other person takes on that task. When someone doesn't feel like changing the oil, I don't mind."

"When we're both just whipped and sad because of the things we've dealt with that day, we order takeout and collapse on the sofa in each other's arms. But those are followed by days of adventure and boisterous laughter. Races to the tops of the mountains, and awe while standing in front of a painting that says everything that I could never put into words." Rylee took a bite from her pizza, then covered her mouth with her hand to add. "It's the dream."

"I don't think it's a fantasy. Although it's aspirational, sure. And communication is key."

"And kindness," Rylee added.

"Always."

"Not always. I'm divorced, so I can promise you, it's definitely not 'always.'"

"How long ago?"

"Seven? No, eight, almost nine years ago. The end came from a revelation that began when I was deployed to Cameroon to help with a natural disaster. I speak French, but I practiced with native French speakers from France. Could I converse in Cameroon? Yes, but it was a strain and exhausting. When I found an English speaker, even one with a heavy accent, it was a relief. This was when people started talking about different love languages back in the States. I wondered if my then-husband had tried so hard to communicate in my love language that he was simply tired, like I was when I tried to speak in Cameroon. Maybe what needed to happen was that I focus on the way he expressed devotion, not how I received it."

"Interesting," Dakota said.

"Your love language is acts of service, I'm right, aren't I?" Rylee asked.

"That," Dakota said. "And quality time. Yours is service, too, or you wouldn't have your job."

Physical touch is up on that list, Rylee thought, but simply said. "Mine are the same as yours."

"Your ex?" Dakota asked.

"Yeah, I thought in our relationship, maybe I was seeing things in a monolithic way. I didn't want to say I knew the only way to love and perhaps we had incompatible love languages and that lack of communication was affecting us —me, he seemed fine—over time."

"Listening."

"So I'm going to call my efforts to engage with him a bid for attention. Like I've seen Tank communicate with you. Tank looks to you, you look back. He walks under your hand, and you give him a couple of scritches. He puts his paw on your foot. That kind of thing."

"We're communicating our affection or information," Dakota said, turning to Tank.

Tank lifted his head to check in and, seeing the calm room and no signal, he lay back down.

"Imagine what would happen if Tank didn't get those returned gestures from you?"

"He'd increase his attention seeking, and then it would fall off. Eventually, he'd stop trying and just go off to do his own thing."

"Right, so after I got married, that's what happened," Rylee said. "It was almost as if my ex thought, 'caught me a fish. It's flopping in my boat, that's all that's necessary."

Dakota's face clouded.

"So after Cameroon, I realized my ex had a love language that he used with his friends, and that his interactions with me were more transactional conversations about running the house and finances. My bids for attention went unnoticed, and eventually, I didn't care anymore. So I left."

Dakota slowly shook his head as a frown tugged at his lips.

For some reason, Rylee felt the need to apologize to the man.

Too much, too soon. Too open.

And yet, she didn't want to play games with Dakota.

Didn't want to waste precious time.

Didn't want to pretend not to think difficult thoughts or that she only wanted fluffy conversations. She and her friends had these kinds of talks, but most of the men she dated weren't up to the rigor.

As she and Neesa agreed on their way to Macadoo's, brainiacs were sexy as hell.

And the sight of the books in Dakota's house was a definite aphrodisiac.

"Forgive me," Dakota rubbed his hands over his face. "I left the conversation for a second as I was using that lens to look back at my own experiences. There's a lot to unpack with what you said."

Rylee sat quietly to invite more.

"My life experiences … Sex," he paused. "Can we talk about sex for a moment?"

Rylee's body reacted with enthusiastic waves of horny.

"Let me narrow that topic because that's too broad, and I'm not throwing you into the sea without a life jacket. Sex as it applies to intimacy." His face flamed red with his hair-trigger blushing mechanism.

Rylee laughed. "Go ahead."

"Thank you. So I had a lot of time to think about a lot of things while deployed to Afghanistan."

She nodded. "Vast vistas of nothing lead to belly-button-lint thinking."

He chuckled. "For the most part, yeah. It was boring with spikes of adrenaline. With my fellow crewmen, I was in a brotherhood. We put our lives on the line for each other. We talked through everything. We laughed. We drank way too much. We roughhoused. We were obnoxious as hell. But the one thing I can say is that there was a deep intimacy that I had—obviously, outside of sex—with my team. And up until that time, all through school—"

"High school or college?" Rylee asked.

"High school for sure, where I was an athlete and got the perks that can seem like a movie trope. But also during my time at the Naval Academy."

"I interrupted you to get a timeline in my head. So I imagine you finished USNA and then qualified as a crewman. We're talking about your early twenties here."

"Exactly. Before I was removed from a society where I had access to relationships with women, I spent little time considering intimacy. And I got my intimacy needs met through sex."

"But that changed?"

A slow smile spread across his face. "I like sex. And I really like the closeness and intimacy I get from being with someone physically. But now I understand that sex is only one way to get my intimacy needs met."

"I like this," she said. "Keep going."

"So intimacy with my brothers came from deep sharing and commitment to everyone's well-being. If something hit my brother's leg, it impacted everyone's capacity to fight. I needed to protect my legs and not become a burden to the team because my injury could make or break a mission and could be the difference between life and death. His leg was the same as my leg. All legs needed to be functioning."

"Why did you leave the Navy?" Rylee asked.

"This AWG gal I knew was involved in figuring out how best to train and configure the special forces for future realities."

"What did she come up with?"

"That everything we know about fighting was about to come to an end," Dakota said. "On the ground, we were about to have drone warfare. In the sky? Potential space warfare where satellites had the capacity to take out other satellites, which could shut down communications and GPS coordinates at strategically delicate times."

"When did she come up with all this?" Rylee extended her hand. "Sorry to be bouncing around like this. It's that I want all the answers at once." She laughed.

"Drone warfare, especially using night vision to look for soldiers? Ten years ago. DARPA started working on uniforms that would thwart the drones from hunting our soldiers."

"That's not new, right? Those have been part of the uniforms for what, forty years or so?"

"You're thinking about the patterns on uniforms, so if someone is using near infrared. Yes, that's been around for a very long time. I'm talking about heat-sensing night vision, and the only way to do that is to use a thermal shield that encapsulates a person's body heat. They did come up with prototypes of ponchos. In the last five years, they've started using them in the field, mostly in Ukraine. Right now, Ukraine is setting a new bar for warfare. We'll never go back to the tactics used in the Gulf wars."

"By using drones, which was part of AWG's predictions," Rylee said.

"Yes. But when I realized that warfare was heading toward gamification, I lost interest. I figured I'd try something different. And then I had my career changed for me, whether I was ready for it or not. I was the recipient of a medical discharge."

Her brow furrowed. "Combat injury?"

"I was on a bridge when it blew. I missed the blast but took the tumble. I broke my back in a couple places when I hit the water. My brothers pulled me out of the river and stabilized me, so I came through in better shape than the potential. The docs fused me together."

"But I saw you run," Rylee said.

"I was in good shape before the accident, and I had a great trainer working to rehab me. It took a couple of years before I could compete again. I still have issues with numbness and tingling in my extremities from nerve damage. That made my fine motor skills under the pressure of adrenaline unreliable. Sometimes my back seizes up out of the blue. And that's not compatible with keeping my team safe and accomplishing my mission, so I bowed out."

"Your ongoing training helps, I'm sure." Rylee had dealt with enough injured Marines that she knew not to offer a drip of pity. They hated it.

"My personality is the thing I fight most. When someone's competing next to me, I push to meet that standard."

"Like running with Cerberus?"

"They're hard core," Dakota stretched long, crossing his ankles. "How did you move from Navy to WorldCares?"

"Much like you did. I was injured. Our packs were hundred-twenty pounds, and I weighed a hundred and sixty when I put on as much muscle mass as I could. I ended up with a back injury—not like you, I didn't break anything. It was just that it wouldn't let me get down next to my injured Marines as fast as I needed or wanted to. I wasn't willing to risk their safety for my bad back."

"No more sliding into base."

"Yeah. Well, that is a loss. I liked being out there and getting my hands on my boys first. And sexist or not, I think a female face hovering over in dire moments probably reminded them of mom when they were sick as kids. Stereotypically, it's mom who was cleaning up the puke. But case studies show it's stylistic. Women tend and befriend, and that empathy, I think, goes a long way to the Marine being optimistic about their outcomes."

"Mindset is crucial."

"How did you get involved with the Secret Service? You had to pass their physical standards test, so that tells me you're doing okay. And I'm really glad about that."

"I got my law degree with an emphasis in financial and monetary institutions—something to keep my mind busy while I was working on my rehab. The Secret Service was recruiting, and it seemed cool." Dakota picked up the pizza box and held it out to Rylee.

"No, thank you. I'm full. Putting you back into the conversation where I broke in and meandered about."

"I like to meander about in conversations. It means that there's more to explore and dig into."

"But not all conversations, right?" Sometimes, Rylee just needed to get to the point and have a solid outcome.

"No. When I'm on task, I want the information to be clear and concise. Give me the facts and the action steps, boom, I'm out the door."

Good. Same page, Rylee thought. "We were talking about intimacy. How do you fulfill those needs now?"

"Friendships. Mostly Tank, to be honest."

"A brother that you can cuddle." Rylee thought she might consider getting a dog. She'd wait for her diagnosis to see if she'd be around to care for one.

"When I got Tank as a puppy, my training mentor, Joe, taught me that you had to be precise with the dogs during training and real with them when you weren't. The dogs knew their humans' anger, joy, sadness, the whole emotional spectrum, even if the human didn't know what they were feeling. Joe had me do dog therapy. I started talking through everything with Tank. We'd lie down together, and I'd process my day. And as I told the story, I had to let emotions bubble up and ride out in my words. Joe insisted that, over time, Tank would learn to trust me more. Our connection would become deeper because I wasn't masking in front of him."

"Yeah, well, you were trained for stoicism, so I bet that was a challenge," Rylee whispered. Could this be real? A man who owned his emotions and could talk about them? Good job, Joe.

"Truly a challenge." He looked down at the floor, thoughts obviously jostling around in his head. He brought his gaze up slowly. "I was away for work for a couple of months while Tank was training with Cerberus, and, man, the homesickness was real." He moved his hand to his heart. "A blessing and a curse. To love and to know that in all probability you will lose the one you've given your heart to? Yeah, even the shadow of that pain can be intense."

"You know," she whispered so as not to churn the air in what felt like a sacred space, "it's rare that someone would say something that vulnerable to me. Men, in general, don't seem okay with exposing the places where they could be wounded. I've noticed that they like to keep their shields up. This level of sharing isn't something I'm used to outside of my close-knit friends circle."

"Too much?" Dakota asked softly.

"New is all. And if I'm being honest, I'm a little off kilter, but only because I don't have any practice with a man speaking about their emotions. With men, I usually discuss practical steps that need to be taken, possibly a debate about a movie or a book."

"Game theories?"

"Usually not. Typically, it's things that are a type of parallel play—let's go kayaking, let's catch a show, let's play a game. This is new." Rylee gestured between them. "I like it. Thank you."

And suddenly, Rylee was exhausted. She felt the energy drain from her body.

"You're worn out."

"I'm sorry." Rylee shifted around. She didn't want this evening to end. But a week of sleepless nights from the painful tingling in her hands and feet, along with everything else, caught up to her all at once.

Dakota came to a crouch, then he gathered up the pizza boxes and trash, "Tank and I should get out of here and let you get to bed."

"Stay?" she asked.

He stilled.

Rylee tipped her head back to catch his gaze. "I'd like you to stay."

"I have a gym bag in the car. I'll be right back."

Tank lifted a brow but didn't move.

While Dakota was gone, Rylee let her head rest on the chair cushion and closed her eyes. She heard him come in and lock the door. Heard him move into the bathroom and brush his teeth. Heard him wander into her bedroom.

"Rylee," he whispered, "time for bed." He pulled her arm around his neck. "Shshshsh, you don't need to wake up." He scooped her into his arms and carried her to bed.

In the dark room, she was a mere shadow.

"Do you want to change?" he asked as he lay her down.

Rylee reached out, resting her hand on his chest. "Can I wear this?"

Dakota tugged off his T-shirt and handed it to her.

Rylee undressed, dropping her things in a pile beside the bed. "Mmm, this is warm and soft, nice. Thank you." She lay back, and Dakota tucked the covers around her.

"Do you want me in here with you?" Dakota crouched beside her and swept the hair from her face, kissing her lightly. "Or do you want me on the couch?"

"Here." She wiggled over to make room for him on that side of the bed. "Can Tank be on the bed?"

"No, but he can lie beside you so you can reach him." Dakota signaled to Tank around the bed, where he plopped down with a satisfied sigh. "What do you want me to wear? I can leave on what I'm wearing now, or I have gym shorts."

"Whatever you normally wear," Rylee murmured.

He hesitated.

"Yeah, if you sleep naked, that's okay too. I'm asking you into my bed, Dakota. After all, we caught up on the first two months of dating in one night."

He chuckled. "Oh, so that's what we were doing?"

"If you're okay with it. And if you'd like," Rylee lifted her hand to point toward the bathroom, "I have condoms in my medicine cabinet."

20

———

Rylee

Saturday

Rylee was lying awake in bed, trying not shift around restlessly because she didn't want to wake Dakota. It felt wonderful that he had scooped around her in his sleep. And the arm that rested over her, with his hand gently on her shoulder, felt protective.

But her phone buzzed on the nightstand, and it was Hailey's ringtone.

"Hailey, hi," Rylee whispered.

"Sorry if I'm waking you. There was an Earthquake in the southeastern Anatolia region of Turkey fifteen minutes ago. It was a 7.6 at the epicenter with a severe regional impact. Iniquus has a contract with a university whose students were conducting a spring break archaeological dig outside Öncüpınar, a town of about a thousand. If you're looking at a map, the nearest city is Kilis."

"Okay, I'm pulling that up and looking," Rylee said as she put the search in the bar, doing her best to spell what had sounded like "Oncu-pinar." She spelled took a jab at spelling it. "On the Syrian border?"

"That's it. When our computer picked up on the quake, the students were setting off their SOS buttons on the Iniquus app. They're buried in the rubble at their hotel."

"Okay, what do you need from WorldCares?" Rylee put her feet on the ground. Dakota was fully awake, listening attentively.

"I'm calling to offer you a ride. Are you spooling up a team?"

"I haven't gotten a call from Logistics yet," Rylee said.

Dakota got out of bed and pointed to the bathroom, lifting his brow to ask if she wanted to go first. Rylee waved him in.

"This is what we have," Hailey said. "Cerberus Team Bravo is gearing up with the K9s to find our people and do an extraction. We have access to a jet through McKayla Pickard Gideon, Cerberus Bravo operator Ash Gideon's wife. She uses it for humanitarian runs around the world. It can hold our team and yours, plus equipment if you're sending out a single fast-response team."

"I'll take you up on that. Even if we're sending out more teams, their transit will be slower. Better to get our people mobilized."

"We're requesting that you send an extraction with crush injury team."

"That would be Quebec for crush stabilization. But we don't have a surgeon who goes with that team. You know this. It's just getting them out, stabilizing, and handing them off. Will you have medical?"

"We don't have those capabilities. This all happened minutes ago. We reached one person in the group by phone. They said their hotel was one of the more modern buildings in the area. Most people live in concrete houses that aren't up to modern earthquake standards. I'm working the lines to see regionally what we can do for emergency medical care. But given their architecture, we have to assume the hospitals will be swamped. There is a U.S. military base to the north."

"So how close can the jet get us to this town?" Rylee asked. "Do you know anything about road damage?"

"We'll be working with the Turkish government along the usual channels to allow us to land and operate outside of the normal procedures. I'm calling you before I speak to them so I can share a roster of potential rescuers we're bringing in. My goal is to get us landed right outside of town, so we have limited need for the roads. We don't have satellite images available yet, but I'd imagine landslides are cutting off roadways."

"Does this region meet our stability criteria?" Rylee asked measuring the kilometers to the border.

"I can send you the intelligence we have on the region to the east. We have this flagged orange for increased risk of cross-border interaction."

"This is exactly why we work with the CIA. I'll call Casey Andrews. Could you put him on the plane roster?"

"Absolutely. The more we know, the safer we are, especially in this area.'

"What about getting supplies in?" Rylee asked. "Do you know about trains to bring in our refugee housing?"

"There's a train that passes right through the village. Beyond that, I don't know. The scope of Iniquus's mission is to account for everyone on our list and, in whatever state they're in, we transport them to an American hospital somewhere in Europe. After we accomplish that goal, we'll reassess to see where our K9s will be most helpful."

"I tried to pull up news on the impact, and there's nothing yet," Rylee said. "What time are you flying out?"

"McKayla's plane is on the West Coast," Hailey said. "When I looked at public airlines, once we get to Turkey and take ground transportation, flying directly into a municipal airport a half mile from the village cuts the travel time at least in half, even with waiting for her jet to arrive. The pilot says they can take off within the hour. Here it will be refueled. There are no seats, which works for us. Think of it as a high-end military cargo flight. You can stretch out in a bag and get some sleep. There will be a refuel in Amsterdam to make sure the plane doesn't require servicing in Turkey. But yeah, before we offered the space to any other service, I wanted to reach out to you."

"I really appreciate this, Hailey. Let me get down to WorldCares and spin up the logistics machine. We'll talk to Turkey and see which area medical teams might be available. Give me the numbers you have. How many protectees do you have? How many in the village?"

"We have twenty-one. The most precise village population I have is from two years ago, and there were thirteen hundred."

Rylee's doorbell rang. Dakota was in the shower. Rylee

pulled on Dakota's T-shirt and her sweatpants, and she went to see who it was, saying, "Okay, you know how this works. Let me get the government to send us a request, so we can show up and do our work. How many teams do you think?"

"I'd send Oscar and Quebec to start. Quebec on the plane, though, please," Hailey said.

It was Neesa at the door. "Oscar just came in from Colombia. They're on R&R."

"Okay, Mike then?" Hailey asked.

Rylee pulled the door open. "Agreed. Neesa's here. Let me bring her up to speed, and we'll stay in touch. I do need the cargo capacity ASAP, please." And Rylee ended the call.

"Nice T-shirt," Neesa said with a wink.

"Isn't it?"

"Have fun last night?"

"Neesa, why are you here?"

"Mandy and I were going to Dos Chicas for breakfast when we got a call from Logistics. They need to spin up fast-response teams for a major seismic event in Turkey."

"I was just on the phone with Hailey. They're deploying Cerberus Bravo. I have first steps. Wait, you weren't going to ask me to brunch? It's literally two blocks away."

"When Mandy drove by, I saw Dakota's car, so I figured if I knocked on the door, you'd be busy." Neesa elbowed her. "Or *gettin' busy*. I wasn't going to interrupt."

"You know Dakota's car?" Rylee looked up and down the street.

"I saw you drive off on the Day of the Dead, Potomac version.

"Okay. Where's Mandy?"

"Parking and coming here. She has her work computer —here she is." Neesa lifted her hand and waved. "Mandy! We're here. Let's go, girl. This is supposed to be a fast response team."

As Mandy jogged up, Dakota came out of her bedroom dressed and shaven, Tank by his side.

Rylee walked over to him. "Sorry for the early morning chaos." She rubbed a finger down his jawline.

"I saw a package of razors in your medicine cabinet last night. I hope you don't mind."

"Help yourself."

"You're spooling up?" he asked.

"Earthquake along the Turkish-Syrian border," Neesa called out. "Good morning. This is Mandy."

"Has everyone eaten?" Dakota asked as the women walked into the living room.

"No one," Rylee said, heading toward her kitchen. "Is there any leftover pizza?"

"There is. But why don't I dig around and get something on the table for you?" Dakota asked.

"Yes, please," Neesa said. "Prioritize the coffee, though. Thank you, Dakota."

"I'll get that done, then I'll take off." Dakota picked up the coffee pot and held it under the filtered waterspout on her fridge. "Once I have you all fed, I need to run Tank before he gets the zoomies."

Rylee came up on her toes and kissed him. "I appreciate everything."

Neesa and Mandy were already setting up their computers at Rylee's table.

Over eggs and toast with roasted vegetables and coffee,

Rylee left a message for Casey Andrews, letting him know he had a spot on the forward team and to please call her as soon as he got the message.

"Azaz is minutes away on paper. It's quite a bit farther to get to a regulated border crossing," Mandy said.

"How is the stability in Azaz right now?" Neesa asked.

"Volatile. The intelligence report says various armed actors are posing political and security risks. They use words like fragile."

"That's never good," Neesa said, nibbling on her toast.

Dakota leaned over Rylee, dropping a kiss on her lips. "I'll text a check-in later. I don't expect an answer, I know things are about to get busy." He turned to the others. "Good luck, ladies." And off he went with not a single "Look at me! Look at me! moment."

Neesa noticed it, too. "What? No 'I'm the god of scrambled eggs' remark?"

"Concentrate," Rylee said.

"As far as I'm concerned, he is the god scrambled eggs. Delicious." Mandy took a bite, then put down her fork. "Okay. Active conflict zone. Three major players are fighting it out. Economic strain. Currency instability." Mandy paused. "I don't see anything in the reports indicating that it's spilling over the border into Turkey."

"Are you going, Rylee?" Neesa asked.

"Yes. As we planned."

"You have a go bag?" Mandy asked.

"They outfitted me the other day, I'm set."

"Okay. I'm heading to the warehouse to organize supplies and load the truck." Mandy closed the lid on her laptop. "Let me know the second you have information about the space and weight that's available to us in the airplane hold. I'll get the truck headed to the right hangar."

"Thanks, Mandy," Rylee said. "And I'll have the cash in my bag with me."

"Logistics is already rocking and rolling," Neesa said. "But we'll head to the office to lend them support. We'll stay in close communication."

Mandy headed out the door.

"I don't love the idea of walking around with fifty grand in my backpack," Rylee said.

"As long as you treat your backpack like it's full of plane snacks and nothing more interesting, you're golden. Or you could go the other route. You could get security to handcuff it to your left wrist. If they want the money, they'd have to chop your hand off to get it."

"Gross. And also, no," Rylee said. "They could simply unzip it, take the money, and leave me holding the bag."

"Ha, I see what you did there. Very clever. I'd be clever, too, but your boyfriend doesn't know how to make his coffee thick enough for my taste."

"Not boyfriend. But if there's ever a next time, I'll make the coffee. I'm sorry you suffered."

"You need to take a shower. That's his shirt, isn't it? So you did the dirty with Dakota, huh?

Rylee walked back to the bathroom, leaving the door open so she could talk to Neesa while the water warmed up. "Jasper?"

"Not yet. He's acting the gentleman, and I both like it and don't like it. Slow is probably for the best." Neesa pulled Rylee's armchair around to face the bathroom and sat. "So give me the low-down on Mr. Dakota Kayne. Oh, hey, did you know what his call sign was in the military? Raisin."

Rylee pulled the T-shirt over her head and held it to her nose to smell Dakota's clean scent. The smell of spices and soap. "Raisin? What? Why?"

"Raisin Kayne. Jasper's call sign was ghost."

"Okay, because?" She folded the T-shirt and put it on her shelf, then tugged her sweatpants off and dumped them in the hamper.

"Jasper sounds like Casper?" There was a shrug in Neesa's voice. "I got distracted and never asked. Okay, so spill. To me, Dakota seems like a good guy. You can see it on his face. Easy going, friendly, kind."

Pulling on her shower cap, Rylee stepped into a cloud of fog and turned the showerhead to massage so she could lean into the wall, and it could pelt her butt and thighs that were sore from yesterday's crawl across the Iniquus field.

"Yeah. I like his ready smile and that his smile hits his eyes, not just his mouth."

"Genuine," Neesa said.

"Sincere without the weight that word usually carries. I like that his dog is so thoroughly devoted to him." She poured some liquid soap onto her palm.

"I'm told that one should always trust a dog. Dogs hate me, so I'm assuming that saying is accurate. Why am I hearing hesitation?"

"Yeah, well, good guy. He's different. Forthright, no games, seemingly no agendas." Rylee worked the soap over her skin, wishing that this morning had been slower and that she had woken in Dakota's arms, they had another tumble, then they were showering together.

"Now, I hear a 'but?'" Neesa said.

"But I'm not used to that. I don't like to expose so much of myself to a stranger."

"This is when you reflect on the conversation, right?" Neesa asked. "At the time, it's good?"

"Very comfortable, zero red flags." Rylee adjusted the water stream to something gentler so she could rinse. "He just throws me off a bit."

"Pulling damned teeth, here. How so?"

"It was maybe too comfortable? It was maybe too much like we were already friends?"

"So you've friend-zoned the guy and slept with him anyway?"

"Not at all. Nope. Quite the opposite. He's … that was … I had an exceptional time last night. I was relaxed. My brain was stimulated. And things moved naturally forward."

"Well, shit, girl, he stimulated your brain." Neesa cackled. "I bet you threw him down and jumped his bones."

"Exactly what happened. Look, Neesa, it's just bad timing. There's a lot on my plate, figuring out the attrition at work, this new horrific shadow with the counterfeit money and all the ramifications there, and with my upcoming diagnosis. I might be undergoing treatment or participating in a medical trial. Yeah, bad timing for a new relationship. In their newness, relationships take up headspace and emotions, energy that I don't have to spare."

"Not sleeping?"

Rylee turned off the water, reached for a towel, and dried herself. "According to my watch, yes, some, but it seems to me that all I can do is relax my body into a restful state and try to distract myself from the going-to-sleep sensations in my hands and feet."

"But other than your life is chaotic right now, what do you think?"

Rylee, wrapped in the towel, moved over to her underwear drawer and plucked out a pair of hip-huggers. "He's a fully actualized grown-up, which is nice. I can't remember feeling this safe."

"Bad timing, though." Neesa turned the chair to face Rylee as she dug out a tactical outfit for the day. "When would the good timing be?"

"Oh, let's see. I have a diagnosis. I've been someone's guinea pig, and everything bad is reversed, so I'm not constantly distracted by my body. WorldCares isn't in danger of losing its integrity, so we don't risk thousands, if not millions, of lives over the next decade. And we have a solid group of people who aren't floating job to job but learning, growing, then teaching the next generation."

"So what you're saying is that you can have love and happiness when all the world is utopia. That sounds like something to take up with a counselor. People deserve love and happiness." Neesa turned away so Rylee could drop her towel.

"Intimacy." Rylee stepped into her panties, which rolled annoyingly against her damp skin.

"How's that?"

"We were talking about how Dakota discovered there was a big difference between sex and intimacy, and intimacy comes from close, caring relationships."

"He told you that on the first date?"

Rylee leaned over so her boobs could fall into the cups of

her bra. "Was it a date? Yeah, I guess it was. Yes, then not the first date that was scampi." She hooked the band and adjusted the straps. "Second date was pizza."

"Oh, girlfriend, he is head over heels for you."

"You think?" Rylee tugged on a WorldCares T-shirt. "I'm decent, you can spin back around. Flipping this around on you. Jasper?" She shook out her pants, then stepped a foot into the leg.

"In love!" Neesa dunked her head back and raised her hands toward the ceiling in a move that shouted hallelujah.

"Ha." Rylee jumped the waist over her butt and buttoned the top.

"I'm not kidding," Neesa said, looking Rylee straight in the eye. "I'm going to marry that man.

21

———

Dakota

Saturday

"Where are you?" Jasper asked over the speaker phone.

"In my car, heading out to run Tank, why?" Dakota rolled to a stop at the red light.

"Kumar's a hound dog on a scent."

"That's never good. Hey, start with Benny."

"He's going home tomorrow if everything goes as planned. Boggles the mind that he was dead on a Metro platform, two strangers jumped on his chest, and now he gets to go home and be with his family."

"It makes me believe in miracles. So why's Kumar working on a Saturday morning?"

"Yesterday, when you and Rylee were taking your sweet time swaying across the field at Iniquus. I called him to let him know about the two names that showed up in all three of the WorldCares events that also had a counterfeit episode."

"Correlation is not causation," Dakota said, pressing the gas and easing onto the turnoff for the park. "But I can tell that got him jazzed."

"Kumar's got us busy. Put all your weekend plans on hold."

"Okay. Hey, did you know that WorldCares is spooling up? Rylee's going to deploy with team Quebec to be eyes on the ground."

"She's not thinking she's going to single-handedly take down the counterfeiter, right?" Jasper asked.

"We know she could. We saw her—well, I saw her—deck a guy at the bar. But she has no authority. I don't think her going has anything to do with our case at all. I think she's observing to better understand what her people are up against in the field to provide better support. Your turn, what does Kumar need?"

"He took that information Iniquus provided from the camera footage to a judge and asked for an opportunity to do a walk-through of Lewis McLeod's house with a K9, and if the K9 indicated in any area, that we have the right to search it for any paraphernalia associated with counterfeiting."

"He has the search warrant in hand?"

"Yeah," Jasper said. "He's over there now."

"Okay. I need to run Tank because he's Tank and he needs running. And then I need to go home and put on a suit because my showing up in my jogging shorts is a poor representation of the Service."

"Which is fine. We have a little latitude since the guy's out of town."

"Turkey?" Dakota asked as he parked.

"Israel for Spring Break is what his social media says."

"Do we trust it?" Dakota asked.

"Time and location stamps in the data all look right," Jasper said. "Look, I think on this one, since it's not out in public, you can't loop Reaper into the mix."

"Where is McLeod's place? Are we talking apartment building?"

"House in Fairfax that is considerably more expensive than what you'd think could be afforded by an adjunct professor," Jasper said.

"Yeah, what does he teach?"

"You're going to love this." Dakota could hear Jasper's smile. "Fine art."

"And that jazzes you because Benny just showed us those bills that the art major made by gluing Bible paper together," Dakota said.

"I see the symmetry," Jasper said.

"I can get to Fairfax by ten hundred. Do you want to text me the address?" Dakota pulled into a parking space and cut the engine. "You've got to have a cop team together. Otherwise, Kumar can break down the door. My breaching days were over when I said farewell to the Navy."

"On it."

"Alright, Tank," Dakota said after he hung up. "Here's the schedule. Because of the time constraints, instead of going on a long run, we'll go at it hard, catch our breath, then Fifi's mom said you can go over and play this morning. I know! Fifi! So while you have a date, I'll get spiffed up, then it's right back in the car and out to Fairfax. Ready?"

And just as he said he would, Dakota and Tank were waiting outside a craftsman-style house with a professionally landscaped yard at exactly ten hundred.

The car in McLeod's garage was this year's model. It was impossible to say if this was relevant to the case. The man could have inherited a stack of cash, won the lottery, or sued the shit out of someone. There were a lot of reasons the guy could be living beyond his paycheck that weren't criminal.

Kumar pulled up to the curb and wandered over. "So this is the beast." He held out a hand to be sniffed. "Does he bite?"

"With two hundred and fifty PSI. Go ahead," Dakota said, "stick your hand in his mouth."

Kumar slid his hands into his pockets.

"Tank can smell a drop of gas in a pool of water. Do you think he needs you to stick out your hand to smell you? Pet peeve. No one needs to do that for any dog. Just stand there and let them decide what they want to do."

"Good to know," Kumar said. "So he can find specific chemicals. Can Tank also find people associated with those chemicals?"

"Cerberus was training him so that if he found counterfeit currency, it might be possible to track back to the human who had touched it and left a scent. There are a lot of variables to his, or any dog's, ability to do that. So it depends. There's some danger there, too. When the counterfeit gets passed by drug dealers, it can get enough substance on it, Fentanyl, what have you, that it could put Tank into a life-threatening situation. I always carry Narcan for him." Dakota raised his chin to indicate Jasper's car turning onto the block, followed by two police cars. "Here we go."

"Dangerous as hell," Kumar said. "Can you imagine messing around with the drug cartels like that, giving them fake money?"

"The dealer may be third or fourth in line before you get to the pharmacist."

"Still." Kumar lifted a hand to greet Jasper. "Hell of a chance."

"I don't think people involved in the industry see a golden future. Most of them I know don't see themselves living very long."

"I've got the cops," Jasper said, climbing from his car. "You want to pull out the warrant, so everyone knows what's allowed here?"

Kumar pulled it from his file so Dakota and Jasper could read it, then pass it to the officers.

"His social media said he was engaged to a Colombian woman. He's hitting above his weight with this one." Kumar pulled out his phone and showed a picture of a gorgeous, tall twenty-something young woman next to a gaunt-looking middle-aged man with a ring of curly hair. "That's Lewis McLeod? No, man, that doesn't make sense at all," Jasper said.

"Did you look into the girlfriend's background?" Dakota asked.

"I'm working on it. Today, we're starting with Tank's sniffer. A bit of a fishing expedition because Lewis McLeod may have zero to do with the printing and just do distribution."

"Or he could have zero to do with any of it," Jasper said.

"Or he could be a victim just like WorldCares," Dakota said.

"You're trying to rain on my parade. And here Veer and I were nice enough to go out and have a last-minute beer with you, Jasper, on the off chance that Neesa would show up."

"No one's raining on your parade, Kumar. And that's got to be the most grandpa phrase I've heard in a while. Go on and call the police up to knock on the door and see if anyone's home," Jaser said. "We may get lucky, and the cat sitter is here."

"I can watch Tank work, right? I'm going to watch." Kumar signaled the police.

"That's fine, just keep a distance," Dakota said. "Oh, hey, Jasper said it looks like Benny is going home tomorrow."

The police were pounding on the door.

"That's good news because Veer's been on my case about my salt, and my exercise, and stop with red meat already. When was the last time I got my cholesterol checked? We're signed up for a couple's CPR class. I told her I have to do all that stuff, well, most of it, with the job."

"She's scared for your well-being," Dakota said as the cops used a battering ram to break the door open. "It's nice to be so loved."

"It is," Kumar agreed.

Dakota pulled the tug towel from his bag and held it under Tank's nose. "Tank, time to work. Find chemical."

They moved through the house in a choreographed pattern. If Tank was missing a section, Dakota would point it out.

First floor, clear.

Second floor clear.

Attic clear.

"Nothing at all?" Kumar looked frustrated.

"He showed some interest in the bathroom and the hamper," Dakota said. "I'm going to take him down to the basement. And if we don't get anything down there, we can come back and revisit the bathroom."

As soon as Kumar cut through the padlock and opened the door that led from the kitchen to the basement, Dakota knew they had bingo. Tank's whole body changed posture.

"Yup, here we go," Jasper said, rubbing his hands together.

Down the stairs, Tank immediately went to a series of cabinets and alerted.

Kumar had to use bolt cutters to get through the locks.

But there it was, shelves of chemicals, inks, copper plates, rolls paper.

Dakota looked over the items, and it was a full setup for producing counterfeit. The only way Tank would have hit on these scents was if they used the same chemical products used in Colombia or Peru.

Jasper came up behind him. "Looks like he has a Colombian connection. This is their formula." He gestured along the shelf with an open hand. "And these are the same types of plates they just confiscated in the Diaz arrest."

"Theory?" Kumar asked.

Dakota held out the towel for Tank and started their tug-of-war celebration. "Yeah, I have one. I'll bet you the

Colombian girlfriend was in one of his classes, and she made a play for him. Brought him home to see her beautiful country, and there, our good professor had a life-changing event. What that is, I'm not going to guess. But then he uses his art skills to make the plates, and the Colombians, in return, teach him what else he needs to know to produce his own cash stream, and it's a happy family."

"I'm liking this theory," Jasper said. "Keep going."

"From the looks of the professor," Dakota said, "he isn't brave by nature. He may know how to make counterfeit money, but using it? That's a whole different ball game." Dakota dragged Tank's towel to the left, then the right. Then let Tank sit into his haunches and try to pull it from Dakota's grip. This was one of the reasons Dakota hit the gym and lifted heavy weights.

That bite was no joke.

"He would have been warned that he couldn't go to shops in his own area hand them a fake hundred for his purchase and get back real bills. Just like our little art student did when she was traveling all summer to stay ahead of the Secret Service," Jasper said as he documented the materials and packaged it up as evidence.

"Right," Kumar said, "so he takes it a step further. He wants to take it out of the country and trade it for US dollars. He lets people with integrity do the switcheroo. Once he leaves, no one's going to charge him with anything. Those crimes happened in a foreign country in a disaster, there are bigger worries."

"Twenty-dollar plate here," Jasper said. "Maybe he started small to test the theory with WorldCares."

"Ballsy to go after Iniquus, though," Kumar said.

"I highly doubt he did," Jasper said. "What happened with Iniquus was they were given that money along the way by one of the charitable groups buying something from them."

"There's the hole in this theory." Dakota let go of the tug towel so Tank could toss it around and shake it. "How did McLeod know that there was cash to be had at disaster events?" He turned to Kumar. "It's an important piece. See how long he's been doing his photography of disaster events. Maybe he was around the cash and remembered it. Maybe he was a victim in a mass disaster or had family who was. Okay, I'm taking Tank out of here."

"Dakota, before you go," Jasper said. "Let's talk Turkey."

"Yeah?"

"Kumar, you said McLeod is in Israel, right?" Jasper stood and walked over. "Easy proximity to the earthquake disaster and WorldCares."

"What are you thinking?" Dakota asked. "Cerberus Bravo is heading over on a private jet owned by McKayla Pickard Gideon. Hailey's organized it and invited World-Cares' team Quebec and Rylee to fly with them."

"Bajillionaire McKayla Pickard got married?" Kumar whistled. "Somebody's a brand-new rich bastard."

"She married an operator with Cerberus Bravo," Dakota said.

"Either way," Jasper said. "Iniquus wants this problem solved. Hailey might be able to get you and Tank on the flight. Take some camping gear. Bottle of water and some MREs. You and Tank keep an eye out for our art friend. Sniff around people's tents as you walk by."

"Why do you think he keeps showing up where World-Cares is?" Kumar asked, leaning a shoulder into the wall.

"Simple," Dakota said. "Whoever is doing this needs to be easily recognized. He needs to have earned the people's trust. Hey, John Doe, can you sit here with my supplies while I run to the can? He can't simply wander from group to group. He has to adopt a group so that he can hear the scuttlebutt. 'Hey, careful with your cash, someone's dumping phony money.'"

"What did Rylee call it?" Jasper asked.

"Devil cash?" Dakota said. "As soon as he hears rumblings about counterfeit money, he attaches to one of the other disaster groups. Neesa and Rylee said cash is king, but the U.S. dollar is the pope. He probably has no idea his face is on film. The WorldCares body cams are integrated with their radios on their shoulders."

"You think he'll bite?" Kumar asked. "He's pretty close in Israel."

"He'd have to have a way of knowing which teams are going where," Jasper said. "Friend? Ally?"

"WorldCares has an up-to-date website," Dakota said, bending to take the towel back from Tank, who was lying on the cement floor, gnawing on it. "Their being wheels up for Turkey is already on their front page. They need people to know where to donate their dollars. So if I were a betting man, I'd lay a wager he'll be there. If—and this is a big if—he has the counterfeit currency with him to exchange."

"Call Hailey over at Iniquus," Jasper said. "See if you can't get your ass on that plane."

22

———

Hailey

Sunday

The plane had made it as far as Amsterdam.

While they were refueling and changing to a tactical aviation team that was comfortable going into an orange zone and camp on the plane until the Iniquus protectees were evacuated, Rylee went inside to use the bathroom and buy a salad and some fruit.

It would be a while before she'd have access to fresh produce again.

She jumped out of line when her phone rang, and she saw it was Casey Andrews's number.

"Where are you?" Rylee asked, scampering away from the crowd to stand in an empty corner.

"I'm not telling you," he laughed.

"Well, I'm in Amsterdam, and I was told we're waiting for another passenger. I hoped it would be you. Is it you?"

"I'm sorry, but no," Casey said. "Langley caught me up on the shit show you and the Secret Service are putting up with. Sorry about that. Listen, until it's solved, Langley doesn't want me to wear your logo or connect with your people."

Rylee gasped. "Are you being serious right now?"

"Operational integrity. I can't get called into a courtroom. My name can't go into anyone's news article."

"No." Rylee moved her hand to her throat. "I understand that. I would never knowingly endanger you. But selfishly, I feel like your not being with us is putting my team in danger."

"Was my showing up part of your risk calculation, Rylee?"

"On paper? No. In my head, absolutely. WorldCares classifies the village we're heading toward as orange. With the breadth of the quake impact, I'm concerned."

"Could you reroute to a different assignment?

"We've agreed to work in proximity with an Iniquus team, and we're on their plane with our supplies filling the hold. So sure, we could bail, but that might burn bridges of trust. We go into the orange areas. Everyone knows there's risk in this job."

"Look, it's not up to me. I can't go. But I can pull the intelligence I have on the area and send it to you to share with your team and Iniquus. Iniquus goes in contractually, which means they'd crawl under flying bullets to save their protectees. It won't change anything for them except an awareness level, and possibly your adrenaline load. Sorry, they're calling my plane. I've gotta go. I'll send that information on. Stay frosty."

Rylee blinked at her phone.

Well, shit.

Closing her eyes to compose a text that everyone would understand but wouldn't reveal anything to those outside the loop, Rylee texted Hailey and Neesa: **Refueling in Amsterdam. Heard from our friend who wears the WC logo. He can't deploy with us until this $ issue is solved. He will share what he knows about the area.**

When her phone rang, Rylee expected it to be Neesa. Instead, she saw John Madoc's name. "Hey John, if you're calling because your ears were burning the other day, I was thinking about you."

"Hello, Rylee. You were?" John asked.

"I saw while scrolling that Madoc means fortunate or blessed, and I was very happy for you."

"I am both a fortunate man and very blessed. And hopefully you will be, too."

"How is that?" Rylee asked.

"I had someone drop out of our study on Friday, and I've entered your name. You should aim to be in London by Wednesday night to acclimate to the time zone."

The dead air was thick between them.

"Rylee?"

"I'm here. I'm lost."

"Your doctors from Browning Neurological Group sent your diagnosis and medical files to us. Your profile fits exactly into the parameters of this study. I'm glad I had my computer set up to flag your name so it wouldn't get missed or shuffled into the pack. You popped right up."

"Hold on a second," Rylee's throat squeezed tightly, barely allowing sound to form. She looked at her recent incoming calls from an unknown number that came through on Friday, when she'd left her phone with Neesa and Hailey so she could rub her thighs on the Iniquus field.

She had to lean forward and pant to find a breath.

Not cancer. Not dying. Just slowly degenerating.

"I have MS, then," she whispered with the phone back to her ear.

"Wow," John said. "I'm mystified how I'd get this diagnosis first. Am I the one breaking the news? I'm so sorry, Rylee. Truly. But, of course, you're not surprised."

"Good to hear it from you, John. Glad to know. If I were going to pick someone to tell me the news, it would be you. And so, yes. Yes, absolutely, I'll be where you need me to be when you need me to be there. Right now, I'm in Amsterdam, we're getting refueled to head to Turkey."

"Business? This would be an unfortunate time for a vacation there. The news out of the area is devastating."

"I'm with one of the WorldCares teams responding to the earthquake. But I'll go and do a few days' work, get on a plane and head your way."

"Not last minute, though, okay, Rylee?" John's voice was stern. "This is going to sap your energy. I want you here two nights before you do this, so the jet lag isn't so rough and so you don't have flight issues and miss this window."

"I can do all that. Thank you."

RYLEE SENT A SECOND TEXT: **Neesa, I heard from John Madoc. Apparently, I missed the diagnosis call. It's MS. I need to be in London by Wednesday night to get the prick on Friday. I'll let you know if I need help**

arranging my exfil. I didn't ask any questions and don't have any answers besides that my guinea pig day is set for Friday. No idea if there's a recovery time. After all the effort to get to this, I'm still in shock.

RYLEE DECIDED to loop Hailey in. If Iniquus was flying out before Wednesday, she'd like to catch a ride to a European hub.

"Rylee, I'm so sorry you're going through this." Hailey's voice was pure sympathetic support. "I had no idea. Listen, I'll do everything I can from my end. We'll get you where you need to be in time."

"I'm not stepping on your op here. I can have my team figure it out. I just wanted to be on your radar." Yeah, the compassion in Hailey's voice dug into the squishy, tender part of Rylee's psyche. She was awash in emotions, and that was no way to deploy.

She needed to get squared away, or she'd be a deficit to her crew.

"I'm sending you all the best wishes."

"Thank you. I think I see …" Dakota and Tank must be the extra passenger they were expecting on the plane. "Yes, Dakota's heading this way." Rylee was glad to leave the conversation and step away from the sympathy Haley showered on her. "He's huge compared to the other passengers."

"Good trip. Keep me in the loop."

"Will do. Bye." Rylee raised her hand and waved toward Dakota.

A sense of relief washed over her. And her only thought was *he's here.*

WITH BAGS of snacks for the trip, Rylee and Dakota headed out the door onto the tarmac with Tank between them.

Dakota stopped by the baggage cart to see that his supplies had all made it over to McKayla's plane, then they walked up the steps together to settle on her sleeping bag, where she'd eked out a little private space for herself toward the back of the plane by the toilet.

As the attendant turned off the lights and the teams settled into their sleeping bags, Rylee and Dakota ate in silence so their murmuring wouldn't disturb anyone as they snuggled down with their pillows.

Soon, every single responder—be they from WorldCares or Cerberus—was sleeping.

"Get while the getting's good" was the phrase that came to Rylee's mind.

Once they landed, everyone would be hard at work saving lives.

Rylee was restless with all the changes of direction Amsterdam had revealed.

But now, as snores filled the cabin—K9 and human alike —Dakota took Rylee into his arms to cradle her and whispered into her hair. "I saw your face when you were on the phone in Amsterdam. Would you be comfortable telling me what's going on?"

How much did she want to say here?

It wasn't that she didn't trust Dakota to be supportive. It

was more that she didn't trust herself. It wasn't a safe time to be vulnerable. You don't go into a battle with your heart on your sleeve.

"I'm feeling emotional. I got some news from various sources. Some very good—a reprieve to be honest. Some things that give me hope. Some that have me on edge concerning this mission."

He sat still and waited.

"I'm not ready to share yet. I'm still a bit shell-shocked."

Dakota tightened his arms around her. "Silence? Talking? What could help?"

"We could talk."

"I'd like to pick up on the conversation we were having over pizza at your house if you're good with that as a topic."

"Okay," Rylee said.

"When I asked you about the wrong person, we dove into game theory, and I'm not sure I heard your answer."

"The wrong person? Someone who sees me as unequal. Which isn't quite right. There are things I do well and things I suck at. I would hopefully share some of the averages and the strengths with someone, but it would also be nice that where I fall short," Rylee held out a palm to indicate Dakota, "play on words intended, that someone taller in that domain can you know—"

"Reach that shelf without straining and just hand it to you. Meanwhile, you're closer to the ground—"

"I can grab things from the lower cabinets and pass them up. I am not that short, by the way. I'm taller than the average woman. It's just that you're an outlier on the height chart. Bet it sucked when you were three years old, and everyone thought you were seven."

"Very immature for my age," Dakota chuckled. "I have a ton of pictures of me up until I was about seven or so, when I was wearing shirts Mom made for me with iron-on decals that said, 'Big for his age.' 'He's only 3.'"

"Clever woman."

"She is. I like to think that I got her pragmatic, find-a-problem, find-a-solution kind of thinking."

"Because your dad?"

"Dad's a band-aid kind of guy," Dakota said, his tone low and private. "He'll slap a quick fix on things if absolutely necessary and then move on to do the things that caught his attention next. He's very busy in his head. He likes a good chair and his pile of books over anything. Our lives were run on a strict schedule by my mom, who made lists for lists."

"Yes, that's what I don't want. There's a term for it."

"Micro-managing?" Dakota offered.

"Hey," Rylee said, "I micro-manage for my job. It saves lives."

"You're co-director of an international NGO," Dakota corrected. "You've got to be amazing at the details."

"I am, actually. And there are two women, me and Neesa, who share the role. And some people might think, 'Yes, every woman I know micro-manages her household. She knows where everything is, what needs to be done, she's got it all figured out, and the dad shows up as if that is his only role.'"

"Showing up. Yes, that's the role my dad played," Dakota said.

"You've probably seen on social media the viral post about the woman who had an amazing Christmas all laid out. Every wish met. Everything was glorious and festive. In the video, the dad said it was his favorite time of year. Then one of the kids points to the empty stocking. 'Why is there an empty stocking?' 'Oh,' says the mom, 'that's mine.'"

"Empty?"

"Her husband loves Christmas because he gets all of the joy and zero of the mental load and physical work. She was cut out of the joy but carried the entire load. Not only the load, but she's also responsible for the outcome. Everyone's happiness lands in her lap. Their disappointment is her failure. Her disappointment goes unnoticed."

"I'm not on social media much," Dakota said. "I didn't see it. But I can picture it because I'm sure that's what happened every year in my house growing up. My sister and I would make something special for each of our relatives. Simple things, I remember one year I dipped fat pretzel sticks into chocolate and then got to decorate them with sprinkles. I had a great time doing it. I remember how proud I was and how everyone praised my good job. It was mom's good job figuring out that it would be happily received if it were made by a little kid."

That image charmed Rylee. "How old?"

"Four? Maybe five? I never remember my dad or anyone wondering how we could make Mom happy." He paused. "Man, that hits hard."

"She plans. He follows. Our culture expects women to have unrealistic amounts of energy to remember everything about everything for everybody, while the partner simply shows up knowing all will go well."

"It's unfair at best and borders on abusive—emotional abuse."

"I agree. And I brought this up because you asked. And I assume you want me to tell you the truth."

"Always," Dakota said.

"On the 'What I don't want in a relationship' list is for someone to assume that planning and forethought are gender roles. In scientific studies, that's simply not borne out."

"No, she's shackled with it."

"I mentioned the end of my marriage came from the love language issue. But this was another big one for me. It helped to end my first marriage. I was deployed to Afghanistan, and I'd get back to base happy to read messages from home. My messages from hubby weren't, 'How are you? I'm thinking about you and sending you love.' They were, 'Who's the plumber?' 'Did I have my cholesterol checked?' 'You didn't remind me that it was my sister's birthday. Did you have a gift and card ready for her somewhere?'"

"That's extreme."

"You think? I don't know."

"Yeah, that's bad. Are you wondering if I ascribe to that way of living?" Dakota asked. "I wasn't paying attention, now I will. What I can tell you is that I live on my own. I haven't forgotten a special day in years, maybe because I've learned to set alarms not just for the day, but also for the day when I need to make preparations. I travel a lot, I have to think ahead." He stilled. "You have me reviewing my life."

"How does it look?"

"The last lady I was dating, Rose, has two kids. She was always tired. Now, that I'm looking back on that—and I have a feeling that I'm going to have to do a lot of looking back and thinking this through—her emotions would catch quickly."

"Short fuse? Overly emotional?"

"Exhausted, I think. Just before our relationship ended—it ended amicably—her kids' pet died, and she was hysterical on the phone asking me to please come and take it to the garbage bin at her apartment before the kids came home, since she had no place to do a burial ritual with them. In the light of this conversation, I could hear it in her voice that she was cooked. She didn't have an ounce more to give."

"I'm glad she had someone to call. If she was—as you called it—cooked, can you imagine what might have happened if you'd said no? In that moment, she had to have great faith in your integrity."

"That's really nice of you to say."

"I met a woman named Rose," Rylee said. "She looked like she was at the end of her rope. Like she didn't have anything else to give. And yet, she gave me a lifeline. When she flashes in my mind, I send her something in the air. Do you believe in that?"

"I think I need a better idea of what you're describing," Dakota said.

"I think of someone, in this case Rose, and I know she was wrung dry, so I send her a smile, or I send her a thought like, 'I hope something happens today that makes you feel special.' Or 'I hope some unexpected good comes your way that eases things for you—an empty parking spot close to the door, a whole street of lights that turn green, a spare twenty in your pocket so you buy yourself some chocolate.'"

"That's very sweet. Do I believe in it? Yes. Tank and I

communicate in pictures that we send back and forth. You know, Tank picked you out of the crowd at the race and wanted desperately to meet you. Tank fell in love with you at first sight."

Rylee swallowed back the thick emotion that clogged her throat. "Thank you. I can't tell you how much that helps me right now."

Dakota grasped her chin and tipped her head up so he could kiss her gently. "I asked what you didn't want in a relationship." He released her, and Rylee settled back against his chest. "I'd like to know the other side of that coin. What do you want from love?"

"Love?" Rylee's voice was soft, so it wouldn't carry to the others. "Simple things. I want to pile my fork high, so he can taste what I'm tasting. I want him to hold something out and say, 'smell this.'"

She could feel Dakota's smile.

"Nothing mean. Good scents. Interesting scents. 'Can you figure out what this reminds me of?' scents."

"Mmm." He tucked her under his chin and dropped a kiss.

"I want him to point his finger so my eye sees what he sees and when I don't know what he's pointing at," Rylee wrapped her hands over his forearm to hug him to her, "I want him to draw me into his arms, hold me against his chest so I'm looking out from his viewpoint, and he leans in and whispers, 'There just over the breaker, the sun is going to disappear in three, two, ahhh."

He stilled.

"I want to share all the sights and sounds and scents, the sensations that weave our imaginations and our stories together to form a whole cloth under which we can wrap ourselves on cold nights and say, 'Remember that sunset?' and we are both back there in the moment."

"A whole life of that," Dakota's voice was a warm rumble.

"It takes a long time to build what I want."

"Worth it, though," Dakota said.

"Yeah," she sighed. "I think so. Into the sunset."

"It's glorious. I'd like to watch it with my someone."

"Me too. The right person at the right time."

23

Rylee
Sunday

As soon as the plane landed, Cerberus Bravo was in motion. Packs on their shoulders, tools in their hands, booties to protect their dogs' paws, they jumped into the backs of three pickup trucks that waited for them then raced the team toward the hotel that had collapsed around their protectees.

Good job, Iniquus Logistics, that flowed like water.

That was the standard that WorldCares strived for. Every minute of delay could cost a precious life.

Bravo asked that WorldCares clear their gear and supplies out of the plane because Cerberus would camp in the passenger area and set up their first aid station there. And the pilot and staff would remain with the plane throughout. If they needed to conduct an emergency evacuation to save a life, they would take off without hesitation or warning.

As WorldCares got busy setting up the tents and moving supplies, an elder who could speak Arabic wandered over to speak to Rylee. He said that he helped staff the tiny airport and wanted to let the responders know their building had some cracks, but was holding up. The rescuers were welcome to use the toilets and showers they had available.

Another pickup pulled forward. This one held the local leader who would take George, Quebec's tactical lead, out to get a visual of the situation and make plans aligned with the locals' needs and wants.

WorldCares didn't show up to step on toes.

They were there to put their expertise to work.

And because volunteers—who always arrived, desperate to help save their friends and loved ones, their fellow villagers—didn't always know what to do, there was usually an educational component. Sometimes, the best of intentions could lead to complications or further disaster.

Before they landed, George had come back to her area of the plane to ask Rylee not to help. They had a system, they had roles as a team, and even something as simple as opening a box could mess things up. "Glad to have you observe and take notes."

"But stay out of your way," Rylee said.

"There is actually a way to free someone up to be able to sleep, and that's to stay in the supply tent. Boring as hell, I warn you. I also warn you not to move or rearrange anything in a way you think would be more efficient. It's already efficient because everything is in the same spot, it always is."

"I get that," Rylee said. "Hands off. Twiddling my thumbs. What about when I need to sleep?"

"Tie down the flaps and sleep across the entrance. That's not to say you won't be woken up. If we've made contact with someone in the rubble, we're not asking them to wait until we have a good snooze before we dig them out in the morning. We keep going."

Dakota had accepted her offer that he and Tank sleep in the supply tent with her. Rylee figured that Tank would alert her to anyone trying to sneak in and stick some counterfeit bills in her pack.

And so, while the worker bees flew about putting up the tents and shuffling supplies in what seemed to be miraculous time, Rylee stood out of the way.

Dakota got busy wandering amongst the backpacks and supplies on the off chance that things weren't on the up and up from the get-go. By doing an initial sweep, he could testify in court that he had done his due diligence.

Dakota had Tank sniff everything.

Then Tank got a pair of booties, and the two of them took off to see if they could lend Cerberus a hand digging out the people trapped in the hotel collapse.

Rylee, trying to stay out of the way, decided to head over to the tiny municipal airport to see if their hangar areas would be a good place to use for a medical team if Mandy was successful in finding a disaster medical assistance team routed their way.

Everyone was trying to get their hands on medical supplies along with field-deployable doctors and nurses. Mandy said to expect a medical unit from Egypt by Tuesday. That was the same day that WorldCares Team Mike would arrive. Later than expected. But, after reviewing satellite imagery of the village, Logistics decided to bring in heavy equipment to move cement walls and lift roofs.

Was that too many days?

Yes.

Given the scope of the disaster zone and the number of people affected, it was fortunate they were able to connect their supply cars to a train and head in the right direction. Everyone was scrambling for limited resources and access to open delivery routes.

Standing in the yawning opening of the hangar, Rylee thought it would be adequate for maybe a hundred people.

The elder, who had escorted her over, showed Rylee the three shower stall areas, with their slimy-looking cement floors and rusted showerheads. Compared to Afghanistan, this was luxe. The toilets were the variety that had ceramic footrests while you squatted over a hole, then filled an orange plastic jug with water from the spigot to pour behind you. The TP was tissue paper-thin. Rylee would remember to bring her own roll with her when she needed the facility. It was nice that she wouldn't be squatting over a hole she dug in the dirt.

Her mini tour brought her to the glass tower with the controller. There, she was looking through his binoculars to see what she could of the village. As soon as the tents were in place and the solar powered link panels were up, Rylee would check on the latest satellite imagery.

From this vantage point, what she saw were buildings that crumbled from the violent shaking.

They looked like the ruins that remained after the dust of battle settled.

Rylee's nervous system remembered the horrors.

The controller said those who made it out of their homes slept just over the hill, safe from aftershocks, but now that Quebec was set up, they'd move the camp closer in.

"Have you had any aftershocks?" Rylee asked. The language they shared was Arabic.

"One big. One small."

"We don't have a large number of refugee tents with us until Tuesday. I believe it's fifty. But those are fifty families that won't be out in the open. They're pretty stable despite aftershocks."

Looking east, Rylee saw the dust churn up, and her body clenched. In her memory, she was back on the battlefield, tending her wounded Marines when over the hill came another round of insurgents, and devastation followed.

With shaking hands, Rylee handed the field glasses to the controller. "Any idea who that is or where they're coming from?"

After looking for a long moment, the controller said. "That's east. The only people who are east of us are the Syrians. Two pickup trucks. Six men."

"Weapons?"

"There are always weapons. Come, we will go welcome them."

Rylee was hyper-aware that she was walking around with a backpack filled with $50,000 in cash. It was a vulnerability, and yet she had nowhere to stow it.

Reshaping her countenance to meet the norms for women in this part of the world, Rylee adopted a stance of dignified modesty as she stood at a respectful distance from the controller, yet close enough to be under his male protection.

Rylee had learned a thing or two about survival as a woman in the Middle East.

"*Assalamu alaikum*," peace be upon you, the driver said as he exited the first pickup, rifle in hand.

The others clustered by the trucks, watchful.

"*Wa-Alaikum As-Salam*," and upon you, the controller responded.

The driver's gaze landed on Rylee. So she took a step forward and placed her hand on her heart. "Rylee Jones, I'm with WorldCares. We've come to help," she said in Arabic.

"Yes, we saw the plane and came to tell you of the destruction on our compound that was wrought by the earthquake."

"I'd like to hear. Shall we talk inside?" Rylee gestured to the hangar, and they all gathered in a circle, sitting on the cement floor. Quebec must already have the satellite connections up, because when Rylee pulled her computer from her backpack, she was able to access an intake portal.

"We have come because our people suffer," the leader said.

"Can you show me where this is on the map?" Rylee pulled up her latest satellite image. And as the leader pointed to a spot, she zoomed in, looking up and down the dirt road with the crushed building. "This damage is from the earthquakes?" she asked.

"Yes." The leader was staring at the image, and Rylee passed him the computer. "You can look around. It might give you a better idea about where to put your rescue efforts."

When he handed the laptop back, Rylee put the coordinates into the computer program. "How many people are usually in this compound?"

"A hundred and three."

"How many have been accounted for?"

"Fifty-seven."

"Do you have dead?"

"Among the fifty-seven are three dead."

"What are you doing with the bodies?" Rylee asked, and he didn't respond. "Do you have cloth for shrouds?" Rylee knew there was a supply amongst the boxes.

"This, I have," he said.

She continued down her list documenting the man's responses to what resources they could access: water, food, and sanitation.

"This is very limited. Perhaps a day or two as our storage room was crushed and the wells caved in."

"Do you have access to medical help? Bandages, ways to clean out wounds? Diapers for the babies?"

He did not.

"Do you understand that you should not just dig people from under the buildings because crush injuries kill?"

The crush injury question went unanswered, so Rylee pulled up a series of pictures to help her explain. The first picture showed a man with his legs trapped by a wall. "Listen, this is very important. A crush injury is life-threatening because all the toxins build up in the area that has no circulation." She flipped to the next photo, showing the helpers applying tourniquets to both the man's legs and then lifting the rocks. "If you release the injured body part from under the weight, all the toxins flow into the body, and it can be deadly." She turned to the next set of pictures showing the steps of applying a tourniquet. "You know how to tighten it down so there is no blood flowing?"

"Yes, I know this."

"If you don't have medical help on hand," Rylee said, "the best you can do is tourniquet the limb and get them to the hospital as fast as possible. The longer you take, the more likely an amputation will be necessary to save that person's life. As fast as possible." She turned the page and showed a man writing in pen on the skin next to the applied tourniquet. "Make sure you write down the time that you put on the tourniquet right on the limb so the doctors will see and know what they can safely do. It's very important."

"You will send a medical person back with us," the leader announced.

"We don't have anyone like that. We have search dogs and shovels."

"This is what we need. You must share your supplies with us."

"I agree you need supplies. Our supplies are arriving on the train around lunch on Tuesday. We will have food, sanitation, and water to share. We will have medical supplies on the train. I know it's a long time to wait. We are waiting, too. But everyone needs to be helped. You will come back on Tuesday with your trucks, and we will share what we have."

The man glowered at her as if he didn't believe her.

So Rylee pulled up a satellite connection to video call Mandy. Then Rylee handed her phone to the leader with a translator open.

"Mandy, here's the situation."

While Rylee and Mandy worked out what could be done with supplies, the leader's combative stance hadn't changed.

Rylee was frightened by the rifles. The men could shoot them all dead, take all the supplies they had on hand, and escape across the border.

"The supply train is getting there mid-morning on Tuesday," Mandy said.

"Tuesday, that's farther out than I'd hoped." This was performative, and Mandy would recognize that and play along.

"I'm really sorry. The whole region is impacted. Supplies are flooding in, but transportation routes are limited. Bridges, tracks, and roads aren't passable. The good news is that they expect the track to be cleared by Tuesday morning, and we have our supplies on that first scheduled train. I had calculated for a large population." Mandy was stellar with her explanations. "We can share supplies, and if necessary, I can arrange for a second delivery. But, sir, so you understand, we are not authorized to cross the border into Syria. And even if we were allowed, it could only be at an official crossing area. Reports from your area indicate the border is very difficult to navigate right now. The chances of our getting the items to you would be very small. I'm not encouraging you to break any laws. But any collection will have to happen on the Turkish side of the border. Can you do that?"

"We will do that," the leader said once he read the translation.

"Tuesday around noon," she said again. "When the train gets there, you will need to give our people a bit of time to sort your supplies out. But I am putting together a rescue package for one hundred people. You said one hundred?"

"One hundred. Tuesday."

"Thanks, Mandy. I'll report in later." And Rylee closed the lid on her laptop, tucked it into her pack, stood, and, with hand on heart, she bowed. "I must get to my tasks. I will see you on Tuesday in the afternoon." Then she extended her hand toward the trucks, indicating it was time for him to go.

Rylee thought that had gone about as smoothly as possible. She stood in the doorway with the air traffic controller, watching as their cloud of dust faded.

He was sweating and shaking when he looked at Rylee and nodded. "Good. Good," he said in English, and Rylee didn't know what to make of that. It might be the only English word he knew.

As Rylee retreated to the main supply tent, she saw that George was back, rallying the team, giving them instructions, and handing out maps.

It was time for Rylee to be sentry.

She wasn't sure how she felt about being the only one in their camp.

But there she was. And there she'd be.

With a vague lift of her hand, so George knew where she was, Rylee went into the supply tent to call Neesa back.

"It's six in the morning, your time. Have you had coffee?" Rylee asked.

"Girlfriend, I have a new IV set up with a timer, so an hour before I need to open my eyes, it drips directly into my soul. Actually, Jasper's here. Not here, here. He's in the shower. "

Rylee smiled. "Good for you."

"Yup, very good for me. You doing okay?"

Rylee told her about the encounter with the Syrian and how she had a good case of traumatic response when she saw the pickups approaching with the armed men in the back. "It quite literally set my nerves on fire."

"Tell me what that means," Neesa said. "Your symptoms are worse?"

"Yeah, if I had a dial, I'd say the buzzing is usually about a two. But right now it's a five, maybe six."

"Practically, what does that mean?"

"The buzzing is as high as my knees. My feet feel a little numb. Not that it's breaking my stride. It's just worse."

"You should leave."

"Okay. I'll jump on the next mule that walks by and trot on out. This is a disaster zone, Neesa." She took a breath. "That was rude. Yes, I know what you're going to say. You asked if I could handle it, and frankly, that was at the beginning of last week. Look at all the shocks I've taken to my system. And these men that I spoke with, their loved ones are under rubble. Of course, they're desperate. The thing that set me off was a war memory, nothing that they did."

"Where are Tank and Dakota?"

"I don't know, but they're sleeping in the supply tent with me. I always feel calm when Dakota's around." Rylee focused on the stacks of MREs in the corner. "It feels wrong that I'm here with the boxes and nothing to do. I'm here to observe the responders, not sit in a tent."

"Okay," Neesa said, "but by sitting in the tent, you can see if anyone is sniffing around for the wads of cash in their absence."

"Frankly, the money seems stupid when I'm here amongst life-threatening situations."

"You're staring at a tree instead of seeing the forest."

"Honestly, the forest slid down the side of the mountain with the soil," Rylee countered, "and is looking like giant pickup sticks lying everywhere. These are lives, not trees."

"Still try to see the forest here. Your job is to figure out whether there is an exchange of counterfeit money for real US dollars. And as you do that, you're protecting future rescues."

"No. That's Dakota's job. My job is to stop the attrition. Alright, I know you've got your spin class before work. I just wanted to return your call. Love you."

"Get some rest, I love you back. Wednesday is coming."

24

———

DAKOTA

Monday

RYLEE AND DAKOTA had zipped their sleeping bags together so they could sleep in each other's arms.

Tank was in his crate, lying on his back and snoring.

"Jasper spent the night with Neesa last night," Rylee whispered her gossip.

"Mmm, do I want to know that?" Dakota chuckled as he pulled Rylee tighter against him and whispered in her ear. "I'm going to tell you a secret about Jasper. We don't meet weekly at Macadoo's. Jasper didn't think it was professional to ask Neesa out, though he thought they had a spark. So when she was walking down the corridor behind us, Jasper set up the event in the hopes that Neesa would come, and once he saw her in an off-hours setting, he could talk to her as a private citizen."

"Clever. Neesa took the bait, hook, line, and sinker. But

what if she liked Jasper, but she had judo lessons that night?"

Dakota moved to the side as Rylee kicked her feet. She did that throughout the night. Last night and the night at her place. "Then Jasper would have licked his wounds and worked on overcoming a broken heart."

"They're cute together," Rylee said, flipping over and pushing her ass into his hard-on, then pulling his arm over her so they spooned.

Because this was a community tent and anyone could come in at any time, it was a blissfully torturous position to be in. "Tell me what you think about our many brush passes before we finally met. Veer said it was Fate's hand."

"Veer is?"

"A woman you didn't meet because you kicked some guy's ass and left before we could toast you."

"Fate's hand keeping us apart, you mean? I mean, if I was always running off in the other direction …"

"Don't finish that sentence. I kind of thought of it as flirtatious," Dakota ventured. "Like, I don't know, teasing foreplay. No, that sounds awful and isn't the right sentiment."

His phone pinged, and Dakota reached for it, squinting at the screen. "Huh."

"What's that?"

"A Navy brother in Utah texted. I guess it's dinnertime there. He said he ended up as a volunteer when the search and rescue team was out looking for a missing solo hiker. The hiker just got pulled out of quicksand at Arches National Park thanks to the guy's phone having an emergency satellite connection."

"Is the hiker okay?" Rylee asked.

"He was extracted and hiked out, so I assume so. Mace, he's a guy on Cerberus Bravo, has a K9 named Diesel. Have you met him yet?"

"They did a round of names. I haven't memorized them all yet."

"His wife, Tara, got stuck in quicksand once. Luckily, she knew what to do, so the drunk people around her didn't pull her legs off. That's the closest I've come to knowing someone in quicksand."

"I don't know what to do." Rylee kick-kicked her legs. "What do you do in quicksand? What do you do if it's your dog in that mess? You can't go in after him, and isn't it a bad thing to flounder? Of course, a dog would struggle."

"Wow. That's a horrific thought." Dakota focused on Tank and went completely still.

Rylee reached out a hand and gripped his arm. "In the Kevin Bacon scenario, I am now three people away from knowing anyone who has ever encountered quicksand. You have to figure that's pretty rare."

Dakota didn't take his eyes off Tank when he gave his slight nod.

"You had a rush of thinking, 'What would I do if anything were to ever happen to Tank?'"

Dakota turned back and smoothed a hand protectively over her hair.

"I get it. It's terrible to think of something happening to someone. It's worse if you're in a position where you have vowed care and safety. It's almost unbearable when they're suffering, and there is shit-all that you can do about it."

"Who are you thinking about right now?" Dakota asked.

"My dad. He's had MS since I was a kid. You saw him, he's in a wheelchair now."

"I'm sorry that's happening."

"Yeah. I'm the medical person in the family. I've made a second career of poring over the scientific studies and trying to get him into trials."

"No success?" He smoothed his hand down her arm, then pulled her hips so he could wrap himself protectively around her.

"Not for him."

"But someone?" There was a niggle of danger that prickled Dakota's scalp.

"As of yesterday? Me."

"You." His heart slammed into his ribs. "Why you?" His voice had deepened and grown husky, rumbling from his chest. "Why you, Rylee?"

"I went through testing this week. And I got my results. It's MS. But—" She patted his arm. "Squeezing, too tight."

Dakota had to force himself to soften.

"I am all set up for a really promising experiment. A guy with the British Army that I knew in Afghanistan is now working on experimental CAR T-cell therapies in London. And he knew I was looking for a trial for Dad. He clued me in that a group in his building was looking for volunteers."

"For your dad, though."

"He was too advanced," Rylee said.

"But you're not? This might work for you, right?"

"Fingers crossed. Over the last year, I've had mild symptoms that come and go, pins and needles, and numbness in my hands and feet. I was pretty sure that I knew what it was. It was harder to convince a doctor to take a closer look. They thought I should take up yoga."

"Yoga. Does that help MS symptoms?"

"Not at all, but you know, it should calm a hysterical woman suffering from the ravages of anxiety."

"I don't understand."

"Having never lived a woman's life, you wouldn't," Rylee said, gently. "Doctors know very little about women's bodies. Science was done on men for men up until the last couple of decades. So when women show up with symptoms that don't immediately ring a bell because the symptoms are different from men's with the same condition—"

"Like Neesa was saying, a heart attack was felt differently?"

"Exactly. So women show up and say, 'Hey, here is a list of my symptoms I'm experiencing.' and the doctor writes 'whiney woman' or 'difficult' on the chart, notes the issues, and they do absolutely nothing to fix the situation."

Dakota was mystified by what Rylee was saying. He believed her. He'd heard his friends complain about the frustration of medical care. Nothing this bad, though. You don't mess around with something as degenerative as MS. You treat it ASAP.

"Cut out caffeine and take up yoga?" Dakota tried to match her matter-of-fact delivery. But inside, his body was in full protective mode. He'd move mountains to help her get better.

"Cure all. Panacea for all that ails us, sad, weak females." He felt her grimace against his arm, then she said, "Sorry that sounded—"

"Like it should, dripping with disdain and frustration. I can't imagine how you deal with the gaslighting."

"The most dangerous one was that time I went to the doctor with severe stomach pains, and they said my leggings were too tight."

"What was it?"

"Ectopic pregnancy."

"What?" Dakota's face hardened. "You didn't die, which I'm very grateful for. How did you survive that shit?"

"I went home, changed into a sack dress, and went to a different hospital."

"Do you think if a guy walked in with severe stomach pains, they'd have suggested it was from his pants being too tight? Disgusting."

"Yeah." Rylee kicked her legs again.

And now Dakota knew that it probably had to do with the discomfort of neuropathy. He'd experienced that a bit since he'd broken his back. But it wasn't something that got worse with time. "So you have the diagnosis, how are you feeling?"

"Jostled."

"Are you worried about being part of a study?"

"To be honest?" Rylee asked. "No. not at all."

"But you're *here*."

"Might as well be. I'm a flight away from London. I'm leaving Wednesday morning. That will give me a day of downtime to rest a bit and a safety window if something unexpected happens. I get the prick on Friday."

The ground beneath them rumbled, and Dakota pushed himself over the top of Rylee, bracing himself on his forearms to shield her.

A moment later, all was still.

"Aftershocks," she whispered.

25

———

Dakota

Tuesday

"He's there," Kumar's voice boomed triumphantly over the phone.

"What do you mean he's here?" Dakota said from the top of a rubble heap.

"McLeod's got a newsletter on his website. One just pinged in my in-box. He was in Israel taking photographs, and Israel was sending a response team on a boat. Somehow, he wiggled himself on. He didn't say where the Israeli's went to help, but McLeod said he was heading to the Turkish-Syrian border south of Kilis. Sound familiar?"

"Is there a date? I mean, I've been here. He hasn't stopped by to say hi."

"You said there are still standing buildings?"

"Standing and habitable shouldn't take up the same

space in your mind. Though no one was able to convince the folks to stay out. Until the tents get here, it's shelter."

"When is that, do you think?" Kumar asked.

"This afternoon. I had planned to go help Team Mike, but now I think I have to stick around and try to find McLeod."

"Are the teams finding people alive?" Kumar asked.

"It's a mess. The students that Iniquus went after are all alive. They've worked about a dozen out from the tangle of building material. The ones that are out are all living on the plane. Bravo has food, water, and air supplies going to the others. They're good at what they do. Patient. Doing it right."

The ground rumbled beneath him. It was a very strange sensation.

Every time the Earth shifted, so did the walls and rubble in the village.

Dakota moved away from the debris pile onto the roadway.

The Earth reverberated again.

This time, it was aggressive enough and long enough that he crouched to the ground and put out a hand for stability.

Screams erupted from the village, and Dakota couldn't tell if it was fear or pain. Both. It had to be both.

"Got to go," he called into his phone, then hung up.

He dialed Rylee. She was in the supply tent, and this morning she was having trouble walking. She thought that she probably fried her circuitry over the last week. But this just wasn't the environment to be immobile.

"I'm fine," she said. "A couple of boxes shifted."

"Okay, I'm going to help in the village. Call me if you need anything. Help getting to the restroom or whatever."

"I'll pee in a bag. I'm not taking someone off rescue for something that stupid. But thank you. Go. Goodbye."

A damned amazing woman. If he didn't know better, he'd think he was in love.

Did he know better?

Could this be love?

Whatever the label, it was cellular and intense.

Dakota had never felt this way about anyone ever, nothing even close.

"What do you think, Tank? Too soon to name it?"

"Hey, Dakota," George called over to him. "Can you take this down to AJ?"

Dakota grabbed the webbing, checked the direction George was pointing, and took off at a steady jog.

He was in a new part of the village. This had all been standing this morning. That last tremor must have been the shake that collapsed this street.

Dakota hated that Kumar had called him. Hated that he knew McLeod might be around. That meant Dakota needed to focus on his mission, finding McLeod and trying to find the counterfeit money on him to tie him into the distribution. He'd prefer helping with he rescue.

Dakota's phone rang, Rylee. "You're not going to believe this," she said.

"Quicksand?" He shot for levity since he'd learned that was her and Neesa's coping mechanism.

"Close. Hailey called me. Guess what she discovered."

"McLeod is here."

"You knew?" Rylee sounded disappointed.

"Kumar just got McLeod's newsletter. Did you see him, Rylee? Is he at the camp? You said Hailey." Dakota jogged past people standing in the bare patches, their hands on their heads, shocked by the new circumstances.

"Iniquus has contracts with most of the major universities. So on the off chance he was on their roster, she checked to see if McLeod's school had an Iniquus contract."

"Does it?"

"Yes. So when students or faculty travel, by contract, they're covered for extractions. His college doesn't cover him for kidnap insurance, just extractions from dangerous situations or medical emergencies."

"So how did Hailey know that he's here?"

"When they travel, the participants have to sign in to their app and let Iniquus know when they'll be out of the country. The app sends updates and advisories. She checked to see if he was still in Israel, and McLeod updated last night that he was in Turkey, specifically our little village. She's very excited. His place didn't have an address. But the app did register a coordinate when he was updating his status. I'm texting that to you."

"But you haven't seen him."

"No."

"Keep the money with you," Dakota said, "like on your back. Listen, more people will be heading your way. The village took a big hit with that last tremor. Things are a lot worse than they were."

Dakota stretched out his hand to give the webbing to AJ, who snatched it and ran toward a backyard.

"I wonder if it affected Team Mike and the train rails. They should be getting into the station soon. The airport staff are rallying vehicles and people to help transport the supplies back to our camp. If anyone asks, our tents are all fully occupied now, and people are wandering over with rugs and blankets, making do. Sanitation is a situation. And the first aid station in the hangar is also full. Egypt can't get here fast enough. Mandy didn't tell me how they're getting here. I'm assuming a container ship. That takes about twenty-four hours."

Dakota looked at the string of GPS numbers that pinged in his messages. "Thanks for the update. Hey, Rylee, Bravo has McLeod's coordinates, right?"

"Yes. Hailey put McLeod on their roster. They have twenty-two to evacuate. They've pulled out fourteen."

"Okay, I'm going to go see if I can't take one off Bravo's list for them. I'll check in later."

It wasn't an easy path to get to the red pin on his map.

When he got there, he found a family huddling together in the backyard, in shock.

Pulling his pack from his shoulders, Dakota dragged out his bottle of water. One by one, he helped them tip their heads back and rinse their eyes, hoping to protect them from corneal scratches, starting with the baby cradled in his mother's arms.

Then he encouraged them to drink and clear their throats. One by one, he checked them over for breaks or bleeds and concluded that they hadn't been hurt, though their hair and skin were caked in dust and they were obviously in shock. At this point, there was little he could do to stabilize the family other than point them toward the airport, where there might be enough water for them to wash.

Tank had lain out of the way like a good boy, but his tongue was out, and he was stress panting.

As soon as the family left, Dakota moved over to crouch by Tank, checked Tank's video camera, and then checked his own. If this was where McLeod was supposed to be, everything they found might be evidence in a court trial.

"Do you want to show me what's wrong? Tank, show me."

Tank stood, shook, and trotted over to what had once been a one-story building. The walls in this back corner had been painted bright Kelly green. The bedcover was purple with silver threads. There was an overturned chair and broken glass visible.

Dakota looked to make sure Tank hadn't pulled off one of his booties.

Tank's snoot was working hard as he chuffed the debris. This was the part of their work that concerned Dakota: all the things Tank would pull into his system, all the ways it could harm him.

Coming back to the same spot for a third time, Tank sat and looked at Dakota. He alerted that a scent was detected.

Dakota lifted the slab of wallboard and set it aside. There he found a backpack.

Aiming his camera to capture his search, Dakota unzipped the top and pulled it wide. There he found McLeod's passport and cell phone. There were snacks and half a bottle of orange soda. Some cords. Earphones. A leather-bound journal held shut with a loop closure.

"McLeod!" Dakota called. "McLeod, rescue. Can you hear me? Call out or bang something with a rock."

Dakota stilled. He didn't trust his ears, damaged through

the years by explosives, but he could trust Tank. So he watched to see if Tank swiveled his ears toward a sound.

Nothing.

"McLeod! Rescue! Call out!" he stilled again.

Again, nothing.

But Tank's nose stretched out toward the journal. His nose chuffed the air. Responding to Tank's whine and a stomp of his foot, Dakota opened it.

There, he found that the pages had been glued together, and a hole had been neatly cut out of the middle. In the cavity was a banded stack of what appeared to be hundred-dollar bills.

Hundred-dolla' bills, ya'll.

Dakota walked out of the space onto clearer ground, where he pulled Tank's reward towel from his backpack, though it felt absurd to be high-pitched celebrating amongst the destruction.

To Tank, the search for chemicals was a game. It had to be fun and happy to keep Tank excited to go to work.

With McLeod's pack dangling from his shoulder, Dakota made one last call. If McLeod was in the house, it would take Bravo's expertise to successfully extract him.

Hopefully, the guy was safely walking through the village, focusing his camera lens on the brutality that Mother Nature could inflict.

The phone made Dakota question that possibility.

Dakota joined Bravo to let them know what he'd discovered about McLeod. He stuck around to replace Mace on the hotel rescue, as Mace and Diesel jogged up the street to sniff-search the rubble at McLeod's rooming house.

To his elation, Dakota was there to help widen a hole and drag five desperate students out to the fresh air.

It must have been hell to be trapped for days that way.

Now that Dakota had his evidence, he could set his mission aside and put 100% of his efforts into helping the teams pull people into the light.

26

Tuesday

.

"Dakota, are you with Bravo?" Rylee asked over the phone. She was in military mode. All the emotions that wanted to spark were set aside. She'd deal with them later. Right now, she was riding on intuition and the sense of danger that rippled the air.

"Affirmative."

"Is Ares available for me to go on speaker phone and give some information?"

"Yeah, give me … Yes … Yo, Ares," she heard Dakota shout.

"Ares here."

"Dakota here."

"Rylee here. I need to let you know a couple of logistical details that might have a bearing on your mission. First, the

Egyptian medical team is at the Mediterranean port. They are approximating their arrival to be tomorrow morning. Second, the last tremor triggered a rockslide to our west, blocking the train tracks. They have a work crew clearing it. But most of the equipment they would need is already in service. The supplies that WorldCares was bringing in to support the village are on the train on the other side of the slide. That includes our heavy equipment. Ares, Hailey was coordinating with my team to bring in anything that you requested. I'm not sure if you were depending on that equipment to get your people out. I have no ETA. Push comes to shove, we might be able to arrange for an overland expedition to pick up specific items, but it would be a difficult expedition."

"Thank you," Ares said.

"Uhm." Rylee scraped her teeth over her lips to stop their buzzing, nerves, not MS.

"Go on, Rylee," Dakota said.

"When we arrived, I told you all about the Syrian group that is in dire straits when their compound collapsed on the other side of the border. I offered them support from that supply."

"Listening," Ares said.

"I told them to come back on Tuesday afternoon. I'm expecting them soon. On my team, George is aware. He's sending one of the crew that needs a scheduled rest back to the tent, and I'm going to the tower to watch for their approach. I'm the only one from WorldCares who speaks enough Arabic to effectively communicate. But I have nothing to offer them, even less than I had when we got here. Our supplies are very low."

"You're concerned," Ares said.

"I am. They were armed with semi-automatic rifles. I'm not suggesting anything other than that they are trying to survive. And survival often means doing what's necessary. As you know, we are not armed. My understanding is that you are not armed either. I thought you should be aware so that contingency plans could go into place. For us, all we can do is press on with our rescues."

"You're heading to the tower now?" Ares said.

"I am."

"Keep me in the loop," Ares said.

"Wilco," Rylee said, clamping down on her training. She could sweat all she wanted, but she'd still do her duty.

"Ares out."

"Rylee, are you able to walk?" Dakota asked.

"Yes. Much better. Tingling, no numbness. I'm good."

"Here's the plan. I want you to make the tower your spot for now. If you're okay with it, I'm going to leave Tank with you. That way, I can focus on getting the last of the students out. We're close. We have one more section to dig through. Are you down with that?"

"Of course."

"Tank and I are coming to you there. Quickly gather food and water for two or three days, a first-aid kit, our sleeping bags, and your backpack. If you're sentry, you need to be in the eagle's nest."

"Two or three days? For you, right? My logistics team is arranging transportation. I have a flight to London tomorrow."

"It's the basics that I always have with me. You'll be on

your flight tomorrow if you're not on the Iniquus flight tonight."

"What's my time frame?" she asked, glad to have a task and a destination. Sitting in the damned tent, unable to see anything, cut off from being of service, had been miserable.

"I'm ten minutes out," Dakota said.

The gathering was seamless. She had everything neat and organized because, honestly, what else did she have to do with her time? Rylee figured Tank's crate would be important, and that had taken a minute to collapse.

Dakota called out. "It's me," and Tank offered up a bark, so Rylee knew he was there, too. The zipper scratched as it slid up the flap. And there he was, Dakota in full combat mode, latent strength, fierce concentration. He must feel it in the wind the way she did.

Rylee pointed at her pile of their things.

Dakota handed Tank's lead and their pillows to her. "Food and water?" he asked as he slung the bags over his shoulders.

"Seventy-two hours of MREs, water pouches for hydration, baby wipes for sanitation."

"Good." He bent and pressed a kiss onto her lips. It was the kind of kiss that assured her that she wasn't alone. That they were a team. "Let's roll." After moving through the tent flap, Dakota put Tank's crate on his head and heaved the duffle onto his free shoulder.

"What's in your backpack?" Dakota asked as they hustled away fast enough to make time, but not so fast that they'd stir fear amongst the refugees.

"An e-reader, a solar power bank with a backup crank. A shit ton of cash. A flask of rum and four diet colas."

"Good planning."

"Did you find McLeod?"

"No, but I did find his backpack. Guess what he's got hidden between the leaves of his journal."

"It was him, then. Well done, Secret Service."

"Group effort," Dakota said, his head on a swivel.

"But you can't find him?"

"Iniquus has him on their roster. They'll do a thorough search job. If he were in his guest house, though, that last tremor collapsed it."

"Shit."

"You okay?" Dakota asked. "Hanging in? Is this too fast?"

"Why do I feel like I should be running?"

"There's a lot of fear and desperation riding the air," Dakota said. "Anyone in a desperate situation with firearms is a risk factor. It makes sense that our warning systems are pinging. Not just us. After Ares got off the phone with you, Bravo heard the news and went into turbo mode. They weren't exactly lollygagging before. So it's a significant push."

"How should I handle this? I think you being there puffed up like GI Joe would be a mistake."

"You might be right about that. We don't need any *mano a mano* shit, and my Arabic isn't great. I speak Pashto and Dari." They'd made it to the hangar. Quebec had done a good job of setting up a clean, efficient space to provide care for the injured until Egypt could get there. Villagers were staffing it, and apart from the sounds of human distress, it was as good as one could hope for under the circumstances.

Dakota walked through the door, peeked into the

shower room, the toilets, then stood and listened at the stairs. "Rylee, release Tank. Tank, forward,"

Tank clattered up the stairs.

"As soon as Bravo has their count, they can take off and get their people out. I think that's their plan. When they go, you go. You have a date in London."

"You?" she said.

"I'm going to work with Bravo. So for right now, we need you to be our oversight. If there were a satellite, Iniquus would have it up and be advising. That is not what was happening when I came back to the camp."

"I looked earlier, we're in the wrong location right now, it's north of us. Time should change that and another satellite will come in line."

At the top of the stairs, Dakota dropped the bags and nodded at the man sitting by the radio.

The controller looked from Dakota to Rylee to Tank to the bags.

In Arabic, Rylee said, "The train isn't able to get through today."

The controller's face hardened.

"Are you expecting a plane?" she asked.

"No."

"Perhaps you'd like to go home?" she asked. "I can manage here."

Again, he looked from her to Tank to Dakota, then nodded and hustled down the stairs.

"You have money, Rylee."

She patted the strap of her backpack.

"Leave the pack here, put a strap of money in your hoodie pocket. Take Tank with you if you go and talk to their leader. Trust Tank, he'll do the right thing. Okay? So if the men come, you apologize. You explain. You tell them the new timetable. You give them the money and say that perhaps this would help them find resources already in the area. That's the only thing of value that you have right now."

"I agree that's a good plan. And you're going to go and help get the students. Then, our duties here will be complete."

"What did George say?" Dakota asked. "What does Quebec want to do?"

"He said this is nothing new. They'll just keep at their job. It was a village of thirteen hundred, so it's a monumental job for a team of fifteen. But the villagers have been exceptional."

"Agreed." He pressed a kiss into her forehead and held it there. "I am so damned impressed by every damned facet of you. I'm the luckiest guy in the world to have met you."

She laughed, and the stress eased.

She had this.

She did. She had it.

"It's hard to hear him walk away, Tank. For now, it's just you and me all alone in the tower. Shall we take a look to see what we can see?" She picked up the binoculars, and there it was, the cloud of dust coming over the horizon.

She picked up her phone to tell Dakota, "Company's coming."

27

———

Rylee

Tuesday

Rylee, with Tank at her side, went down the stairs and walked out to the pickup trucks.

Hand to her heart, she used the area's formal greetings, words of welcome, and friendship. The words that conformed to the requirements of hospitality.

She spread a blanket, and they sat.

Then she pulled out her meager offerings from her bag, pouches of water and packets of trail mix.

They were patient as they moved through the rituals.

But now it was time to break the news. Rylee opened her computer to the pictures she'd saved of the landslide on the tracks. She showed the leader and explained the delay.

"My people are dying for lack."

"I'm sorry for your suffering." Tank sat at her back, guarding her six. Dakota was right. Tank knew what to do.

"The people here are struggling, as well. This is a terrible disaster. I do not have the supplies that I wished to share with you. I do have this to offer." She pulled out the cash, held it on the palms of her hands, and offered it with lowered eyes to convey the humility of her gesture. She maintained the posture until she felt someone pick up the money.

"It is my hope," Rylee said, sincerely, "that with U.S. currency, you will be able to purchase supplies from your neighbors. This strategy has proven useful in such circumstances. And that is why I have this available for such emergencies." She hoped it sounded like all the money she had to give. It was looking probable that her own team would need the rest to scrounge up food and potable water. Their own supplies were dwindling quickly.

Rylee stood and put her hand over her heart. Then she extended her hand toward their trucks to signal it was time to go.

The leader called, Rylee turned to see the men coming out of the hangar and from the direction of the camp.

They'd been conducting reconnaissance.

Hopefully, they now realized, she was right; there was little here. And many to serve. They'd have to wait for the train to get through.

She went back up to the tower to watch the trucks head across the flat dirt, holding the binoculars steady until the last puff of dust disappeared over the horizon, then she called George to make her report. "I think you handled that as well as possible. It's probably good."

"Are you finding people?"

George's voice was tight. "Right now we're finding bodies."

One of the benefits of being in the tower was that the keening was muffled. So much grief. So much pain. It was bad enough, man's inhumanity to man. Why did it seem so much worse when it was Mother Earth who caused the destruction?

"Okay, George, I'm in the tower keeping an eye until the sun goes down."

Her next call was to Ares, where she answered each question as precisely and dispassionately as she could.

And finally, she allowed herself to call Dakota and let the warmth of his voice blanket her and soothe her nerves. "Stay in the tower. Keep Tank with you. We've started pulling out the last of the students. We've got contact with all twenty-one now. Three of the Bravo guys went after McLeod at his last known location. I don't think Bravo is going to wait on that rescue. It sounds like they'll take off as soon as the students are all on the plane, and come back for the team and McLeod if he hasn't been found. I'm going to go remind Ares that you need to be on that flight. Make sure your phone is charged. I'll call you when there's movement. Stay safe."

She almost heard it in his voice. Did he just hold back an "I love you?"

Rylee closed her eyes. She was mistaken. It wasn't what she imagined of the vibrations in his tone. She remembered all the people and things that had connected them, all the physical exertion and intense feelings that she'd gone through, and when you do that with someone, you are cemented for life.

And just like she was thinking of Benny and Bean Counter, Briefcase, and even Jesus and his kayaks. She wished them well.

Dakota and Tank were now cemented to her, too.

And she was pretty sure that was true for Dakota as well.

And yet …

And yet.

"What are you thinking, girl?" Rylee muttered to herself. "A man takes you to bed, makes you see fireworks, and you start to swoon like you're a character in one of Neesa's bad romance books that she reads aloud so everyone can have a good laugh."

With Tank lying at her feet, Rylee picked up the binoculars, made herself as comfortable as she could on the worn-out chair, and began her vigil.

RYLEE'S first clue that there was a problem was a series of screams that cracked the night.

Her phone rang, and she snatched it up. "Here!"

"Rylee, take Tank, leave everything else except your pack with your passport, and run for the plane. You have to run."

"Wilco. Out."

Dakota's words were rocket fuel. She snatched up her backpack and Tank's lead, and she was thundering down the stairs.

"What in the world!" she shouted as she reached the open doors of the hangar.

The moon that night was round and full, and it hung low to the ground, reflecting off the pale, packed dirt. Not bright enough to read by, but certainly bright enough to see the old pickup truck parked in the front.

A man in his desert robe stood in the truck bed, his semi-automatic rifle aimed.

Rylee came to a screeching stop, dragging Tank with her as she shifted into a shadow.

The caregivers hovered protectively, using their bodies to shield their loved ones as the rifles swept the space.

No shots had been fired, but the menace was enough to cow the people.

Two other men, rifles at the ready, covered their comrades who pulled supply boxes from the back, running them forward and loading them into the back of their truck.

They yelled instructions to each other in Arabic.

Panic was contagious. It spread like oil on water, then caught fire.

As the men turned to the back of the hangar for more boxes, those who could were running into the night.

Rylee turned to see two other trucks parked by World-Cares' main supply tent, where one of her responders had been sleeping.

Had he escaped?

Already disoriented and traumatized by the recent earthquake, the villagers were now running across the wide expanse barefoot in their nightwear. Fathers with children on their shoulders and elders on their backs. Mothers with kids dangling from their hips, hunkered low so that their bodies shielded their children.

Shadows of people in terror.

Rylee hadn't heard a single shot.

Bullets were unnecessary when people were exhausted

and had no reason to fight. They'd escaped the tumbling buildings with their lives. Why would they risk that precious gift now?

Some children stood, sobbing, separated from their families in the tumult.

Rylee was lifting them and thrusting them in the arms of fleeing adults as she spun them and pointed them toward the rise of land to the north. Once over that incline, they'd be out of a bullet's trajectory.

Rylee twisted toward the sound of a young woman screaming *'no'* as one of the men with rifles dragged her toward the truck. She sat back on her heels, trying to use her body weight to break his grip.

Tank shot from Rylee's side with his lead dragging behind him.

Rylee raced after Tank to protect the girl, shouting "Stop! Leave my sister alone!" in Arabic.

The man turned toward Rylee as Tank leaped into the air, biting down on the rifle hand.

This was one of four men at the hangar. All of them had rifles.

The three others were surely racing forward as their comrade screamed in agony.

Rylee got her hands on the man's rifle and twisted it out of the man's grip as Tank shook his arm viciously.

Lifting to her knee and planting a foot for stability, the rifle butt pressed to her cheekbone, Rylee swung the barrel from left to right, trying to spot the others. She lowered the rifle to one man's chest; partially hidden behind the box he clutched.

"Come here and take your brother," she called over the sound of the screaming man to her side.

Rylee didn't know anything about combat-trained dogs, but she thought that if the kidnapper would lie still, Tank would stop the attack.

Though his screams dragged at her attention, she didn't look their way. She was focused on the man with the box who was in her sights. If he dropped the box, he could swing his rifle to aim at her.

If the box dropped, she'd have to shoot.

Rylee curled her finger into the guard, letting the pad of her finger slide into the curve of the trigger. It was muscle memory.

There were so many people, a missed shot could hit an innocent.

She sniffed and steadied her nerves, slowed her breath. There could be no wobble despite her buzzing tingling fingertips.

If he dropped the box, she'd squeeze back on that trigger. *One. Two.*

"Come and get him before he's ripped to shreds," she called.

The man leaned forward as if he was going to set the box down.

One. Two. The command repeated in her mind as Rylee yelled, "No. You and that box, come here and get your brother. Come here."

The man looked around for backup. Rylee didn't shift her gaze.

The man beside her was begging for relief.

Still, injured villagers ran, and hobbled, and dragged themselves away.

The man with the box lifted his shoulder to protect his neck as he took a sidestep, and another.

As he reached them, he freed a hand to reach down.

His comrade clung on.

"Tank, let him go. Good job." Rylee called down.

She could feel Tank's eyes on her. She knew he registered the rifle at the ready.

Tank spun around and plastered himself to her side. Intense and solid.

The man balanced his box in one arm, holding it in place by his chin, and with the other hand, dragged his comrade, bleeding and whimpering, to the pickup.

Here was the danger point.

The moment when the box went down, and the man turned. If he lifted the rifle, she had to shoot. *One. Two. Rifle lifts. She shoots. One. Two. Cause and consequence. One Two.*

Out on the runway, the whine of the airplane engine intensified, the engines roared, and Rylee knew she'd missed the window that Dakota opened for her when he told her to run.

The plane was flying away without her.

28

DAKOTA
  Tuesday

THE WINDOW HAD BEEN SHORT. Iniquus logistics oversight, apprised of the possible threat out of Syria, had been monitoring the situation using satellite images that had just come back online.

Oversight counted seven pickup trucks using a military formation moving from the direction of the border and five klicks out.

Ares reached out to the breakoff team that Dakota had attached to as they worked to extract McLeod from the bathroom, where he'd thrown himself into the bathtub. The ceramic sides kept the ceiling slab from crushing him.

With the comms open, the team formed a plan.

At the collapsed hotel, the team was so close to getting the hole through the wall large enough to reach that last pocket of students.

The pilot was preparing for flight.

With no visible big guns mounted onto the trucks, oversight would make the call for the flight crew. As soon as the insurgents pulled within shooting range, the plane doors would be closed, and the plane would take off with the people on board.

They would fly out of range and land on the highway at a safe distance.

Meanwhile, it was unlikely that the insurgents would want anything from the crushed village. Bravo team members on the ground would hide in the wreckage, wait for the men to take what they wanted and leave, then finish their work and get to the plane once it landed.

While Ares called George - with Team Quebec - to warn them of the dangers and to get their people and rescue supplies hidden, Dakota was desperately calling Rylee.

She *had* to get on that plane.

"Ares," came over the radio. "We're through! We have a solid headcount. We're going to need to carry several of the students. I need one man."

"I've got it," Dakota said, standing and moving before anyone could counter him. He needed to see that Rylee and Tank had gotten on the plane safely. "I'll be back to help with McLeod," he called over his shoulder.

McLeod was his mission. But in this case, his heart came first. No oath or training would keep Dakota from Rylee when she was endangered.

As he raced, toward the hotel, he thanked the Fates he'd thought to leave Tank with Rylee.

He trusted his dog.

"Dakota, here!" Ares shouted over to him. "Can you take him?"

The student stood on one foot, clutching at a friend, steadying him.

"Is she okay to run?" Dakota asked of the friend.

"Good to go," Ares said and slid back into the ruin.

Dakota turned to the kid. "This isn't the most comfortable ride you've had, but at least you'll be out of here." He ducked his shoulder to align with the kid's hips and put one arm between his legs. Then, pulling an arm, he had the student across his shoulders, partially held in place by Dakota's pack.

"Grab my wrist," he told the woman. "I want you looking down at the ground where my headlamp is shining. We're moving fast. Don't trip."

The woman was asking questions about how far away the gunmen were as they jogged. And Dakota had to tell her to save her breath and focus on speed.

Dakota was gritting his teeth against the pain that shot through his back, radiating from the surgical site of his fusion.

It was bad. Each step sparked Dakota's nerves.

Over the comms, Dakota heard. "The trucks are at the airport. The insurgents have dismounted."

"Ares here. Push on with the students. Go. Go. Go. Team McLeod, hunker down now. Out."

"Faster," Dakota called. "You can do it. It's a sprint, and then you're on board."

The woman gripped harder, leaned forward, and, just as Tank dragged Dakota through the K9 charitable mud race, he pulled the woman at a pace she probably didn't know she could run.

Bravo loaded the students onto the plane with Mace and Bear to provide first-aid stabilization. They left their K9s on the plane.

No Rylee. No Tank.

Dakota tumbled back to the ground with the other Bravo team members. They turned to race back to McLeod as the steps were pulled up.

The door slammed shut, the plane already taxiing.

With a roar, the jet took off almost vertically.

Dakota had never seen a passenger jet being flown tactically before, but the pilot got the airport and tower between it and the insurgents, then kept the plane low while it moved over the horizon.

Dakota raced toward the tower.

There, his breath stopped as he found Rylee on a knee with Tank at her side.

Somehow, she'd pried a rifle loose from the insurgents and had them in her sights as the men leapt onto the back of a pickup, pounded the cab roof, and the truck took off.

The light from his headlamp caught on a pool of blood around Rylee's knee, and Dakota's heart left his body.

"Rylee, it's Dakota," he called.

She was in combat mode, hard-focused on the task at hand.

He didn't want to startle her when she had her finger on the trigger.

His hands were out, and his muscle memory had him sink into a low profile.

"Rylee, it's Dakota," he raised his voice.

Her eyes didn't waver from her target until the truck was out of range, then she looked down at Tank, over to the puddle, and up to him.

Dakota wanted to race forward and scoop her into his arms. He wanted to check every square inch of her to figure out why there was so much blood.

He held steady. "Rylee, you have your finger on the trigger of a rifle. Put the rifle down."

She looked down at the rifle and seemed to unwind from the intensity of whatever had taken place.

Laying the rifle down, she tried to stand and fell to the side, shooting a hand out to catch her weight.

Dakota was beside her in a flash.

He stretched her out and was patting over her, looking for the source of the blood.

"No, no," Rylee protested, "not my blood."

A young woman was on the ground sobbing an elderly woman had her hands on the woman's shoulder.

Dakota saw no blood in that direction.

He'd heard no shots fired.

"Tank took down one of the comrades. That's his gun. This is his blood. Tank's tooth must have severed an artery in his arm."

"Okay, but what?" Something was obviously wrong.

"My legs went numb. I can't feel my feet."

Dakota scooped Rylee up in his arms and carried her toward the ruins. He hadn't had an update about the others in the area. Though the direction of the motors told him the insurgents had taken what they wanted.

His steps were shortened as his back spasmed from the exertion of digging for days.

Rylee had her arms around his neck and rolled toward his chest, keeping her weight tight, which made things easier.

It would be easiest if she were over his shoulder in a fireman's carry, but the hell he was going to do that. This is where he wanted her, pressed against his heart.

As they reached the village edge, Bravo was gathering along with a few WorldCares responders. Dakota recognized their leader, George.

From up the road, McLeod, the shithead, covered in plaster dust, stumbled forward.

"McLeod," Dakota told Rylee. "That's the last of the Bravo protectees."

"They're protecting him?"

"As far as the U.S. airport, they are. The Secret Service will be waiting for him. For now, Rylee, he's just an American citizen. He's not a criminal. He has nothing to do with counterfeiting."

"Got it. We don't need him running."

George stepped forward, "Rylee, are you okay?"

"Fine. Little problem with my leg, that's all." She patted Dakota's chest. "So I hitched a ride. Is our team okay?"

"Just another day on the job. We'll keep working on getting that child out. When it's daylight, we'll assess the camp."

"Can you reach into my pack and take out the cash?" she asked. "You may need to wheel and deal to get a ride out to the train and get hold of fresh supplies."

Dakota let Rylee's legs hang long as he held her to his chest, and George accessed the backpack.

That she was considering practical next steps was a testament to her *sang froid.*

Once the pack was zipped again, Dakota scooped Rylee back into his arms and turned to Ares. "Do we have a plan?"

29

———

Rylee

Friday

The plan had been easy.

Anti-climactic.

Ares had purchased a pickup from a man who had been working to dig his fellow villagers from the rubble. Team Bravo had transportation during their mission.

Dakota had placed her in the passenger seat as if she were made of glass.

This wasn't how she'd been treated in her life, as precious.

It was interesting. Rylee could get used to it as long as it didn't come with the expectations that she was weak.

Ares was at the wheel, focused on driving by moonlight over the road toward the highway where McKayla's jet had landed and was waiting.

Dakota and Tank were in the back with the others.

Onto the jet they climbed.

Off they flew.

Rylee and Dakota parted ways at Heathrow.

There was an ache in her heart when Dakota lifted her onto the wheelchair, knowing he would fly on. But physically, Rylee was fine. Her foot had regained sensation; she could walk. "Dakota, you're hovering."

"Get used to it," he said.

Rylee bent to kiss Tank goodbye. "All the steaks when I get home. All of them. I'll cook for you and Fifi."

With her hand on Tank's head, she tipped back and accepted a kiss from Dakota that, if Rylee read about it in her fantasy novels, would have been described as a kiss that claimed her as his.

And she hoped that Dakota felt that same sentiment from her.

Cemented.

That was what happened in desperate situations.

But this kind of cemented relationship was a world apart from the other connections she'd made in her life.

The sun had circled the Earth.

And here it was, Friday.

She was sitting in the hotel lobby, waiting until it was time to ask the doorman to hail her a cab.

She hadn't heard from Dakota since Heathrow. Of course, he'd been flying, then had to deal with McLeod's arrest.

It was after midnight in the States.

And with that thought, her phone rang. Rylee snatched it up with anticipation and found Neesa's name on her screen.

"Dressed and ready?" Neesa's voice was bright.

"Just wondering what's happening with Quebec."

"Yeah, I heard from Mandy that you were involved in an event," Neesa said. "The team is fine. Morale is high. They're on task."

"Good to know, but that's how Mandy categorized my last night in Turkey? An event?"

"Why? How would you describe it?" Neesa's voice edged with worry.

Rylee took a minute to bring Neesa up to speed.

"I bet it felt like it went on for hours, but we got a readout from Iniquus Logistics and the whole thing, start to finish, was less than twenty minutes."

"Yeah, it felt longer," Rylee said.

"So I have good news. Team Mike and the equipment have arrived, and Quebec is taking a rest day unless they get called to a compression injury. But Egypt is there, and last report, they were busy setting up their field hospital."

"Perfect," Rylee said.

"Jasper already told me about Shithead McLeod's arrest. That's his prison name. He's not in prison, but jail. The Secret Service convinced the judge that he's a flight risk. If he could print his own money, there was no reason not to flee. Nothing to hold him back."

"I hope he rots there," Rylee said.

"Okay," Neesa said. "Catch me up on you. You arrived on Wednesday as instructed."

"Can you believe it?"

"What did you do to relax yesterday?" Neesa asked. "I couldn't get you on the phone."

"I turned my phone off while I indulged in the hotel spa. I picked the full-day package. And after I was rubbed and buffed, I just wasn't in the mood for words. I went to bed."

"Full day, that sounds exactly right."

Rylee stuck with the gossipy banter so her emotions didn't surface. "They were confused by the dirt and blood in my hair," Rylee said.

"Imagine that."

Rylee smiled at Neesa's signature deadpan delivery. "They tsked over my raggedy nails."

"A given."

"I had plenty of hair on my legs for the wax," Rylee said, stretching her leg long and seeing the angry red dots that would go away in a day or two.

"Dakota goes for the wild woman who runs with the wolves."

"No complaints," Rylee said. "And Tank seemed to think we had an affinity, both being furry as we are. My god, that dog. Hero. Dakota, too. Both of them."

"You, too," Neesa said.

"Me, too, I guess. Feels weird to think of myself like that. So I won't."

"I'm sure if you told Dakota he was your hero, he'd feel the same," Neesa said.

"True." Soon, Rylee would have to say goodbye. Soon, she'd be in the taxi heading toward the hospital. John wouldn't be there. His wife thought she was in labor.

So Rylee would go through this alone.

"So, pampered …" Neesa nudged.

"Yes, and I had a big salad for dinner. This morning I had some porridge."

"Good. Rylee, it's human to be nervous. This is a moon

walk. A new step into science. And you're taking it. I'm proud of you."

Rylee swallowed.

"You talked to John about what to expect?" Neesa asked.

"I'll be at the hospital for the day. I'll be tired. They have a doctor in the States who will order the blood work they're watching, and I'll fly back at six months and a year for scans and prods. And honestly, so I can cuddle John's new baby, who should arrive any time now." Rylee stood. "It's time. Thank you for distracting me for these last minutes."

"You've got this."

"Yes, I do." Rylee slid her phone into her pocket, squared her shoulders, and walked toward the door.

Taxi. Reception. Into a blue cotton hospital gown. Propped up in the bed.

Now, all she had to do was wait.

Rylee turned to the knock on the door. And there Dakota stood, with a bouquet of bright flowers in his hands.

It was déjà vu.

"Neesa said you were in D.C." Rylee squinted. Was this real?

"I was, but only to hand over McLeod to Jasper and Singh at the airport. I went back in and repurchased the first flight to London, so I could be here to support you." He moved into the room and set the vase on the windowsill where she could see it, then leaned over for a kiss.

"My god," Rylee said as she suddenly realized, "I knew you'd come. I knew you'd be here." She'd just been holding her breath, waiting.

"It's scary to be one of the first." Dakota pulled a chair to sit by her bed. "I didn't want you to go it alone."

"It is. Admittedly, I am a little wigged out. Better now, though." She reached for his hand, and they laced their fingers.

The nurse walked in with IVs on a cart. "Ready?" she asked cheerfully.

"Let the guinea pigging commence," she said brightly, but Rylee turned worried eyes to Dakota and squeezed his hand tighter.

He brought their hands to his heart. "You've got this, Rylee. And I'm not leaving your side."

EPILOGUE

Dakota's yard was filled with baskets of pink flowers.

White wooden chairs were lined in neat rows over by the arbor where Jasper and Neesa had taken their vows.

A three-man band was set up on his deck while the wedding attendees gathered on the slate patio.

Neesa stood with her back to the women as she raised her bouquet for the toss.

Rylee stepped forward with a grin on her face.

When Neesa counted down, "Three. Two. One." And tossed the flowers over her head.

Rylee used her tall stature and the length of her arms to whip the flowers out of the air before the single women could grab them for themselves.

Neesa turned around with a grin to see who had won.

"Rylee," she scolded. "You and Dakota got married last month. Why are you out there catching the bouquet?" she turned to Dakota. "She's done with you already?"

Dakota slipped his hand in Rylee's and raised their hands

over her head to show off the brand-new gold band. "Can't get rid of me, Neesa. Rylee and I are golden."

"It's not for me." Rylee laughed as she turned and pressed the flowers into Kumar's hands. "Kumar wants to get married next. I thought he needed a little magical help getting Veer and him to the altar."

Veer was laughing.

Rylee held up a finger, then plucked a single flower from the center. "And one for Tank, so he gets his happily ever after with Fifi." She looked over to where Tank and Fifi lay side by side in Fifi's yard, watching the wedding. Turning back to Neesa, Rylee said, "Also, you're terrible at tossing. I was standing over here, minding my business."

"There's a reason I sit in an office and crunch numbers," Neesa said.

Jasper came to stand beside his new bride.

Neesa raised her voice. "I know many of you think that Jasper and I met when the Secret Service was hot on the trail of a counterfeiter, who risked WorldCares' reputation and therefore our integrity and viability. WorldCares is both my job and my passion. I believe it's the reason I was put on this big, beautiful, dangerous Earth. That horrible man, I'm pleased to tell you, has started his new life in a prison jumpsuit and will be processing his poor choices for the next seven years. All that's to tell you that Jasper and I, my maid-of-honor, Rylee, and her husband, Dakota, all set out together on a very unusual journey. And I suppose some part of me has to begrudgingly thank that horrible man for being evil."

The crowd chuckled.

Neesa turned and smiled at Jasper, then turned back to the guests. "For those of you who don't know the whole story, though, Dakota and Rylee, Jasper, and I were all caught up in the machinations of the Universe one crazy week two years ago. During that week, Jasper and I met over a telephone call when his dear friend Benny was suffering from a broken heart." She looked up at Jasper with a soft smile. "I fell in love with the sound of a stranger's voice on the other end of the phone. The steadiness and love that voice held for Benny was the fuel I needed to keep up the fight." She turned to Benny. "I would like to thank Benny for being well and being here with us. I know it's typical for the bride and groom to have the first dance. But I'm going to be perfectly honest, Jasper is a great dancer, and I cannot untangle my feet. So we've decided to request that Benny and Martha do us the honor of dancing our first dance while we stand over here and sway. Martha and Benny, Dakota and Rylee, will you honor us?"

The music started.

"Did you know she was going to do that?" Dakota asked as he pulled Rylee into his arms, and she lay her head over his heart. "Look at poor Martha's face."

"Too many emotions all at once. Do you remember when we were on the plane to Turkey and I told you I wanted years and decades of sunsets?" She tipped back to see Dakota's eyes. "That's what you're seeing on her face. All the things. All the years. All the good, all the difficult, and all the terror-filled. All of it."

"We're going to have that," Dakota said, wrapping her tighter. "We already have. You were a successful guinea pig, and now you have a bright horizon in front of you. In front of us."

"And it's going to be an amazing life."

THE END

Readers, I hope you enjoyed getting to know Rylee, Dakota, and K9 Tank. If you had fun reading *Tank*, I'd appreciate it if you'd help others enjoy it too.

Recommend it: Just a few words to your friends, your book groups, and your social networks would be wonderful.

Review it: Please tell your fellow readers what you liked about my book by reviewing *Tank* at your favorite retail store. If you do write a review, please send me a note at hello@fionaquinnbooks.com. I'd like to thank you with a personal e-mail. Or stop by my website, FionaQuinnBooks.com, to keep up with my news and chat through my contact form.

If you would like to know the reading order of the World of Iniquus books, flip the page to find a chronological reading list.

The Next Book in
The World of Iniquus Chronology:

Acting on Instinct
Cerberus Tactical K9 Team Delta

Make sure **Acting on Instinct** is on your reading list!

WORLD OF INIQUUS NOVELS
IN CHRONOLOGICAL ORDER

Year One

Weakest Lynx (Lynx Series)

Missing Lynx (Lynx Series)

Year Two

Chain Lynx (Lynx Series)

Cuff Lynx (Lynx Series)

WASP (Uncommon Enemies)

Year Three

In Too DEEP (Strike Force)

Jack Be Quick (Strike Force)

Relic (Uncommon Enemies)

Mine (Kate Hamilton Mystery)

Deadlock (Uncommon Enemies)

Instigator (Strike Force)

Yours (Kate Hamilton Mystery)

Open Secret (FBI Joint Task Force)

Thorn (Uncommon Enemies)

Gulf Lynx (Lynx Series)

Year Four

Ours (Kate Hamilton Mysteries)

Cold Red (FBI Joint Task Force)

Even Odds (FBI Joint Task Force)

Survival Instinct (Cerberus Tactical K9 Team Alpha)

Protective Instinct (Cerberus Tactical K9 Team Alpha)

Defender's Instinct (Cerberus Tactical K9 Team Alpha)

Danger Signs (Delta Force Echo)

Hyper Lynx (Lynx Series)

Danger Zone (Delta Force Echo)

Danger Close (Delta Force Echo)

Year Five

Fear the Reaper (Strike Force)

Warrior's Instinct (Cerberus Tactical K9 Team Bravo)

Rescue Instinct (Cerberus Tactical K9 Team Bravo)

Hero's Instinct (Cerberus Tactical K9 Team Bravo)

Striker (Strike Force)

Marriage Lynx (Lynx Series)

Guardian's Instinct (Cerberus Tactical K9 Team Charlie)

Beowolf (Iniquus Certified Cerberus Tactical K9)

Red Line (CIA Color Code)

Sheltering Instinct (Cerberus Tactical K9 Team Charlie)

Shielding Instinct (Cerberus Tactical K9 Team Charlie)

Year Six

Radar (Iniquus Certified Cerberus Tactical K9)

Trusted Instinct (Cerberus Tactical K9 Team Charlie)

Acting on Instinct (Cerberus Tactical K9 Team Delta)

Whiskey (Iniquus Certified Cerberus Tactical K9)

With more Iniquus novels to follow!

For the most up-to-date list, go to FionaQuinnBooks.com

ACKNOWLEDGMENTS
MY GREAT APPRECIATION

To my publicist **Margaret Daly**
To my cover artist, **Melody Simmons**
To my editor **Rossana Tarantini**

To Cookie at the Greensboro North Carolina Police Department.

To my Street Force, who support me and my writing with such enthusiasm and kindness.

To all the professionals who shared their knowledge of working K9s, especially the various Virginia search and rescue teams.

Please note: This is a work of fiction, and while I always try my best to get all the details correct, there are times when it serves the story to go slightly to the left or right of perfection. Please understand that any mistakes or discrepancies are my authorial decision-making alone and sit squarely on my shoulders.

Thank you to my family for your love and support.

I send my love to my husband. This year has been quite the adventure.

And, of course, thank *YOU* for reading my stories. I always smile joyfully as I type this sentence. I so appreciate you!

Fiona Quinn is a USA Today best-selling author, a Kindle Scout winner, Amazon Top 40, and an Amazon All-Star.

Quinn writes suspense in her Iniquus World of books, including Lynx, Strike Force, Uncommon Enemies, Kate Hamilton Mysteries, FBI Joint Task Force, Cerberus Tactical K9 Series: Alpha, Bravo, Charlie, Delta, and Certified Cerberus Tactical K9, the Delta Force Echo series, CIA Color Code Action Adventure, and now, an Iniquus cookbook!

She writes urban fantasy as Fiona Angelica Quinn for her Elemental Witches Series.

And, just for fun, she writes the Badge Bunny Booze Mystery Collection with her dear friend, Tina Glasneck, as Quinn Glasneck.

Quinn is a Canadian author rooted on the shores of the Atlantic, where she lives with her husband and children. There, she pops chocolates, devours books, and taps continuously on her laptop.

Visit: www.fionaquinnbooks.com

COPYRIGHT